TEEN PREGNANCY:
SOCIAL AND ETHICAL ISSUES

Edited by James Wong and David Checkland

Teen pregnancy and parenting are widely considered to be a social problem. These original essays, arising from a conference at Ryerson Polytechnic University, explore the many factors affecting how Canadian society responds to, and creates, the phenomenon of teen parenting. The contributors bring expertise from diverse disciplines, including education, social work, sociology, history, and philosophy, to address matters of social policy on the issue.

The study's new findings, the interdisciplinary approach, and the Canadian focus make this unique gathering of facts and ideas an essential resource for students of sociology, health and women's studies, philosophy, urban youth culture, and public policy.

James Wong is Assistant Professor in the Communication Studies Program at Wilfrid Laurier University.

David Checkland is Associate Professor in the Department of Philosophy at Ryerson Polytechnic University.

EDITED BY JAMES WONG AND
DAVID CHECKLAND

Teen Pregnancy and Parenting: Social and Ethical Issues

UNIVERSITY OF TORONTO PRESS
Toronto Buffalo London

© University of Toronto Press Incorporated 1999
Toronto Buffalo London
Printed in Canada

ISBN 0-8020-4215-5 (cloth)
ISBN 0-8020-8070-7 (paper)

∞

Printed on acid-free paper

Canadian Cataloguing in Publication Data

Main entry under title:

Teen pregnancy and parenting : social and ethical issues

Includes bibliographical references
ISBN 0-8020-4215-5 (bound)   ISBN 0-8020-8070-7 (pbk.)

1. Teen mothers – Canada. 2. Teenage parents – Canada. 3. Teenage mothers – Canada – Case studies. 4. Teenage mothers – Services for – Canada. I. Wong, James, 1955– . II. Checkland, David, 1951– .

HQ759.64.T425 1999   306.874'3   C99-931445-9

University of Toronto Press acknowledges the financial assistance to its publishing program of the Canada Council for the Arts and the Ontario Arts Council.

University of Toronto Press acknowledges the financial support for its publishing activities of the Government of Canada through the Book Publishing Industry Development Program (BPIDP).

Canadä

Contents

CONTRIBUTORS vii
ACKNOWLEDGMENTS xi
INTRODUCTION: JAMES WONG and DAVID CHECKLAND xiii

1 Teen Parenting and Canadians' Values SUZANNE PETERS 3

2 What Do We Know about Unmarried Mothers? SUSAN CLARK 10

3 Day-to-Day Ethical Issues in the Care of Young Parents and Their Children MIRIAM KAUFMAN 25

4 'On My Own': A New Discourse of Dependence and Independence from Teen Mothers LINDA DAVIES, MARGARET McKINNON, AND PRUE RAINS 38

5 A Critical Feminist Perspective on Teen Pregnancy and Parenthood DEIRDRE M. KELLY 52

6 Teenage Pregnancy: Social Construction? IAN HACKING 71

7 How Should We Live? Some Reflections on Procreation KATHRYN PYNE ADDELSON 81

8 The Construction of Teen Parenting and the Decline of Adoption LEA CARAGATA 99

vi Contents

 9 Changing High-Risk Policies and Programs to Reduce High-Risk Sexual Behaviours   MAUREEN JESSOP ORTON   121

10 A Round-Table Discussion of Teen Parenting as a Social and Ethical Issue   151

11 On Choice, Responsibility, and Entitlement   DAVID CHECKLAND AND JAMES WONG   176

Contributors

Kathryn Pyne Addelson holds the Mary Huggins Gamble chair in philosophy at Smith College. She is the author of numerous articles and two books: *Impure Thoughts: Essays in Philosophy, Feminism, and Ethics* and *Moral Passages: Toward a Collectivist Moral Theory*.

Lea Caragata is assistant professor in community development and social policy at Wilfrid Laurier University, where she teaches in those areas as well as feminist analyses of social work practice. Her current research focuses on social construction, civil society, and social movements (especially as related to social and economic marginalization), as well as international development. She has also developed and managed social housing for homeless and marginalized people and was a senior administrator and policy analyst at the Municipality of Metro Toronto.

David Checkland is associate professor of philosophy at Ryerson Polytechnic University in Toronto. He has written on the topic of decision-making capacity and decisional authority.

Susan Clark, on secondment from Brock University in St. Catharines, Ontario, is executive director of the Nova Scotia Council on Higher Education. She joined Mount Saint Vincent University in 1972 and was one of the academic deans at the university from 1979 to 1990 and founding director of the Institute for the Study of Women. From 1990 to 1997, she was academic vice-president at Brock University. A sociologist educated at Liverpool University, McMaster, and the University of British Columbia, Dr Clark's research interests have been in women's work and social policy.

Linda Davies is associate professor in the School of Social Work at McGill University, where she teaches qualitative research, mothering and social work practice, and child welfare. Her research and publications are on the social reproduction of mother blaming, particularly in child welfare, and the social construction of teen motherhood and youth protection.

Ian Hacking is university professor of philosophy at the University of Toronto, and also in the Institute for History and Philosophy of Science and Technology there. His most recent books are *The Social Construction of What?*, *Mad Travellers: Reflections on the Reality of Transient Mental Illnesses*, and *Rewriting the Soul: Multiple Personality and the Sciences of Memory*.

Miriam Kaufman is a pediatrician specializing in adolescent medicine at the Hospital for Sick Children, Toronto, and associate professor, University of Toronto. She is author of *Easy for You to Say: Q's & A's for Teens Living with Chronic Illness or Disability*, co-author of *All Shapes and Sizes: Promoting Fitness and Self-Esteem in Your Overweight Child*, and editor of *Mothering Teens: Understanding the Adolescent Years*. She is completing a new book on adolescent depression.

Deirdre Kelly is associate professor in the Department of Educational Studies at the University of British Columbia. Her research interests include the sociology of education, feminist studies and schooling, and teaching for social justice. Her books include *Last Chance High: How Girls and Boys Drop In and Out of Alternative Schools*, and *Debating Dropouts: Critical Policy and Research Perspectives on School Leaving* (with Jane Gaskell). She is currently completing a book on teen mothers and the politics of inclusive schooling.

Margaret McKinnon is associate professor in the Faculty of Education, University of Ottawa, where she teaches qualitative research and educational psychology. Her research interests include mothering, schooling, and work education. She has published articles related to the social construction of teen motherhood, social services for teen mothers, and schooling and mothering.

Maureen Jessop Orton is director of the Ontario Study of Adolescent Pregnancy and Sexually Transmitted Diseases and research associate at the Faculty of Social Work, University of Toronto. She was formerly assistant professor at McMaster University's School of Social Work. Her interests include human sexuality and research and development for problem prevention. The Ontario Study (co-directed with E. Rosenblatt, 1980–93) has published four reports to date.

Suzanne Peters was director of the Family Network of Canadian Policy Research Networks Inc. (CPRN). Author of *Exploring Canadian Values*, an analysis of the values and principles Canadians articulate in looking at trade-offs in the social policy arena, she also created *The Society We Want*, a public dialogue among citizens that CPRN co-ordinates with twelve national non-profit partner organizations. Her untimely death as this volume neared completion is a loss to us all, and we dedicate the book to her memory.

Prue Rains is associate professor in the Department of Sociology at McGill University, where she teaches qualitative research, deviance, and social control. Her research interests include ethnographic studies of deviance and social control, particularly with respect to youth and women. She has published on maternity homes (including *Becoming an Unwed Mother: A Sociological Account*) and juvenile justice policies and institutions.

James Wong has taught at the University of Toronto and at Ryerson Polytechnic University. He is now assistant professor in the Communication Studies Program, Wilfrid Laurier University. His research interests lie in the areas of philosophy of the social sciences, epistemology, and ethics.

Acknowledgments

We have many people to thank for their part in making this volume possible. First and foremost we want to thank the contributors for their diligence, patience, and commitment, both at the initial conference and during the editorial process. A more pleasant and engaging group would be hard to imagine.

We would also like to thank all the participants in the round-table event, and those who attended and participated in the May 1996 conference, 'Early Parenting as a Social and Ethical Issue.' That conference was supported generously by Janssen-Ortho Inc., the Ontario Secondary School Teachers Association (Local 14), and Proctor and Gamble Inc., to whom we are most grateful.

A grant from the Office of Research Services at Ryerson Polytechnic University has helped support this publication. Errol Aspevig, dean of Arts at Ryerson, and Betty Harlow, chair of the Department of Philosophy there, provided both invaluable encouragement and financial support for the conference and the volume. Initial research for this project was also made possible by a Social Sciences and Humanities Research Council of Canada Post-Doctoral Fellowship to James Wong. Reviewers and editors for the University of Toronto Press provided many helpful suggestions.

Introduction

JAMES WONG AND DAVID CHECKLAND

A thinker is very much like a draughtsman whose aim is to represent all the interrelations between things.

Ludwig Wittgenstein, *Culture and Value*

This volume presents multidisciplinary perspectives on teen pregnancy and parenting as a social issue. For some time already this issue has been getting political and scholarly attention in the United States, but increasingly it is also being discussed in Canada and other countries. This book grew out of a conference on the same theme in May 1996 that was organized through the Ethics Centre at Ryerson Polytechnic University in Toronto.

Teen (single) parenting is widely considered to be a social problem. One pressing question is: What should social policy be on this matter? Despite wide agreement that teen (single) parenting is undesirable, people differ strongly when it comes to appropriate policy responses. Another question is: What factors are relevant to the justification of any such policy, and how are they to be thought of, weighed, or compared in coming to conclusions? Matters raised by this second question are too often taken for granted or left in the shadows of public debate. Concern to bring underappreciated aspects of the so-called social problem of teen parenting to light motivates much of this volume. Part of its usefulness, we hope, lies in the appreciation of connections, discontinuities, and analogies that an 'album' of different perspectives on the subject can stimulate. In the course of this, we hope, there are opportunities to rethink just *what* (and *who*) the problem is.

We make no pretence to have balanced all possible, or even the most prominent, perspectives, either political or scholarly. But neither is the volume intended to be polemical or one-sided. Rather, the perspectives herein are, we think, best seen as different ways or stages of thinking through what it would mean to be, in the philosopher Bernard Williams's phrase, persons 'equipped with a more generous range of human values' trying to understand and respond to teen parents and teen parenting.

There are a number of excellent U.S. volumes on teen pregnancy and parenting. This volume, however, has an avowedly Canadian focus; all but one of the contributors are Canadians, and the research and analysis herein generally has in mind the Canadian context. This is significant, because Canada has not had the same correlations among and between poverty, residence in inner cities, welfare 'dependency,' and race that have been prevalent and much discussed in the United States. Moreover, though it may be becoming less true, public debate and public institutional responsibilities have been conceived and enacted differently in Canada. As Michael Rachlis has pointed out, Canada has constitutionally avowed 'peace, order and good government' over 'life, liberty and the pursuit of happiness.'

This volume is an attempt to think afresh about teenage single parenting (most of which is done by young *women*, of course). While a public policy perspective informs most of the work contained herein, the reader will not find much detailed discussion of, or recommendations regarding, specific public policies. (Maureen Orton's chapter in this volume is the exception.) Rather, most of the chapters are concerned, in various ways, with the prior matter of the adequate *framing* of a policy issue. Some of the chapters are explicitly concerned with aspects of the issue obscured by currently fashionable approaches and discourse (e.g., Caragata, Kelly, and Davies). Some offer empirical data relevant to any policy. Such data raise questions of significance and interpretation (e.g., Clark, Peters, and Caragata). Others look anew at the general question of how we assign responsibility and costs (e.g., Addelson). There is also a personal reflection on a particular kind of experience with teen mothers (Kaufman). Perhaps most remote from the public policy perspective, Ian Hacking's contribution raises a philosophical question about the meanings of the currently fashionable phrase 'social construction,' used in discussions of this issue.

It is readily apparent that there is more than one issue lurking in the phrase 'teen single parenting.' The issue most hotly debated in the United States, parts of Canada, and recently within the Labour government in

Britain is that of entitlement to welfare benefits. Concern about this matter is evident in a number of the chapters, as is the frequent, though contingent companion phenomenon of 'reform' – the demonization of the dependent. But the following matters also deserve attention: the question of 'prevention programs,' especially sex education in the schools (discussed by Maureen Orton); the matter of public funding for other support services, most obviously day care, but also public health and/or child welfare follow-up, and parenting education and support (see the Round-Table Discussion); the question of enforcing paternal support or involvement; the issues of adequate information regarding, and access to, abortion and adoption (see Orton and Caragata); and, finally, the larger issues of education and/or training and economic opportunity (see Round Table). The kind of attention we give these matters, however, is deeply affected by our judgments about responsibility, character, and opportunity.

Why has the issue of teen parenting arisen *when* it has, and *how* it has? The age at which it is 'normal' to begin raising children has varied across cultures and times. What is relatively new is not that some teenage girls and women get pregnant. Rather, what is new is *single parenting* by larger numbers of these very young mothers. Contrary to what some people assume, this rise in teenage single parenting reflects no great rise in numbers of births to young women. In fact, the birth rate to teens in the United States reached a peak in the 1950s and levelled off below those 'baby-boom' rates in the mid-1970s (Luker 1996: 3–8). In Canada, the birth rate for teens reached a peak in the 1960s and levelled off to less than half that rate in the 1980s (see Statistics Canada 1994: Table 14B). What is new is that an increasing percentage of babies have been born 'out of wedlock' over the past three decades generally, and the surrendering of such children for adoption has come to be chosen far less frequently by pregnant teens than either abortion or the keeping of the child (see Kelly and Caragata). These changes have occurred, to be sure, in a wider context where many attitudes, laws, and institutions related to, or having an impact upon, sex, procreation, and the family have changed hugely and swiftly. The mutual implications of these varied changes is not always obvious, and there is an ongoing need to connect policy discussions with a wide range of facts as well as with the lived experience of those affected by, and contributing to, such changes.

At times it is hard to tell what concerns people more: that young women are becoming parents too early (too early for what? for their own good? their children's? society's?); that they are doing it as *unmarried* or single parents (which may be seen as a problem inherently – as illegitimacy – or because of its consequences in so-called social costs); or that they are doing it before they are economically ready to be self-supporting (and hence become what some call dependent on state resources). Is the concern driven by submerged worries about the so-called decay of the family as a social institution? Or, about the so-called abuse of government welfare policies? Is such concern grounded in issues of justice and personal responsibility, or elsewhere? Is it a beneficent concern for the individuals affected, perhaps guided by paradigms of human development? Or is it an interconnected set of attitudes and assumptions more complex and variable than any of these alone? Are assumptions about the extent and nature of the so-called problem and its causes warranted by the evidence?

The question of the *causes* of increased teen parenting, and its further consequences or *effects* can only, one might think, be addressed through empirical research. Yet, in social matters, we often cannot await detailed scientific knowledge. This is partly because of the complexity of the phenomena studied and the contestability of the methods of study. But it is also partly the result of the practical need to act despite limited information or unclear analyses. Moreover, some causal claims *seem* both accessible to common sense and, at the same time, not easily tested by formal methods. As a result it is often the first task in approaching a position on, or dispute over, such an issue to try to identify what assumptions are being made, and to compare these with available evidence. (See Addelson's discussion of what she calls 'considering overall outcomes.')

Evidence alone, however, only takes us so far. One of the main themes of this volume is that the territory demarcated by what has been called by some 'the social problem or problems of teen parenting' is complex, and in a number of ways. Academics are expected to reach such conclusions – indeed, are often suspected by others of creating complexity for their own ends. Perceived complexity, in turn, often becomes either a bar to social and/or political action, or a reason to act in relative ignorance under the banner of 'common sense.' Yet we hope that no serious reader of this volume will want to lay a charge on the authors of manufactured complexity. Nor are the authors represented here guilty of employing expertise in ways that might tend to shift policy issues out of the realm of public reflection and into the hands of supposed experts. Quite the opposite is the case, we suggest.

The complexity addressed in this volume is not, for the most part, highly technical or a matter of arcane knowledge of social causes (though some of that is needed, and some of the needed knowledge is here). Rather, it has a specific character too often passed over: it is *moral* complexity produced by a sense that a number of different sorts of values and issues must be distinguished and given their due if we are to clarify and justify social policies in this area. Despite how it is often presented, this felt complexity is not simply *political*. That term is often taken to suggest that the problem is basically a matter of society *choosing* between internally consistent but competing visions of the issue. Choices must and will be made, of course. But prior to that there is the task of sorting through tensions, conflicts, and priorities among and between different sorts of values. Here the greatest enemy of the true and the good is probably oversimplification or the sense that we cannot reconcile or balance different interests and values. We wish to stress that this 'sorting,' to be responsible, requires a degree of reflection and self-critical evaluation as well as overt debate.

The issue of teen parenting also should bring to the forefront the needs and status of adolescents and 'youths,' a group towards which political, ethical, and social theory have generally been ambivalent. Adolescents are poised between the legally full autonomy of adulthood and the dependent, non-autonomous status of childhood. Psychologically, adolescents – perhaps especially female adolescents, given the changing conceptions of women's rights and roles – are also in a 'no man's land' that has been neglected in public discussion. Developmental paradigms and common sense (by now influenced deeply by such paradigms) locate the adolescent as capable of much that 'adults' are capable of, but at the same time as suspect as a decision maker because of attributed immaturity. Clarifying the appropriate weight to give to developmental considerations unavoidably complicates issues of responsibility, blame, opportunity, entitlement, rationality, and choice.

A 'History of the Present'

For the reasons discussed above, we need what Michel Foucault called a 'history of the present' of the social problem of teen parenting (Foucault 1977: 29–31). In this volume Dierdre Kelly, Lea Caragata, Kathy Addelson, and Maureen Orton all engage in aspects of this. The term 'teenage pregnancy' itself began its career in the early 1960s and only gained popular usage in the early to mid-1970s (in particular in the United States). Prior to that, 'illegitimacy' was the dominant term and perceived problem. First in the United States, and subsequently in

Canada, teenage pregnancies were established as a social problem warranting state intervention. The publication in 1976 of the influential monograph *Eleven Million Teenagers: What Can Be Done about the Epidemic of Adolescent Pregnancies in the United States,* by the Alan Guttmacher Institute (the research arm of the Planned Parenthood Federation of America), was a watershed in establishing 'teenage pregnancy' as an *urgent* social problem in the United States requiring social and state interventions (see Nathanson 1991; Solinger 1992; Luker 1996). 'Teen parenting' has succeeded or supplemented 'teen pregnancy' as the foremost issue as it has become apparent that increasing numbers of young women are choosing what was once the rarest and either bravest or rashest option: keeping and mothering, most often outside marriage, the children of their teen pregnancies.

It still may seem implausible that a term such as 'teenage pregnancy' could mask important value issues and assumptions until one notices a point made by Miriam Kaufman (this volume): despite a strong tendency for women to delay childbearing into their thirties in industrial cultures, no one speaks of an 'epidemic' of parenting by older women. In an earlier time order, *illegitimacy* and its cognate terms 'unwed mother,' 'illegitimate children,' 'promiscuity,' and the like wore their value commitments rather more on their sleeves. Illegitimacy was a bad thing, a social and personal evil. The introduction of terms like 'teenage pregnancy' (and 'teen parenting' subsequently) reflected a shift from an overtly moral or moralistic point of view to a more scientific, and perhaps a therapeutic, one. Gaining knowledge about these pregnancies, in particular their causes, apparently predominates. Yet teenage pregnancy and teen parenting still carry moral overtones. Their use involves important issues of value that do not simply arise *after* the facts are known, but are partially constitutive of our interests and fact-finding. In social matters it is beginning to be widely appreciated that the use of categories must be reflective and self-critical in order to be defensible.

The current problematic status of these 'youthful pregnancies' (to use Kathy Addelson's phrase) is situated against the background of socially accepted modes of reproduction. Addelson discusses how the definition of the current problem *and* the various solutions and strategies available have been forged in terms of existing middle-class expectations and institutions – the nature of the family and what it is to have a so-called rational life plan, for instance. In the past, many young women could resume the typical life course of supposedly normal young women by masking the misstep of an out-of-wedlock pregnancy through marriage or giving up a child for adoption, or by having an abortion. If a young woman was single and pregnant, it was imperative that she hide the mistake in order to be able to lead a so-called normal life again. This meant either getting married (a 'shotgun' marriage, perhaps), moving to another city or town before she 'showed,' and/or giving birth in a maternity home outside of her prior community. Before the legal reforms in the 1960s and 1970s, safe abortions were beyond the reach of most young women, and much of how people dealt with teen pregnancies involved *masking* their occurrence.

The actual life-course options available to young women at present are much more complex than the once prevalent 'good-girl' life course depicted by Addelson. Rather than a linear progression from school to dating to marriage and family, now many detours and loops are both possible and even typical (see the remarks by Suzanne Peters and Prue Rains in the Round-Table Discussion). Adolescent sexuality is experienced today as far more complex, with available contraception, AIDS, and many other factors very different from the recent-but-distant past. Once pregnant, a young woman's options today include abortion, adoption, and (usually single) parenting. Any of these may be accepted uneasily by a particular pregnant teenager, however, because all are currently morally contested in some way.

Is the Problem of Teen Parenting 'Socially Constructed'?

Some of the work by authors in this volume to rethink the problem of teen parenting by charting its emergence is related to one of the aims of much recent work discussing or attributing social construction: namely, to make explicit historical contingencies that can get taken for granted and that play a central role in structuring our current so-called problems. Yet, despite the popularity of the phrase 'social construction' (it was certainly in the air at the time of the 1996 conference), it is not clear in many discussions exactly *what* it is that is 'constructed,' nor just what it is to construct the thing in question, nor what the implications are if 'construction' is demonstrated. The implication or suggestion frequently is that if some matter is shown to be socially constructed, then current attitudes to it are problematic or defective in various ways. Frequently the target of claims is a set of assumptions or associations that come to cluster around a seemingly straightforward (i.e., not heavily value-laden) term. Freeing a concept of such 'encrustations' is often a central goal of unmasking social constructions, though other criticism may be directed against the very concepts in question.

Yet, as Hacking points out, unmasking is *not* refuting. Social constructionist analyses do not necessarily show that contested concepts or institutions are thereby *defective*; still less do they show that we have better alternatives at hand. They may well be, but for that purpose, additional work needs to be done. Many who speak of 'social construction,' of course, are well aware of this. For several of the authors in this volume, one important role of unmasking is to reveal the ways in which power relations and inequalities are central to, or embedded in, various concepts, institutions, and attitudes. In unmasking connections and associations, especially those related to concepts that centrally structure our options and lives, those connections that can empower as well as those that disempower can be revealed. The appropriate action to take, then, is to examine the *justification* and/or the *necessity* of the relations that hinder or disempower, and to consider various alternatives. This task is only barely begun by such a volume as this.

Conflating the tasks of refuting and unmasking may lead one to a very different sense of 'social construction' – the view that *truth* itself is socially constructed. This, too, may mean various things. It is often taken to mean that truth is a matter of social convention. Construed this way, the claim that truth is *socially* constructed is problematic, for it suggests that truths are determined by what people *think,* as governments in democracies are determined by voting. The issue here is objectivity, in a sense of that term that implies genuine constraints on knowledge claims and maintains some sort of distinction between discovery and invention. The claim that truth is socially constructed is sometimes tantamount to the view that our thinking so (collectively, anyway) makes it so. Whatever the merits or defects of such views, we think it safe to say that none of the contributions to this volume entail or imply such an extreme position.

Ian Hacking believes that claims of 'social construction' have been oversubscribed, if only because they are so often unclear. He seeks further clarity about the nature of such claims in his contribution. As an illustration, Hacking analyses (in the style of analytic philosophy) the possible meanings of 'the social construction of literacy,' finding a surprising number of things that might be meant by uses of that phrase.

The role of the phrase 'social construction' in 'declaring allegiances' is one Hacking greets with caution, if not suspicion. It is one that Lea

Caragata explicitly embraces. One of the allegiances often implied is to the idea of collective responsibility. Without using the term 'social construction,' Kathy Addelson (here and elsewhere) is concerned to show how facing up to our collective moral responsibilities implies 'being honest and clear about the outcomes' (1994: 136) that our institutions, principles, attitudes, and other structures impose on people. Even if such outcomes are not intended by anyone, the thought goes, there is still a sense in which those who benefit from institutions, principles, and attitudes ought to account for their effects. Even when such 'accounting' does not demand restitution or reform, we lack self-knowledge to the extent we avoid it. This is clearly a different conception of responsibility than that typical of much popular rhetoric about teen parenting, where individual choice is the central or exclusive focus (see our paper, this volume).

Equal Opportunity, Justice, and Responsibility

One focus of contemporary policy debate regarding what are called social programs is on reductions in state transfers to individuals. We will call such schemes welfare disentitlement policies. Such schemes are usually motivated by considerations of responsibility and justice. These two connected themes run through several of the contributions in this volume. One way of assessing collective responsibility, though by no means the only one, is in terms of the *justice* of certain situations or outcomes. Entitlement to state aid can frequently be justified on the basis of the prevention or mitigation of injustice. Do 'welfare reform' (i.e., disentitlement) policies meet basic standards of justice? Answering such a question involves thinking through the connections between equality of opportunity, justice, personal choice and responsibility, and perhaps much else. Obviously there is much in this complex terrain that is, in W.B. Gallie's apt phrase, 'essentially contestable.' Rather than conclude that such matters, therefore, cannot be resolved, we would counsel deeper reflection and attention to what generates deep differences. Surprises may await such reflection, and for many these will include changes to oneself and one's views, whether we end up with perfect consensus or not.

As Suzanne Peters reports (this volume and 1996), Canadians almost universally say they believe deeply in equality of opportunity. Yet this concord may mask more than it manifests. It is far from clear that people all mean the same thing by the phrase 'equality of opportunity,' for people may count different things as relevant to that issue. Narrower understandings of equality of opportunity locate natural endowments as beyond the scope of legitimate social concern for justice, though not of charity. Moreover, they usually claim a clear distinction between what is social and what natural. They see equality of opportunity as achieved once formal or systematic barriers to opportunity (especially those based on race, gender, and sexual orientation are eliminated from public institutions. In such an interpretation, justice need not consider the actual resources different people possess, nor the extent of actual freedoms or choices derivable from these, provided there are no formal barriers to the acquisition of other resources, positions, and so on. Wider understandings of equal opportunity may also place certain natural endowments outside of concerns of justice. But they may have quite different views about just what is natural and what is socially produced, as well as about how these categories relate to issues of entitlement. Intelligence, for instance, is very much influenced by adequate diet, stimulation, and nurture. The latter is, arguably, a precondition for later opportunity, and both are clearly influenced by social arrangements. But there is also a strong hereditary aspect, and hence intelligence is often viewed as a 'natural endowment.' Talents and skills are also a complex mix of the social and the natural, and one where we may have little hope of fully disentangling one from the other (see Baird 1994).

Almost everyone will allow that a person's options ought to be 'determined in a fundamental way by ... talents and skills' (Daniels 1985: 33); hence inequalities in outcomes can be just. But many will also recognize social obligations to correct actively for certain arbitrary or irrelevant sources of inequality, at least when they affect shares of primary social goods or, more contentiously perhaps, capacities to actually *use* shares of those goods. The term comes from John Rawls's *A Theory of Justice*. Rawls means it to refer to such things as equality of opportunity, the powers and prerogatives of authority, income and wealth. Focusing on actual freedoms to use one's resources must not, it would seem, go so far as to treat *all* differences as unjust. Such views must distinguish among (1) differences between people that reflect choices of different goals or ends; (2) differences that are purely natural or arbitrary and fall outside concerns of justice; (3) differences in what one can *obtain* from an otherwise fair share of basic goods and/or resources. Many theorists, for example, John Rawls (1971), seem to assume that all individual differences are of the first two sorts. Those who argue for the third sort, for example, Amartya Sen (1993), attempt to show that these do not, upon critical examination, collapse into the first two.

This is not the place to defend or criticize any particular account of equality of opportunity, but merely to point out one place where differences emerge and need further reflection than they generally receive. Whether these differences will remain after reflection and appreciation of the situations faced by others is a matter no one can know.

Inequalities in the conditions necessary for real choice about sex and parenting is the central theme of the chapter by Maureen Orton on the public role in the prevention of unwanted early pregnancies. In her view, a central part of the problems of both teenage pregnancy and early parenting is unequal or inadequate access to information relevant to prevention. Susan Clark's chapter raises the question whether the diminished career and economic opportunities suffered by young parents as a group are, in general, *effects* of early parenting, or of prior causes which partly produce decisions to become a young parent, and which might make such decisions rational for the women involved. Linda Davies and her colleagues explore in greater detail the perceptions of certain teen mothers of the choices they face. While they do not say so, we would suggest that such an exploration sheds light both on the rationality or responsibility of these subsequent choices given their situations, as well as indirectly illuminating the kinds of backgrounds that led them to be in the situations in which they find themselves. The route from appreciation of lived realities to specific policies, of course, is no small issue, and the plotting of such routes is barely begun here.

References

Baird, P.A. (1994). 'The Role of Genetics in Population Health.' In R.G. Evans, M.L. Barer, and T.R. Marmor, eds. *Why Are Some People Healthy and Others Not?*, 133–59, New York: De Gruyter.

Foucault, M. (1977). *Discipline and Punish*. New York: Vintage Press.

Daniels, N. (1985). *Just Health Care*. Cambridge: Cambridge University Press.

Luker, K. (1996). *Dubious Conceptions*. Cambridge, Mass: Harvard University Press.

Nathanson, C.A. (1991). *Dangerous Passage: The Social Control of Sexuality in Women's Adolescence*. Philadelphia: Temple University Press.

Peters, S. (1995). *Exploring Canadian Values: A Synthesis Report*. Toronto: Canadian Policy Research Networks.

Rawls, J. (1971). *A Theory of Justice*. Cambridge, Mass: Harvard University Press.
Sen, A. (1993). 'Capability and Well-Being.' In M.C. Nussbaum and A. Sen, eds., *The Quality of Life*, Oxford: Clarendon Press.
Solinger, R. (1992). *Wake Up Little Susie*. New York: Routledge.
Statistics Canada. (1994). *Reproductive Health: Pregnancies as Rates, 1974–1993* (cat. 82-568-XPB). Ottawa.

TEEN PREGNANCY AND PARENTING

1

Teen Parenting and Canadians' Values

SUZANNE PETERS

The questions raised by teen parenting are questions about the way we as a society construct our responsibilities towards children. Questions about teen parenting are therefore policy questions; they also fundamentally involve questions about values. In policy debates about social issues, the questions are often framed as purely technical questions of, say, how much money we can afford to spend. In fact, however, deep value considerations shape the policy choices we make and condition our understanding of the current political will to take action.

This chapter discusses the findings of a recent project that explored Canadians' values about the kind of society they want, and the ways to achieve that kind of society. What we found is that while Canadians are very concerned about the fiscal bottom line, and about eliminating what they see as ineffective and misguided programs, they still remain committed to notions of collective responsibility and mutual support.

Redefining Canadian Values

The question of what single young mothers deserve speaks to deep values that are at the heart of some of the social changes with which Canadians are currently grappling. The notion of a younger single mother is, in many cases, a litmus test of when and how responsibility is assigned between family and the state. It involves negotiations of boundaries between collective and family responsibility in that most public of private places, the way in which the state provides for families and children. The redefinition and renegotiation of these boundaries now taking place in the public sphere engages Canadians' deepest values about the nature of the family and about the proper role of the state in people's lives, and forces them to appraise those values in the light of the enormous social changes that have been taking place over the past twenty years or so.

This process of redefinition also engages the abundant stereotypes and nostalgic myths that Canadians have about families and the natural reluctance to acknowledge social change. The last thirty years have seen a personal, emotional, and sexual revolution that seems to many to have shattered existing moral boundaries, and transformed many of our social institutions, such as the family. Yet even though these personal and institutional changes are now a fact, most Canadians continue to hold fast to values of personal responsibility or self-reliance and traditional notions of family autonomy and self-sufficiency. Their attitudes to single parents, and early parenting in particular, reflect all of their ambivalence, confusion, and resistance towards these changes.

The idea for this project arose in 1995, when it was announced that the Canada Assistance Plan (CAP) would be replaced by the Canada Health and Social Transfer (CHST). The CHST provides block funding to the provinces for social assistance, education, and health programs, and allows the provinces enormous freedom in how they spend the federal transfer.

These important changes in social policy were being driven solely by the fiscal bottom line, or so it seemed. We felt something more was needed to inform the implementation of these changes and the governing federal and provincial policy structures, some articulation of the kinds of principles that Canadians – not just their governments – might want governing the formation of the structures and the program decisions that were made.

It seemed clear, however, that there were no available data from which we could articulate these principles. We decided to design a study that would develop a counterpoint between quantitative and qualitative research. We would analyse the eighteen multiyear public opinion data bases that touch on Canadians' values, and we would run a series of in-depth focus groups structured to draw out, not Canadians' top of the mind opinions, but their more considered public judgments.

Now, I have a lot of scepticism about public opinion data. That scepticism deepened in some ways as, looking into the polls, it became clear that the questions often change subtly from year to year, or their place is changed in the sequence. Generalizations from the data seem hazardous. However, public opinion polls are the only continuing public record we have of what Canadians have said about their values on crucial issues such as child care and medicare, and it was reassuring to find that many of those values have not changed for Canadians and that they continue to support the social safety net. The public opinion data therefore do tell us something important about what Canadians are committed to.

We thought, however, that we could get a richer feel for where Canadians stood on these issues by engaging people in discussions that could tell us why they took the stands they did and how they saw all the pieces fitting together. Conventional focus group formats do not foster this kind of discussion: either people use the group to ventilate and gripe or they give you a shopping list of solutions that cover absolutely everything that needs to be done.

So, building on methods used in the United States and Great Britain, we developed a process that would put people in the position of having to consider deeper values, the reasons for the choices they make. We gave the participants a set of trade-offs that cut across a range of social issues, such as whether to put money towards prevention or remediation, whether to fund program partnerships or provide smaller programs funded exclusively by government, or often, simply whether to fund one kind of program rather than another.

The participants then made the trade-offs in a deliberative context in which we forced them to develop a process to listen to one another and to think through their own judgments.

Overall, Canadians feel considerable ambivalence. Most of them fear tremendous potential loss and harm in losing social programs. At the same time, they express strong fear of the harm to be done by not reducing the deficit. There is also considerable anger. Canadians are deeply angry about perceived abuses and failures of current programs; they want programs to be more efficient and effective; and they are discouraged by what they see as the inertia of governments. As they struggle with these issues, Canadians are attempting to hold these two things, one in each hand: preservation of the social safety net and fiscal conservatism.

It is this strong sense of the fiscal bottom line that may fuel an impression that Canadians are becoming mean-spirited, and it is certainly what politicians looking to make deep cuts are tapping into. Their strong fiscal concerns do not mean, however, that Canadians are looking for governments that will slash and burn. They are looking for a more refined approach; they are looking for program reform; they are looking for change. But they do not want to disrupt the basic social safety net that they see as fundamentally tied to their sense of their Canadian identity. Our focus groups continued to find most Canadians committed to what they saw as the Canadian values of compassion and collective responsibility. Moreover, that sense of Canadian identity is not just built on not wanting to be Americans – although that is certainly present. It is also based on positive notions of what we can achieve as a society if we operate collectively.

Certainly, Canadians often express a lot of harshness initially. When participants in a focus group first enter the room there is a great deal of top-of-the-mind judgment of the order of 'Cut these programs and get these people shaped up. People have to rely on themselves.' It is only as they consider and listen to one another, and realize the potential consequences and implications of the kinds of cuts they propose, that Canadians soften some of these harsh stances and come to more reflective and compassionate judgments about the kind of social safety net they want. So, yes, there is mean-spiritedness out there, and when offered limited political choices people will vote for governments that promise reform on the fiscal side. But there is another more nuanced picture of what Canadians want, a more reflexive view that they are struggling towards and that they hope policy makers will struggle with them to achieve.

Responses to Trade-Offs

There were several different kinds of responses to the trade-offs we gave them, the responses varying according to the kind of trade-off they were dealing with. Certain trade-offs, particularly in the area of health, produce very polarized responses, for example. Faced with the choice of regionalizing health care services, or having a state-of-the-art centralized service, people will agree to disagree. No amount of deliberation moves them to consensus, or compromise. Someone who says, for example, 'Well I grew up on a farm and when it's my time to go, I just want to go' will not be moved from that position when offered the possibility of state-of-the-art, high-intervention medicine. Those who feel it is important to have a basic primary service nearer their families are unpersuaded by all the benefits that proponents of the centralized, high-tech facility find completely compelling.

Other issues, on the other hand, seem to lead to quick and easy initial trade-offs. One of these is user fees – which explains why this has become a popular proposal in some policy circles. Very often, people will start the discussion by saying, 'That [program] costs too much. We still want to hold onto it, but we should do it by making those who can afford to pay for the service.' After discussion about how much the fee should be, however, and the consequences of putting the fee at one level or another, Canadians generally retreat from user fees. The discussion forces them to reflect on how user fees may stigmatize some groups because they seem not to be paying for something that others pay for, and the fact that user fees may throw up income barriers to certain kinds of groups.

This brings us to those trade-offs that invoke what becomes clear are absolutes for Canadians – principles that they will not trade off against other principles or other benefits. One of these absolutes is accessibility without regard to income, and it shows up repeatedly in the discussions of health care and education. Canadians think of it as the principle of universality, but what they are really driving at when it comes to health care is that there shall be no compromise in terms of our ability to have a system universally accessible to everyone, and, when it comes to education, what they hold absolute is that primary and secondary education must continue to be equally available to all.

Emergent Issues

Trade-offs that involve emergent or transitional issues seem to generate a somewhat different response. Because most of the issues about single parents are emergent or transitional issues, this is also the prevalent response to issues of early parenting. It is the response that people had overwhelmingly when asked about school lunch programs, for example, or about whether to cut welfare rates for sole support mothers or cut job training programs, or about issues related to well baby care versus intensive treatment for infants with special problems. Those issues are all in transition, because our notions about who is responsible for children, and how parental versus state responsibility should be carried out, are in major transition in our country.

Sometimes there are groups, especially when there is a strong leader with a particular perspective, who will refuse to make these trade-offs because they believe 'well, the state shouldn't fund any of those things.' For these people, well baby care is the parents' responsibility, and the private sector can provide the intensive treatment that infants with special problems need as long as the parents receive financial support.

Generally, though, when faced with trade-offs involving these emergent issues, participants will adopt a 'third option' approach: they refuse to let go of either of the existing options, and begin casting around to make up the cost elsewhere or propose an alternative way of dealing with the issue.

This 'third option' approach was invariably the way participants dealt with the issue of school lunch programs. A school lunch program is a relatively good thing for children of parents with low incomes. But people resist the notion of directly providing food at some point in the day for such children, for reasons that have to do with fear of systems that create dependency and a lot of blaming. People accept school lunch programs only because they see them as an effective way to help those children, but they are fearful of directly intervening in families. Rather than abandon the program, therefore, they will say, 'Well, we need to have greater civic responsibility. We need to have those moms in there working the program. Corporations and mothers should work together to make this happen, and the state shouldn't be involved at all.' So there is a notion of collective responsibility in play, but they believe that it can be shaped in some way that does not involve state intervention.

The most difficult emergent issue involved the trade-off between cuts to single mothers on welfare and cuts to job training programs for willing and able adults on welfare. If a group dealt with that issue, they returned to it repeatedly. They wanted to clarify where they stood morally and why they were making their choices. Almost all of them moved to a third option, in the end.

Often, they started off with the most blaming of statements about how women on social assistance had no right to have children, or to have more children. They had clearly bought into the pervasive myth that such women are having lots of children, and having more children to get a bit more money in their pockets.

This harsh view softened once they began struggling with the complex economic and mobility changes facing families, such as the absence of extended family support, the lack of jobs, and the growing proportion of bad jobs. By the end of almost every discussion, participants had come to a new notion of who was deserving and who was not, and had generally broadened the notion of what it is to be deserving. They had also begun to move away from the idea that families could automatically be self-sufficient and self-reliant, and to talk about the state supports that would make income available to these parents. That is what leads me to say there was an enduring sense of collective responsibility.

Here is how one of these shifts occurred. It was in Calgary, with the group that was going to cut both well baby clinics and intensive remedial care and were describing single mothers as 'leeches' and 'lazy.' (It may be true that there is decreased stigmatization of having babies out of wedlock, but there is no decreased stigmatization of the notion that the mother could expect state support for the child, at least not in Calgary.) As the group ended, and after they had already made some shifts in their views, they asked me where I was going next. I replied that I was going to meet with some single mothers on welfare, and that I expected these mothers would be very surprised to hear what this group had said about them, since they feel they are already doing their best, and being as self-reliant as possible.

The group then all sat down again – it was as if the session began again, and they had to talk this through. They said: 'That's all we want for them too.' They then reconstructed their third option on income support so that these women would have a sense that these other Canadians did care about them.

Conclusion

Several of the key principles distilled from our research have been adopted by the interministerial council on social policy reform and renewal. In doing this research, therefore, we have managed to shift policy discourse away from its exclusively fiscal focus to include the Canadian values that are increasingly being expressed as the 'social union' – that is, the values of investment and prevention, of equity and of accessibility, as well as the values of affordability, fiscal conservatism, and program effectiveness. These values also include what I heard repeatedly: that Canadians want to know how their money is spent, and what it accomplishes. And, finally, it reflects Canadians' strong desire for a democratization of the processes that inform the policy debate. Canadians are near to despair over the way that traditional consultations have worked.

2

What Do We Know about Unmarried Mothers?

SUSAN CLARK

For the past decade and more, considerable public debate has occurred on the well-being, rights, and responsibilities of unmarried mothers and their families. These are families where conformity to the ideal family type of heterosexual marriage followed by the birth of children does not occur. Rather, parenthood occurs first and may or may not be followed by marriage. At times, the discussions about these families have not been well informed but have relied on partial and anecdotal information. The most disadvantaged groups of unmarried mothers, for example, the very young teenaged mothers and poor urban minorities, are often the focus of attention, and yet it is difficult to estimate just how representative of all unmarried mothers such groups are. This chapter draws on the results of a large study of unmarried mothers in order to give a more comprehensive view of these families in all their diversity.

The discussion about unmarried mothers takes place in the context of three interrelated issues. First, we are experiencing a change in values and behaviour regarding the formation of families. While different types and forms of family have been with us throughout our history, the number of people who are forming or living in families that do not conform to the ideal type – heterosexual marriage followed by the birth of children – has reached unprecedented levels. This is the case for unmarried mothers and their children. The increased number of such families is undoubtedly responsible for some of the debate about the appropriateness of these families and their well-being, since they are increasingly visible.[1]

The percentage of births to unmarried mothers has increased steadily since the early decades of this century. In 1921, 2 per cent of all births were to unmarried mothers, rising to 5 per cent in 1950 and 13 per cent in 1980. By 1992, 25 per cent of all births were to unmarried mothers. Whereas in the earlier part of the century, the number of such births doubled about every thirty years, more recently the figures doubled in just over a decade (1980–92).[2]

A second change associated with unmarried mothers is that the great majority of them (estimates put the figure at over 90 per cent) now choose to keep and raise their children rather than place them for adoption as was the case for earlier generations. Thus, not only are many more women having children outside of marriage, but new families are formed, thereby creating long-term obligations both within the family unit and between the family and the society of which it is part.

This latter issue is the third element in the current debate about unmarried mothers and their families, namely, to what extent do these families have a claim for societal support. The issue is confounded by concerns about whether the women are making conscious and deliberate choices to have a child and to raise the child without the assistance of a partner. To the extent that this is the case, then it is assumed that such families will be like other families, private entities that call on public support only when circumstances beyond their control have put them into a very difficult situation. There is, however, very considerable concern about young, teenaged mothers. These mothers are themselves still 'children.' The extent to which pregnancy and motherhood are choices made with a full understanding of all the consequences is debatable.

These families can be seen to have a greater claim for societal and public support because they are families formed 'by accident' and by young women who are not themselves adults. In a society that attempts to mitigate the undesirable consequences of accidents and especially on those who are innocent of blame – the children – then, public support should be available when families are living in difficult circumstances and the children are not developing appropriately. Support for these families is, however, often tempered by the notion that in engaging in sexual relations outside of marriage and by not using contraceptives, these young women have behaved irresponsibly and, for some people, immorally. Consequently, at the best of times, support for these families is often grudgingly given. When resources are being cut back, and different groups of people are in competition for the increasingly scarce resources, then the idea of who is or is not deserving of public assistance is more strenuously contested. Unmarried mothers may be seen as less deserving than other groups except for the concern about their children. For the children, there is concern that they have opportunities for development and that these opportunities not be curtailed because of circumstances beyond their control. Somewhat reluctantly, therefore, those engaging in the public and political debates grant unmarried mothers and their children a legitimate claim to public assistance.

Debates about entitlements to public assistance are moral and ethical debates that reflect our values and understanding of the issues under discussion. Facts alone cannot determine who has a greater or lesser claim to public support. Having a good understanding of the issues can, however, help in determining what assistance would be useful. This is turn allows us to determine the resources necessary to offer assistance and the probable consequences of assistance not being given, issues that are part of public policy debates. With respect to unmarried mothers and their children, we have had very little Canadian data until relatively recently. Consequently discussions about the needs of these families have not been overly well informed.

The available information has come from two major sources – general demographic data and anecdotal reports from professionals encountering the families during the course of their work. In particular, the demographic data show a considerable change in the pattern of unmarried births over the past twenty years. In 1977 there was virtually a fifty-fifty split between births to unmarried teenagers and those unmarried women who were older. By 1990 teenaged mothers accounted for just 21 per cent of all births to unmarried mothers. Thus, the great majority of unmarried mothers are not teenagers. These figures, however, hide the fact that because there has been such a large increase in the number of births to unmarried women, we are dealing with an increased number of teenaged unmarried mothers. In 1977 in Canada, 17,096 unmarried teenagers had a child, and 19,161 did so in 1990. Thus, we are faced with about the same number of teenaged mothers as twenty years ago, but they are now a much smaller part of the whole pool. In addition when teenaged women have children, they are more likely to be unmarried than was the case in previous decades. In 1977, for instance, 47 per cent of births to teenaged women were to women who were unmarried. By 1990 this figure had risen to 82 per cent.[3] Part of this increase is because unmarried teenaged women who became pregnant today are less likely to be forced into a quick marriage than in the past. This change likely reflects a greater awareness and understanding that such marriages may be difficult to sustain and the changed values that have lessened (although not eradicated) the stigma attached to being an unmarried mother.

Anecdotal accounts from the medical profession and social workers usually have suggested that young unmarried mothers are having considerable difficulty in coping with their circumstances. Such anecdotal reports are always difficult to evaluate, since it is unclear how common the reported difficulties are and whether unmarried mothers are more likely to encounter difficulties than married mothers. Some families undoubtedly experience difficulties, but the cause of those difficulties may or may not be the marital status of the mothers.

It should be noted that there was a third source of information available in the past, although it did not speak directly to the Canadian situation – research from other countries. In particular, studies and reports from the United States were part of our understanding of the issues. Such reports have, of course, to be interpreted with some caution since the policy frameworks within which each society operates are different (e.g., access to health care) in different countries, and many of the studies involved small samples of the most disadvantaged urban minorities. Just how similar the circumstances of Canadian and American women were was more a matter of speculation than fact.

Concerns about the increase in the numbers of unmarried mothers and the anecdotal reports from professionals led the Nova Scotia Department of Community Services to undertake a comprehensive study of unmarried mothers starting in 1978.[4] The research was designed to overcome the shortcomings of the information then available. It looked at Canadian women in the Canadian context; it included both unmarried and married mothers, and it included a wide age range (fourteen to thirty-four years in 1977) and women in urban, small town, and rural communities.

Between late 1978 and early 1979, throughout the province of Nova Scotia 247 unmarried mothers and 325 married mothers agreed to participate in the study. All mothers had their first child during that period. Over the first eighteen months of the child's life, the mothers were interviewed three times – within four weeks of the child's birth, when the child was about nine months old, and again at eighteen months. In 1988 we went back to these mothers to look at how they were managing now that the child was about ten years old. We tracked 72 per cent of the mothers and asked then to participate in a fourth interview. In addition, we added a further seventy teenaged married mothers to our sample and conducted extensive assessments on 223 children with respect to their social and intellectual development.[5]

These data allow us to address a number of issues related to mothers and their first child. In particular, we can determine whether some of the differences in their circumstances can be attributed to their marital status or their age at the time their first child was born. It should be noted, therefore, that when the mothers are described in the following pages we are referring to their age and marital status in 1978–79 in order to see whether these factors have noticeable effects on the mothers and children despite subsequent changes. At times, we will refer to four categories of mothers according to their age (teenaged or older) and marital status (married or unmarried), always referring to the mother's characteristics at the beginning of the study.

If we look first at the formation of the families of unmarried mothers and children, just over two-thirds (68 per cent) of these mothers indicated that they had not planned to become pregnant. For young women still in high school, 80 per cent said their pregnancy was unplanned. Although the majority of the young unmarried mothers (i.e., those who were nineteen or younger) maintained they had had sufficient information about birth control, a sizable proportion, some 35 per cent, said they had lacked the necessary information. Among those who did not plan their pregnancies, use of birth control was intermittent, and contraceptives were difficult to obtain because the young women had concerns about their parents' or doctor's reactions. Since the contraceptive pill was the only method discussed by many of the young women, their knowledge was, in fact, quite limited.

Pregnancy does not automatically lead to motherhood for all women. Indeed, close to 50 per cent of all teenaged pregnancies are terminated through abortion.[6] The women in the Nova Scotia study, however, gave very little thought to abortion as they were in some way, and for whatever reason, committed to becoming mothers, once they learned of their pregnancy. It is likely, therefore, that these young women are not representative of others in their age group, as for the women in the study, motherhood is seen as a beneficial outcome, despite their own youthfulness.

Adoption was considered by a quarter of the unmarried mothers. Typically, the younger the mother, the more likely such discussion had taken place between her and her own family and the baby's father. Adoption was rejected as an option, out of consideration for the baby and the baby's future development. In addition, while some mothers reported being concerned about how they would cope with their changed circumstances (40 per cent reported these concerns), the majority of the mothers did not have a realistic assessment of how they would manage. Consequently, adoption was not judged as a positive alternative in light of anticipated difficulties.

Marriage was the most frequently considered option and would have been preferred by about a third of the unmarried mothers. These women recognized, however, that their relationship with the child's father did not bode well for the long term and hence remained single.

At the end of the first phase of the study, when the children were about eighteen months old, the researchers were cautiously optimistic about the future of the unmarried mothers and their families. This optimism was tempered by the fact that close to half of the families were experiencing financial difficulties. In addition, many mothers had reported that it had been difficult to adapt to being a parent and to learn all the necessary skills and understandings for dealing with a young child. Nevertheless, the children were being cared for in appropriate ways, were generally developing well, and the mothers reported being quite happy with their lives. In the light of their experiences, however, the unmarried mothers indicated that they would advise other young women to consider very carefully before entering motherhood in the way they had, as being an unmarried mother entailed many difficulties and challenges.

In 1980 the researchers expected that the unmarried mothers' personal and financial circumstances would continue to improve, so that the gap on these issues between young unmarried mothers and mothers who were 20 and older and married would decrease and probably disappear. When the mothers were interviewed again in 1988 and the development of the children carefully assessed, the results showed a complex and less encouraging picture than had been anticipated.

During the nine years since the last interview, 81 per cent of the unmarried mothers had married or entered common-law relationships. Conversely, 18 per cent of the married mothers were separated or divorced. Particularly for teenaged unmarried mothers, early motherhood did not adversely affect their prospects for marriage, since 87 per cent of them subsequently did marry. This is in contrast with the women who were at least twenty years old and unmarried at the time their child was born. These older women were considerably less likely to marry, and ten years after their child's birth 30 per cent of them remained single. When they did marry, they also experienced the highest rates of marital instability of any of the groups studied, followed by the teenaged unmarried mothers who subsequently married. Thus, the unmarried mothers did move towards conformity with the more expected family form – husband, wife, and children – over the course of a decade, although a considerable number remained unmarried, and the marriages of those who had been single mothers were more likely to prove unstable than those of the women who had their child following marriage.

With respect to other dimensions of these families – poverty rates and financial need, educational attainment, employment, and housing – the differences between the unmarried and married mothers had decreased over time, but the gap between the circumstances of these groups still remained and was quite stark. (See Table 1) For instance, over half of the unmarried mother's families were living in poverty in 1988, something that had changed very little during the ten-year period. The unmarried mothers had lower monthly incomes than their married counterparts, spent a higher proportion of this income on housing, and were more likely to have been dependent on social assistance and for longer periods. Despite the fact that the unmarried mothers had lower levels of involvement in the labour force, had experienced more involuntary unemployment, and had considerably lower wages than married mothers, the notion that the young mothers simply relied on social assistance from the time their child was born is not supported. Many of the unmarried mothers were reliant on social assistance at some point during the ten-year period, but they moved on and off the welfare rolls as their family income fluctuated according to their own employment and that of their husbands, if they married. The low levels of income are reflected in the lower levels of home ownership for the unmarried mothers and in the increased difficulties of finding appropriate accommodations, resulting in more frequent moves.

The most significant factor that underlies the continuing gap between the financial well-being of the married and unmarried mothers is education. While many of the unmarried mothers, and particularly the teenaged ones, continued with their education after their child was born, two-thirds of the young unmarried mothers still had less than high school completion in 1988. In an economy that increasingly requires a well-educated workforce, this is a very low level of educational attainment. In contrast, close to 80 per cent of the older married mothers had at least finished their high school education. A low level of education

TABLE 1
Selected economic indicators of mothers

	YUM	OUM	YMM	OMM
Living in poverty (%)	52	54	29	16
Average monthly income (1987)	$1948	$2011	$2327	$3184
Income spent on housing (%)	33	34	24	11
Social assistance (1978–88)				
% received	69	58	43	10
Average duration (months)	38	48	18	26
Completed high school (%)				
1978	11	34	24	70
1988	34	44	41	78
Labour force participation (%)				
1978		34		71
1988		50		62
Hourly wage ≥ $12.50 (%)		7		39
Involuntary unemployment (%)				
1978–88		40		20
Owned a house (%)				
1978	1	9	27	60
1988	48	44	77	87
Average no. of housing moves				
1978–88		3.7		1.7
Children				
Average no. of visits to				
emergency ward (1978–88)	7.1	7.6	6.7	4.5
Average no. of days in hospital	4.5	5.2	1.9	2.8

Source: S. Clark, M. Dechman, F. French, and B. MacCallum, *Mothers and Children: One Decade Later* (Halifax: Nova Scotia Department of Community Services, 1991). YUM: unmarried mother, 19 years or younger; OUM: unmarried mother, 20 years or older; YMM: married mother, 19 years or younger; OMM: married mother, 20 years or older.

results in difficultly in finding employment and employment that pays low wages, and thus the financial difficulties of many of the unmarried mothers and their families. The young unmarried mothers indicated an interest and commitment in furthering their education and, indeed, many had done so. But the demands on their time meant it was very difficult to be a student and a mother.

While concerns about unmarried mothers and their families have taken into consideration the consequences of early and often unplanned pregnancies on the subsequent life chances of the mothers, the children in these families have also been the focus of attention in much of the debate. The issue is whether young unmarried mothers have the knowledge and resources to raise their children so that they are not disadvantaged and become a generation of children, and later adults, who must rely disproportionately on state resources. Whether the mothers are young or somewhat older there is also the question of whether a single person can adequately perform parental duties when this has traditionally been seen to involve two people. During both phases of the study, the mothers indicated their very real concerns and desires to raise and educate their children in the best possible manner. Of the approximately 600 children who were seen in the early stages of the study and the 223 who were assessed in depth in 1988, all were being appropriately cared for, and there were no signs of neglect or abuse. The concern for their children had the paradoxical consequence of bringing the unmarried mothers and their children into more frequent contact with the hospital services. Married mothers reported that the person who gave them the most assistance with the child was their husband. Lacking such support in the early years of the child's life, unmarried mothers turned to alternative sources, one being the local children's hospital. The hospital records indicated that the unmarried mother's children were no more accident prone than the other children, and that the illnesses they presented during visits to the hospital were generally of the same severity as those of the children of married mothers. Unmarried mothers tended to be more frequent users of the hospital services, however, because they had no one else to turn to for assistance when the child was ill. Hospital authorities also reported that the children of unmarried mothers were hospitalized for longer periods not because their illnesses were more severe than those of other children, but because the mothers did not have the support in place to care for a sick child at home.

At age ten, all the children were engaged in virtually the same leisure-time pursuits with the exception of two – taking lessons such as music or dancing and being involved in organized groups such as scouts or girl guides (see Table 2). Because of the costs associated with these activities, the children of unmarried mothers were less likely to be involved in such undertakings than the children of married mothers. The time children spent on other activities was also very similar, since playing with friends and watching television were the two most time-consuming activities for each group of children.

TABLE 2
Participation rates of children in leisure-time activities by mother's original age and marital status

Activity	Married (n)	Unmarried (n)	Total
T.V.	99.4 (313)	100.0 (186)	99.6
Reading	95.5 (313)	93.5 (185)	94.8
Read to	56.9 (313)	59.7 (186)	57.9
Homework	95.2 (313)	90.3 (186)	93.4
Help with homework	89.1 (313)	85.4 (185)	87.8
Play with friends	100.0 (313)	100.0 (186)	100.0
Play alone	83.1 (313)	83.2 (185)	83.1
Organized sport	41.0 (313)	40.3 (186)	40.8
Lessons	45.0 (313)	28.5[a] (186)	38.9
Groups	60.7 (313)	48.9[b] (186)	56.3

Source: S. Clark, M. Dechman, F. French, and B. MacCallum, *Mothers and Children: One Decade Later* (Halifax: Nova Scotia Department of Community Services, 1991), pp. 190–1.
[a] Phi = 16, significance of Chi-square < .001
[b] Phi = 12, significance of Chi-square < .05

Two hundred and twenty-three children were given a battery of assessments relating to their social and intellectual development.[7] Here the issue was to try and determine just how well the children of the unmarried mothers were performing in comparison with the married mothers' children. Each of the four groups of children (grouped according to their mothers' age and marital status in 1978–79) had group averages that placed them in the normal range, indicating that overall, the children were developing quite well. Nevertheless, there was a consistent and disturbing trend for the children of unmarried mothers to perform less well than the children of married mothers on the measures of cognitive development. In many instances, differences in the scores were not large or statistically significant, but the consistency with which the children of unmarried mothers had lower scores than the other children suggests some cause for concern (see Table 3).

In investigating this issue further, it becomes evident that the factor which is most significantly related to the children's cognitive performance is the educational level of the mother (Table 4). In particular, when the mothers have not completed high school, there is a very strong relationship between the lower performance levels of their chil-

TABLE 3
Performance of children on cognitive measures by mother's original marital status and age

	≤ 19 years		≥ 20 years	
	Married (n)	Unmarried (n)	Married (n)	Unmarried (n)
WISC-R				
Verbal IQ	100.1 (59)	97.8 (53)	104.7 (60)	100.6 (46)
Performance IQ	105.6 (59)	102.9 (53)	106.9 (61)	105.9 (46)
Full scale IQ	102.7 (59)	99.2 (53)	106.2 (60)	102.3 (46)
Verbal comprehension	40.9 (59)	38.8 (53)	44.4 (60)	40.7 (46)[a]
PPVT - R				
Receptive vocabulary	100.5 (59)	95.7 (55)[b]	103.6 (61)	99.1 (47)
Basis				
Reading	103.2 (59)	94.9 (53)[c]	104.1 (59)	98.8 (45)
Math	98.3 (59)	94.4 (53)	98.3 (59)	95.9 (46)
Beery				
Visual motor	17.6 (53)	16.9 (45)	17.8 (52)	15.8 (41)[d]

Source: S. Clark, M. Dechman, F. French, and B. MacCallum, *Mothers and Children: One Decade Later*, (Halifax: Nova Scotia Department of Community Services, 1991), pp. 190–1).
[a] $t = 2.07$, $p < .05$
[b] $t = 1.98$, $p < .05$
[c] $t = 2.93$, $p < .01$
[d] $t = 3.44$, $p < .001$

dren and their own low level of educational attainment. Findings such as these would indicate that the mother's marital status at the time the child is born is not the determining factor in the child's subsequent development. Rather, the issue is whether motherhood curtails the completion of the mother's own education. From the Nova Scotia study, we know that young unmarried mothers did find it very difficult to complete high school, and only a minority of them did so. The study also included, however, older unmarried women who had left the education system many years before becoming mothers. These women, in comparison with their married counterparts, had lower levels of educational attainment. But becoming unmarried mothers could not be seen to determine this low educational level, as they had left school many years prior to the birth of their first child. Thus, the Nova Scotia study suggests that there are at least two quite distinct groups of unmarried mothers. One group, the youngest mothers who are still in school at the

TABLE 4
Performance of children on cognitive measures according to mother's current educational level (in years of schooling)

	≤ 11 years	≥ 12 years
WISC-R		
Verbal IQ	95.8 (80)	104.2 (117)[a]
Performance IQ	101.9 (80)	106.9 (118)
Full scale IQ	97.6 (80)	106.1 (117)[b]
PPVT - R		
Receptive vocabulary	104.0 (80)	110.7 (121)[c]
Basis		
Reading	95.2 (78)	103.6 (117)[d]
Math	92.9 (78)	99.3 (118)[e]
Beery		
Visual motor	16.3 (72)	17.7 (107)[f]

Source: S. Clark, M. Dechman, F. French, and B. MacCallum, *Mothers and Children: One Decade Later* (Halifax: Nova Scotia Department of Community Services, 1991), pp. 197–9.

[a] $t = -4.64, p < .001$
[b] $t = -4.24, p < .001$
[c] $t = -3.93, p < .001$
[d] $t = -3.33, p < .001$
[e] $t = -2.86, p < .01$
[f] $t = -3.22, p < .01$

time they became pregnant, find it difficult to continue with their education and take care of a young child. A second group has left the educational system for whatever reason without completing high school and has very low levels of involvement in the system subsequent to dropping out of school. Children born to these women have mothers for whom education has been a low priority.

The children's social development was assessed by both their mothers and their teachers. On four dimensions – being aggressive, overactive, inattentive, and more socially withdrawn – the teachers rated the behaviour of the children of the unmarried mothers as more problematic than that of the married mothers' children. Reports by the mothers do not show the same degree of difference. Unmarried mothers did, however, describe their children as overactive to a greater extent than did the married mothers, but this is the only dimension on which the mothers' assessments varied. These data of their children are difficult to interpret, but it is likely that teachers will interact differently with the children based on their perception of a child's behaviour. It should, however, be noted that the teachers did not document differences in the children's intellectual development according to the family status, although such differences do appear in the other assessments.

The information we now have about unmarried mothers lends support to a number of programs developed to assist these families and points to the importance of maintaining and enhancing this assistance. It must be acknowledged, however, that in developing policies and programs for unmarried mothers, we are dealing with a diverse group of families. We must further acknowledge that some married mothers and their children are also in need of assistance. Consequently, while some approaches should be targeted at unmarried mothers, others may be focused more generally on families with particular needs.

The long-term economic and social consequences of being an unmarried mother, and the higher risk of the children not performing as well as others at school, make these families a legitimate area of concern with respect to our social programs. It is evident that no one policy or program will address the varying needs of families with young children. Further, some approaches require that we act before the families are in the process of being created. As many of the young mothers did not plan on becoming pregnant, and had limited knowledge and access to contraceptives despite having sexual relationships, the importance of young people being well informed about these issues cannot be overstated. Sex-education programs in schools continue to be a highly contentious matter, and yet it is unclear just how effective many families are in dealing with the question of teenage sexual relations. Preventing unwanted teenage pregnancies is one of the most important policy and program initiatives to be pursued. Similarly, access to abortion must be freely available to women who choose that option as a way of avoiding early motherhood.

A second area for policies and programs must focus on the educational attainment of young women. The importance of education to financial security is well documented. That the well-being of the children is also related to the mother's educational standing should be equally well known. Some school boards have begun to respond to students who become pregnant while still in school by providing child care facilities at the school. Such an approach encourages and makes it more feasible for the young women to continue with their education. These high school programs may, however, only take children who are at least six months old and are usually located in just one school in a district. Consequently, the young mother's family plays an important role in maintaining and encouraging her to continue in school and providing additional support, such as transportation to the school. Where the mother's family was able to assist, the unmarried mothers had the best chance of furthering their education. Some young mothers, however, had no family support. In these instances, the high school programs provide an important opportunity not just for the mother's continuing education, but also are a means of teaching parenting skills and ensuring the development of the children. For mothers who have finished with the school system some time prior to having a child, the availability of adult education and training programs is important.

Because there has been concern about very young unmarried mothers, programs that have been available have focused on this group. More by default than conscious planning, therefore, attention has been given to the mothers when their children are very young. Unmarried mothers report that coping with the children when they became toddlers and somewhat older is in many ways more demanding than when the children are young babies. There is, however, virtually no assistance available for mothers with older children except what they might learn from their own families or friends. Knowing how to discipline older children or how to encourage them to learn at school are issues that occur after most of the available programs for unmarried mothers have concluded. This may explain why the Nova Scotia study found the children of both married and unmarried mothers to be progressing well at eighteen months but demonstrating lower levels of intellectual and social developments by nine or ten years of age. As the needs of the child became increasingly complex, the capacity of different families to provide for these needs has noticeable consequences for the development of the children.

As is many areas of social policy, we are faced with the double challenge of trying to remediate the difficult circumstances of the current mothers while at the same time developing preventative programs for young women for the children in the present families. With fewer resources being allocated to educational and social programs, our capacity to deal with children who require more attention and assistance will be stretched. Nevertheless, the negative consequences of young people failing or disengaging from the educational system too early in their lives are far reaching.

Notes

1 Frank F. Furstenburg, Jr., J. Brooks-Gunn, and S. Philip Morgan, *Adolescent Mothers in Later Life* (Cambridge: Cambridge University Press, 1989).
J. Hudson, and Burt Galaway, eds., *Single Parent Families* (Toronto: Thompson Educational Publishing Inc., 1993). S. MacDonnell, *Vulnerable Mothers, Vulnerable Children* (Halifax: Nova Scotia Department of Social Services, 1981). H. MacKay and C. Austin, *Single Adolescent Mothers in Ontario* (Ottawa: Canadian Council on Social Development, 1983). Mott Foundation, *Teenage Pregnancy: A Critical Family Issue* (Flint, Mich., 1981). *Women, Children and Poverty in America: A Working Paper from the Ford Foundation*, Office of Reports, 320 East 43rd Street, New York, NY, 10016, #443, Jan. 1985.
2 Statistics Canada, *Births, 1992*, Cat. #84-210.
3 Statistics Canada, *Births, 1992*, Cat, #84-210.
4 S. MacDonnell, *Vulnerable Mothers, Vulnerable Children*. S.M. Clark, M. Dechman, F. French, and B. MacCallum, *Mothers and Children: One Decade Later* (Halifax: Nova Scotia Department of Community Services, 1991).
5 Ibid., pp. 11–20.
6 Statistics Canada, *Therapeutic Abortions, 1992*, Cat. #82-219.
7 The children were assessed using the following tests: Weschler Intelligence Scale for Children – Revised (WISC-R); Peabody Picture Vocabulary Test – Revised; Basic Achievement Skills Individual Screener; Visual Motor Beery Integration Test; Piers-Harris Self Concept Scale; Achenbach Behaviour Rating Profile, completed by the mother and the classroom teacher.

3

Day-to-Day Ethical Issues in the Care of Young Parents and Their Children

MIRIAM KAUFMAN

Everyone 'knows' that it is bad for teenagers to have babies. They will abuse them, abuse welfare, and be a drain on society. Programs aimed at preventing teen pregnancies may operate with these preconceptions as a basis. Certainly, many people in our society are eager to approach young mothers in public and castigate them for having children. Many of the teen mothers who come to our clinic have been told by strangers: 'You're too young to have a baby'; 'Why should my tax dollars support you just because you wanted to have sex?'; 'Don't you know anything? Your baby will freeze without a hat'; 'If you were my daughter, I'd never speak to you again.'

Do such gratuitous comments help? Is it correct to assume that all of these young women are doing a bad job? Should we return to the 'good old days' when adolescents were not given a choice, but were forced to marry or to give their babies up for adoption? I think the answer is 'no' to all of these questions.

Can We Say That a Teen Parent Is a Teen Parent Is a Teen Parent?

We talk as if 'teen parenting' and 'early parenting' are synonymous, but fitness for parenting cannot be defined by the attainment of a certain age. Also, it is almost impossible to define early parenting on a global basis. We cannot set a standard age and say it is 'too young' or 'old enough' to have a baby. There is much individual variation in abilities. It is also difficult to establish a 'normal' age of parenting based on considerations of child and maternal health. Although we know that younger mothers have an increased risk of a number of problems including premature delivery and eclampsia, these risks seem to be minimized if good prenatal care is provided from early in pregnancy (Grant 1994). There have been theoretical concerns that young women will stop growing if they get pregnant, but there is evidence that this is not the case if nutritional needs are met (Garn et al. 1984). At this time, there are no clear-cut data on which to base a determination of the 'perfect' age to carry a healthy pregnancy. It may well be just after the time when the body has finished growing and has come to the end of peak rates of laying down bone and other tissues, but before significant physical deterioration has had a chance to begin. When we add anecdotal reports from obstetricians that young mothers seem to have shorter, easier labours, we might guess that age sixteen to twenty might be the best time (physically) to have a child.

Cultural norms for childbearing vary widely. In a country or cultural–racial–socioeconomic subgroup where there is a high rate of infant mortality or a short life expectancy for adults, women have children when they are young. There is often a feeling that women must have many children to have a few survive (even though this might contribute to infant mortality), and therefore people start to reproduce young, to increase their chances of ending up with living children. The acceptable age for first pregnancy goes up in cultures with lower infant mortality and also as higher levels of education are expected from young women. In all cultures, people have children when they are adult, or when they are able to qualify as adult (although they may meet all the other qualifications for adulthood, but not attain adult status until they have a child). In cultures where women are expected to get an education, they are not usually considered to be adult until they have completed a certain level of schooling. In Canada, a young woman is often considered to be an early parent if she is not of an age to have finished high school. One of the reasons for the perceived problem of teen parenting in Canada is the clash between this culturally established guideline for the appropriate time to start a family and the norms for the country of birth for the teen or for her parent.

Why Do Teens Get Pregnant? Why Do They Have Babies?

Certainly, some adolescents get pregnant by accident. The accident might be a failure of a method of birth control. It might be due to wrong information regarding effective contraception. There are still teens who think that douching with cola will prevent pregnancy. Many think they can not get pregnant the first time they have intercourse, or if they do not have an orgasm. Some of these 'accidents' occur because young people do not believe it can happen to them. Others have poor access to contraception.

These unintended pregnancies can be reduced through a combination of good sexual health education and easy access to contraception. Access to both of these is limited in most countries at this time. Many jurisdictions in the United States require parental notification if a teen seeks contraception or abortion. In 1996 in Ontario Bill C-91 was defeated. It would have required parental notification for any treatment for an adolescent under the age of sixteen.

Many unintentional pregnancies are voluntarily terminated. But teens who have babies often have become pregnant intentionally, although not usually with *conscious* intent. The pregnancy is meant to fulfil a strong need, often a need for unconditional love. In our practice, we note that several groups of young women are overrepresented in the ranks of teen mothers; including those who have been sexually abused, have been involved with a child protection agency (often as foster children), and those with poor impulse control. Many teen mothers come from a family living in poverty. They are more likely than the average teen to have been doing badly in school or to have a young mother or a sibling who had a child as an adolescent. Many of these young mothers express a need to have someone in their life who really loves them, a wish for stability in their lives, a wish for independence, and a desire to be treated as an adult. They see children as a way to achieve these ends. In addition, some of these young women are in relationships with men who want them to have children. They may have little power in the relationship and believe that these men have their best interests at heart.

Societal Attitudes about 'Early Parenting'

As a society, we believe that these young people should not have children. We try to prevent young people from having children by telling them not to have sex or by presenting them with facts about the difficulties of parenting. If many of these young women are led to a decision to have a child by a background of poverty, neglect, or abuse, we need to correct these root problems in our society to significantly reduce rates of teen parenthood. Judging these young women for their actions, when we as a society have failed to provide a safe environment for children, is like blaming people with cancer for being exposed to radiation or other environmental carcinogens. These adolescents are vulnerable because child poverty is accepted and they have grown up feeling like second-class citizens. They are vulnerable because their mothers have been brought up in a sexist society that has taught them that it is essential to have a man, even if he abuses your children. We need strategies to help them overcome these vulnerabilities, as any major societal changes will be too late for this generation. I think we are ethically obliged to aid these young women who are the by-product of a society in which we are members, and from which we benefit. Even if this is not the case, our society can benefit fiscally when we prevent child neglect and abuse, through the reduction of costs in the police and judicial systems and reduced need for psychiatric treatment.

One of the issues concerning early parenting is whether or not adolescents have freedom of choice regarding pregnancy. Many of those who feel that pregnant young women should not have the right to choose abortion also feel that they should not be allowed to raise children. They often express the view that teens should not be sexually active, and if they are, and become pregnant, they should continue the pregnancy and relinquish the baby for adoption. The reality is, of course, that teens have sex and get pregnant. Less than 5 per cent give up their babies for adoption, as they would have had abortions had they not wanted children. Those who espouse the alternate view that teens should be able to make an informed choice and be supported in that choice, may have difficulty in dealing with the reality of 'children having children.'

What Are the Unhealthy Aspects of Early Parenting?

Adolescents who are mothers live in poverty. If they are not poor to start off with, they generally become poor. It is the exception to escape this fate. It seems that these young women (and the odd father who sticks around) are poor because there are few job opportunities for young people with low levels of education. They are not eligible for the maternity benefits that unionized employees get. There is often only one parent in the household. Many come from poor families that cannot provide enough financial support to make them secure. Many exist on shrinking welfare cheques, augmented by regular trips to the food bank. Waiting lists for subsidized child care are getting longer and longer, and the teen may have to make a choice between staying out of school or using substandard day care. Probably because of increased psycho-social pressures, children of poverty are at higher risk for mental health problems (Offord et al. 1989) and for health problems related to poor nutrition and overcrowding.

Another risk to the health of teen parents is that of sexually transmitted diseases (STDs). By definition, they have had unprotected sex (or they would not have become pregnant), and therefore they have also been exposed to any STDs, including HIV, that their partners carried.

Both infancy and adolescence are developmentally dense times of life. That is, both the child and the adolescent parent are changing at a rapid pace. The developmental needs of the teen and her child sometimes clash, and one or both might suffer as a result. Younger teens have poorly developed abstract reasoning skills (Piaget 1969). This means that they have a hard time generalizing from a specific experience or piece of knowledge and applying general knowledge to a specific situation. Because of this, their children may have difficulty gaining weight because of unusual feeding practices (e.g., we may tell them to cut out the apple juice and they will switch to orange), they may ascribe volition to developmentally normal behaviours ('my two-month-old is waking up crying at two in the morning because he's mad at me'), or jeopardize their child's safety.

Teens may also have difficulty with breastfeeding. They may have poor body image and low self-esteem that lead them to believe they cannot successfully nurse their child. They may be vulnerable to relatives who want to be able to measure what the baby is taking, or who believe that the mother cannot produce rich enough milk. If they have been sexually abused they have learned that breasts are sexual organs, and may feel it is abusive to breastfeed or to enjoy breastfeeding.

It is easy to believe that these difficulties are specific to adolescence, but in fact, adults may sometimes only appear to be more able. Although poor abstract reasoning skills are the norm in early adolescence, there are some adults (about 15 per cent) who do not use sophisticated abstract thinking. Some adults have been sexually abused as children or have other reasons to have low self-esteem and poor body image. It would be absurd to assume that all teen parents will have these problems, or that all adults will be free of them.

What Are the Positive Aspects of Early Parenting?

Young parents may have more energy for their children. They can recover from sleep deprivation more easily than older parents (i.e., those of us who are over twenty-five). They tend to get down on the floor and play with their children. Many of us who work with these families have noticed that babies of teen mothers tend to sit up, crawl, stand, and walk at a younger age. We do not know if this is because they come from younger ova or if there are social factors that contribute. Either way, there are benefits, as the extended family, and the mother herself, often attribute this to the mother's ability as a parent. The family's feedback (spoken or unspoken) and her own sense of accomplishment increase the mother's feelings of self-worth. In my experience, people who think they are good parents tend to do a better job than people who feel terrible about their parenting skills.

Babies of teen mothers tend to get a lot of exposure to the world. They go out with their mothers to visit friends, cruise the malls, or go to school. They may benefit from quality child care offered in conjunction with the education system. Our experience is that those teen mothers who are given adequate support often show an amazing ability to change. They can be loving parents who are eager to be 'good' parents.

What about Fathers?

We all tend to focus on teen *mothers*. I have talked almost exclusively about young women. Boys do not get pregnant and the father of a baby may not even be known. Young men are not expected to take the same level of responsibility within a sexual relationship or as a parent. Many young men grow up in homes where there is a double standard. They are taken care of in a way that their female siblings are not. They may grow up thinking that women (starting with their mothers) are there to serve them, to sacrifice for them. As teens, many young men are given overt or covert permission to be sexually active. They may have later or no curfews, and their fathers may even applaud their sexual 'conquests.' Their parents may encourage them to have blood tests done to disprove paternity when they get someone pregnant. It is not surprising that young men tend to disappear out of their children's lives (or become extremely peripheral) by the time the children are two years old, although we have some wonderful examples of young men who have been very involved with their children.

We must shift our approach to boys and how we raise them. It will benefit them, girls, and our society if they are brought up to take responsibility for their actions and their bodies. This might lead to a decrease in STDs, sexual assault, and teen pregnancy. It seems patently wrong, not just sad or unfortunate, to bring up young men this way. The wrong that is done is not only to the young women who might get STDs, or the sisters who have to live as servants to their brothers, or the people who are victimized by young men who think they have a right to do whatever they please. Bringing up boys to believe that they are better than half the population inhibits their own development and stands in the way of equal and satisfying relationships with women.

Problems That Pregnant Teens and Young Parents Face

I would be the last to argue that adolescent parents should be treated just like older parents. Anyone dealing with these young families needs to be aware of their unique developmental needs, and to tailor care plans to these needs.

We must make sure, however, that we are not basing our care on some of the prejudgments that I discussed earlier. When we think that the care others are providing is unethical or based on incorrect assumptions, we must intervene as advocates for these young people. This intervention may be direct, or it may consist of helping the teen advocate for herself.

Here are some examples of situations in which there was inappropriate differential treatment of teen mothers:

A woman who has been working with the 15-year-old mother of a 7-month-old calls our program for babies of teen mothers. She has helped the mother find child care so that she can go to school. The day care needs the dates of the baby's immunizations. Can she send the mother down to get the dates? She is told that the mother should not come to the clinic that day, as we need to get the baby's record from another department, and it might take more than a few hours to get it. We have some of the immunization dates in a clinic file and give these dates to the worker, but warn her that it may be an incomplete list. Two hours later the mother shows up. She has been told by the worker that she must come down and get the dates in writing. She says that she has missed the first week of school running around doing paperwork for the day care. She expresses her frustration at being told to come to the hospital and states, 'I hate having to talk to a lot of people, and they keep making me go and talk to people who then tell me it wasn't necessary.'

The worker has, for reasons that are not obvious, sent this young woman on a wild goose chase. She has not listened to the mother's clear statements about her needs. She has assumed that she has the right to decide what the teen must do, without explaining why, and in this case, without apparent reason.

A child protection worker calls about a teen mother who has missed a well baby appointment in our clinic three days before. We stress that the baby needs to come in. The worker asks, 'When should I tell her to come?' She is told that the mother should call to make an appointment and replies, 'If she could make appointments she wouldn't be my client.' In fact, as we are speaking, the mother calls on another line and books an appointment for the following week. When told this, she says, 'Well, why did she wait three days to call?'

This baby has a right to appropriate medical care. The mother has the right to learn how to obtain access to this care. This includes being helped to learn how to make appointments and to come to those appointments. It is patronizing for the worker to assume that she will not be able to do this and to make the appointment for her, with no respect for the teen's schedule. If the mother had not called for an appointment, even with a reminder from the worker, it would have then been appropriate for the worker to have let her know that she would make the appointment for her, as the child's welfare must be protected. One could take the view that the worker was trying to help the mother, do her a favour by saving her a phone call. But being able to make appointments for one's child is an important survival skill. Even though it might be easier for the mother to be 'helped' in this way, there will be times when no one is there to do it for her. It is better for her to be encouraged to take this responsibility while there is some supervision, someone who can make sure that she does follow through and get medical care for her child.

It is very difficult for us to protect young people from workers, teachers, or health care professionals who behave badly towards them. But we can do two things to help remedy this problem, without being patronizing ourselves.

The first is to be advocates for young parents. At the most basic level, this involves setting an example by speaking of them and treating them in ways that demonstrate that we see them as individuals with specific needs, not to be lumped into a single set of 'teen parents.' We can identify our own biases and try to change. We can speak publicly about these young people and their needs.

Second, we can help empower young parents. They may think that they deserve to be treated badly. We can help them understand that they and their children have rights. We can help them identify racist, ageist, or sexist behaviour from landlords, teachers, and workers. We can identify their positive parenting skills, and encourage them to rely on these skills.

Dilemmas for Nurses, Doctors, Child Protection Workers, Counsellors, and Others Who Work with Young Parents

Many difficult issues arise in the treatment of adolescents, even those who are not parents. One of the primary ones is that of confidentiality. Teens have the right to confidential care. They can be assured that they can talk openly and that information will not be released without their consent. They should be told the limits of this at an initial interview, that is, that you will intervene (in a way that may breach confidentiality) if they are suicidal, are planning to harm someone else, or report physical or sexual abuse. In Ontario, the latter is reportable only if the victim is under the age of sixteen. Teen parents must also know that they are obligated to safeguard their child's health and safety and that you are obliged to report abuse or neglect. All this seems straightforward, but ethical issues arise. We may have concerns about a teen's parenting skills, but nothing specific on which to base a report to a child protection agency. Further, such a report might ruin a therapeutic relationship that has been established with the adolescent. In this case, the easiest thing is to discuss your concerns with the young person and suggest voluntary involvement with the agency.

Sometimes, a teen has a dilemma where we feel the involvement of a parent or friend could be helpful, but the teen wants no outside involvement. This is commonly the case when a young woman discovers that she is pregnant. She may not want to talk to her mother, even though it is clear that her mother has been supportive of her in the past and would be helpful in making plans. It may be clear to us that the mother will be less supportive if she finds out later, as she may feel hurt that her daughter did not confide in her. Again, all we can do is explore the girl's reluctance to discuss this with her mother. Role playing can be helpful. In the end, it must be her decision.

Other agencies may feel that they have a right to information that would not normally be released without permission. Unless there is a suspicion of abuse, neglect, or suicidality, this information cannot be handed over. Sometimes an agency has teens sign a release form without explaining what it is, or by implying that they will not receive help if it is not signed. A signed paper is not the same as consent, it is just a symbol of consent. If you suspect that a teen has signed a release without actually wanting information to be shared, you should discuss it with her before releasing the information, and only release what she wishes.

Consent is often more of a legal than an ethical issue, but the two can become entangled. Consent laws vary throughout North America, and so does the age at which young people may start to consent to treatment. Various criteria need to be fulfilled if an adolescent wants to consent to or refuse treatment at a younger age. In California, for instance, to be deemed an 'emancipated minor' a teen must have her own place of residence and be self-supporting. Common law in Canada holds that people can consent if they are capable of understanding their disease, the proposed treatment, and the likely consequences of having or refusing treatment, regardless of age. In Ontario, this has been codified in legislation that recognizes that people develop at different rates and that a person may be capable of making decisions about a simple, low-risk treatment, but not capable of consenting to complicated, high-risk treatment.

Ethical issues exist within the patient–physician or client–caregiver relationship. The question of where the boundaries are between young people and ourselves is at the core of many of these issues. Adolescents have a need to understand the nature of their relationships to health care and agency workers. Rigid, 'brick-wall' type boundaries can be difficult as teens want a sense of their caregivers as human beings. They are looking for role models. On the other hand, friendship is not appropriate, given the large power differential in these relationships, based on differences in age, access to information, and in some cases, even the power to remove their children from their care. If the boundary is too loose, the relationship can be misinterpreted and young people may assume they are sharing information as a friend, and then feel betrayed by necessary (even legislated) information sharing. Adolescents with personality disorders often misinterpret friendliness as friendship, and end up feeling betrayed and moving on to a new caregiver. In general, though, friendly behaviour helps adolescents feel more comfortable and boosts their self-esteem. It can be therapeutic for them to feel liked, and worth being liked. The ethical dilemmas may arise if we do not examine and monitor these relationships, asking ourselves, 'Am I hooked on being liked by this young mother?' and 'Am I compromising the care of the child to continue being appreciated by the mother?' Much of the work that I do with these young people stems from my experience as a parent and not from what I learned in medical school. I often ask myself whether sharing the lessons I have learned from my own children is an infringement of the boundary between my patients and me. However, I feel that it is helpful to them when I use my parenting as an example (and not always as a good example). If I say, 'Don't do this, it is bad for your child,' they may feel that I am saying that they are bad, that they do not know what to do. If I say, 'Oh, I tried that, and it didn't work,' there is a level of humour that helps them accept it.

Then there is the whole 'non-judgmental thing.' Many of us have been taught that we should not make judgments about these young people, and we like to think that we do not. But for concerned people, it is probably not possible to do this, and perhaps we should not be striving to be neutral. As role models, we must be seen to be fair-minded advocates of a particular perspective. I do not want to give teens the message that they should strive to be detached, neutral, and lacking in opinion. But the kinds of judgments that are often made about teen parents do not usually help them, so judging cannot be our primary mode of interaction. So instead of saying, 'You're too young for sex,' we can ask, 'What are the good things about having sex? Are there things about sex that make you uncomfortable? What do you think are the dangers?' From a practical point of view, teens are more likely to change their behaviour if they come to a conclusion about it themselves, than if you just feed them your opinion. There are times when strongly judgmental statements are helpful. 'It's not your fault that you were abused,' and 'It's wrong for your boyfriend to be hitting you,' are two examples.

We must also be aware of our feelings with regard to these young people. We may be angry at a young mother for getting pregnant again, or for staying in an abusive relationship. We may identify with their adolescent struggles and feel protective of them. If we know how we are feeling, we can try not to let these feelings negatively influence their care. We can even use our rage, or our tenderness, or whatever we are feeling, to spur us on to action, to find resources, to advocate for changes or whatever may help, either in the particular situation or to prevent its recurrence. It can be helpful to the young person who has experienced the expression of emotion as a negative thing, to see emotions expressed appropriately. We must be careful how we do this. Not only is it important to respect the boundaries between us, especially as we have much more power than our patients or clients, but we must express them in ways that do not burden them. To say, 'I feel upset when I hear you telling your son that he's stupid, and I wonder who you heard that from when you were young,' gives a different message than, 'You really upset me when you talk that way. That's abusive.'

Is It Wrong to Be Offering Care to These Teens?

It has been argued that by offering comprehensive care to these adolescents we are endorsing early parenthood. Some say that we should be telling these young people not to have sex, and if they do, and get pregnant, that they should get the message that what they are doing is wrong. They would get this message by not receiving welfare, day-care subsidies, or having access to special school programs, groups for young parents, or any other special supports. It has even been said that it is the presence of these resources that has brought about the phenomenon of teen parenting.

As I discussed earlier, the definition of early parenting varies from time to time and culture to culture. A short time ago in Canada and the United States young women who became pregnant at an age considered to be too young gave birth and 'gave up' their babies for adoption. In reality, those babies were taken away from them. They were not told that keeping them was an option. Young mothers stopped relinquishing babies, not when they perceived that there were social supports, but when they felt they had a choice. In the past twenty or so years, there has been a marked emphasis in our society towards an ethic of individual choice and decision making, and given this choice, young women have been unwilling to part with their children.

Another result of this societal shift was the so-called sexual revolution, during which young women came to believe that they had the right to the control of their sexuality. The proportion of young women who admitted being sexually active during the junior high and high school years increased, but rates of births to teens actually declined consistently between 1971 (44 per 1,000) and 1991 (22 per 1,000). There has been a bit of an upswing since then, but the birth rate in the fifteen to seventeen age group was still around 25 per 1,000 in 1994 (Wadhera and Miller 1997).

As a consequence of these two developments in North American society, there are many more teen mothers around and visible. This may then make teen parenting seem more normal or acceptable to other teens and may make it easier to decide to continue a pregnancy.

If we were to withdraw services to these young families, we would be punishing young women for having children, and punishing the children themselves. It may be a common theme in literature and religion to be punished for being born, but it hardly seems right. Even with current services, these children are poor, and without our support they would be raised in abject poverty, by young women with no guidance in parenting, destined to repeat this cycle, having their own children while still young.

Conclusion

At the end of all this, do I think that teen parenting is 'good'? No, I do not. There are enormous stressors on these young people. Many of them miss important adolescent milestones and activities. I do not want my own children to have children until they have reached a certain level of maturity and acquired a reasonable level of education. But I am not willing to say that teen parenting is bad. I will not pass judgment on young people who have made difficult decisions, many of whom are doing the best they can. My job is not to decide if they are right or wrong, but to maximize their adolescent development, and their children's safety, development, and health.

References

Garn, S.M., LeVelle, M., Pesick, S.D., and Ridella, S.A. (1984). 'Are Pregnant Teenagers Still in Rapid Growth?' *American Journal of the Disabled Child* 13: 32–4.

Grant, L. (1994). 'Adolescent Pregnancy.' *Journal SOGC* 16: 2221–9.

Offord, D., Boyle, M.H., Fleming, J.E., et al. (1989). 'The Ontario Child Health Study: Summary of Selected Results.' *Canadian Journal of Psychology* 34: 483–91.

Piaget, J. (1969). 'The Intellectual Development of the Adolescent.' In G. Capland and S. Lebovici, eds., *Adolescence: Psychological Perspectives*, New York: Basic Books.

Wadhera, S., and Millar, W. (1997). 'Teenage Pregnancies, 1974–1994.' *Health Reports* 9(3): 9–17.

4

'On My Own': A New Discourse of Dependence and Independence from Teen Mothers

LINDA DAVIES, MARGARET McKINNON, AND PRUE RAINS

The subject of teen mothers is almost invariably framed as a social problem, and much of the contemporary discourse about teen mothers draws on images and the language of stigmatized dependency (Griffin 1993; Kelly 1996; Lawson and Rhode 1993; Lesko 1995; Phoenix 1991a). Teen mothers are spoken of as 'children having children,' and as 'welfare dependents.' Their situation as teenagers who have taken on adult status as mothers is said to pose problems either in the social psychological sense that they have not yet completed the tasks of adolescence (especially schooling), or in the financial sense that they have acquired dependents before becoming independent themselves. And, by implication, they have been abandoned by the fathers of their children, who are unwilling or unable to support them.

Yet perhaps a dichotomy exists between teen mothers' understandings of and feelings about their circumstances and academic and political interpretations of these circumstances. Phoenix (1991b) conceptualized this as 'outsider' and 'insider' views. While 'outsider' discourse reflects preoccupation with issues of dependency, the discourse of teen mothers themselves shows more concern with taking on their responsibilities. The purpose of this chapter is to examine the 'insider' views of teen mothers themselves as they talk about their experiences of pregnancy and motherhood. We look at their considerations around taking care of their children, renegotiating relationships with both their own mothers and the fathers of their children, and establishing some financial stability.

In the course of a larger project focused on services for teen mothers, we interviewed sixteen young women at Linden Place, a weekly community drop-in service for young parents. Nine were 'teen mothers' in the sense that they had given birth to their first child when they were under the age of twenty, four of these, under the age of eighteen. Although the older mothers expressed similar concerns, we will focus explicitly on the interviews with the teen mothers because their 'dependence' is more often at issue.

'Teen mothers' do not remain teenagers forever. At the time we interviewed them, several of our 'teen mothers' were no longer teenagers and many (including some teenagers) had more than one child: one had two children, two had three children, one had four children and one thirty-three-year-old had given birth to seven children and adopted three others.

In order to promote rapport, the actual interviews were carried out by a graduate student closer in age to our subjects than we are. The interview was designed simply to elicit their 'story' and did not explicitly focus on dependence and independence as such. It was only in the process of analysing the interviews that we began to notice the theme of 'independence' in their talk and considerations, and the three contexts in which this theme occurred. These contexts are their relationship with the father of their child, their experience of motherhood, and their experiences of welfare. We will elaborate on each of these.

Relationships with Baby-Fathers

In order to talk about the fathers of these children and the various kinds of relationships our teen mothers had with them, we have borrowed the distinctive and usefully neutral term 'baby-father' from the residents of another setting we are studying.

A common image of the teen mother is that she has become a single mother because the baby-father has abandoned her, walking away from responsibility for the child he has fathered, because he is young or unemployed or simply wants out. One problem with this image, even when it is an accurate description of the baby-father, is that it presents the teen mother as the victim of his decisions rather than as an agent with considerations of her own about the relationship. Contrary to this image, Thompson (1995), Pearce (1993), and Phoenix (1991a) argue that young women may choose not to marry or cohabit for a variety of reasons, including the male's economic or employment status, their own ability to survive economically, the quality of the relationship, and normative expectations about marriage. Our interviews suggest that the teen mothers weighed a variety of considerations in relation to the baby-father and that pregnancy and motherhood became a frame within which they engaged in an active reassessment of the baby-father as a partner and as a father.

In some cases, teen mothers decided to go forward with the pregnancy realizing that this would disrupt their relationship with the baby-father, given his unwillingness to have a child. Faced with a choice between motherhood and the relationship, Pam and Monica, for example, chose motherhood.

I was kind of like on my own because he didn't want me to keep the baby ... He was saying that he was too young, that he couldn't afford having a baby, he wasn't working. I was the only one working ... Pretty much I made the decision by myself. He was telling me not to have it, so it was pretty hard because I knew that if I kept the baby he was going to leave. (Pam)

He was shocked. He didn't want me to give birth, he wanted me to have an abortion. But I didn't want to. He said he was too young for the responsibility and he wasn't ready yet. And he was scared ... I gave him a choice to quit drugs and to quit partying and to look up to responsibility as a father or it's over. And he took the choice that he wanted to party. (Monica)

Other teen mothers, such as Jane and Lucy, refused marriage offers from baby-fathers they sensed were unreliable, in effect ending the relationship:

He wanted to get married but I didn't feel that it would be right for my child because he was never around. And I said, 'Well, what difference would it make if we get married, you wouldn't be around.' So I refused him and he got very angry and pissed off and left. I've never seen him since. (Jane)

He was really happy at first, you know he was like, 'Oh baby, I'm going to be there for you, I love you.' And at the time he wanted to engage me and I just told him, 'No, I'm only 16, I'm going to have a kid, and I just came to the conclusion I don't want to see you anymore, you ruined my life' ... And then when I told my friends that I was pregnant, I got all this information that he is just the kind of guy that likes to go around and get girls pregnant ... like I was just attracted [to him], and the feeling was mutual until I got pregnant. (Lucy)

Motherhood then framed a more complicated set of considerations than the image of the seduced and abandoned female allows. On the one hand, mothers felt that it was important to allow contact between the baby-father and child for the child's sake, even when their own relationship with him had ended. In this sense, they welcomed his involvement with the child which, in the form of child care or gifts, was also support for themselves. On the other hand, when the baby-father's involvement with the child remained minimal, mothers were reluctant to give him any grounds for interfering with the parental responsibility that they, as mothers, had fully assumed. In this sense, they preferred to cut their losses by refusing to accept token involvement or token support.

These considerations were expressed in various ways. Jane, who had ended her relationship with her abusive second baby-father acknowledged his right to limited contact with their child, but made a point of refusing to accept anything else from him: 'I see him once in awhile. I told him, "I don't want nothing from you, I don't want no money, I don't want nothing, I'm not stopping you from seeing your child, but when you do come around to see your child that's it, but you're not taking him out anywhere."'

Dana, a somewhat older twenty-year old, made a point of managing 'on her own' so as to forestall any claims the minimally involved baby-father might make in the future: 'I don't ask him for anything. I'd rather do it on my own because then he can't say, like he won't take me to court because he wants to see his daughter. He can't tell me anything like that because he does nothing for her.' And, after valiant efforts to involve the baby-father more fully, Pam has become increasingly conflicted about his involvement, even for her child's sake:

[It was not] until the baby was five months old that I started pushing him a little bit to help me, because he wouldn't take any responsibility. He would just come around to see her and that was about it. So then I started asking him to buy clothes for the baby but he only bought clothes once and now once in a while he brings me diapers and that's all. [But] let's say I need to go to the doctor's or something, I can't really count on him to baby-sit or anything ... The truth is sometimes I really wouldn't like to see his face at all ... in the beginning he didn't really accept the baby but now he wants to be in her life. I can't really say anything. I can't really tell him you can't ... Some people tell me you shouldn't let him see her. But he wants to be there, so I can't really push him away. It is important to have a father, but if he's going to be around only sometimes, she's not going to feel like he loves her.

As these examples suggest, teen mothers were not simply the passive victims of baby-fathers who left them with a child. Instead, they played an active role in shaping their relationship with uninvolved baby-fathers, sometimes ending relationships with unreliable baby-fathers, sometimes refusing to accept token involvement and the claims this might justify, and sometimes putting up with token involvement for their child's sake.

Not all baby-fathers remained so uninvolved. Commonly, their involvement as fathers was linked to their involvement as partners. This involvement points to a second problem with the image of the teen mother as an abandoned single mother – namely, that teen mothers are not necessarily single mothers (Macintyre and Cunningham-Burley 1993; Phoenix 1991a). Among our teen mothers, two married as teenagers, one to her first baby-father, and the second to her second baby-father. Three others are living in fully committed relationships with a baby-father partner.

Yet even in ongoing relationships with genuinely supportive baby-fathers, teen mothers acted to preserve a margin of independence in various ways. In the most unusual case, Jane (who is still a teenager) does not live with her third baby-father despite their fully committed relationship and fully shared child care; they live in apartments next door to one another, an arrangement that allows him to take care of the baby (especially at night) so that she can pay greater attention to the current needs of her middle child.

In other cases, teen mothers acted to preserve a margin of independence in their financial arrangements with the baby-father. Sally, for example, insisted that her baby-father could not 'live off her' with no job, but also insisted equally that she would not live off him like in 'the old days.' She says: 'Back then, [women] had to stay home and the man had to pay for everything. This is not the old days, this is now. This is the '90s. If you have a guy that helps you, supports you, OK, you're lucky. But then if you don't, you've got to do it your way ... [Others] ask me are you married, who pays the rent, is that you or is it him ... Does it matter? Do I have to sit on my bum all day and my husband gotta go to work? I don't like that. I don't want him to support me. If I wanted that, I would've stayed home.' And although she and the baby-father share expenses, she insists on keeping her name on the lease and paying the rent.

Nelly, who regards her two-year live-in relationship and upcoming marriage to her baby-father as a partnership, finds the prospect of financial dependence on him troubling: '[To] have a husband that's supporting me – I'd feel weird because I've been supporting myself like mostly ... Because so far I've been supporting him all the time. So it's kind of equal ... I got him out of this bad situation so, but for him to support me all the time I would feel uncomfortable. I'd have to help out somehow with something, you know.'

The considerations these teen mothers had regarding their relationships with baby-fathers suggest that they do not expect to depend on baby-fathers financially, and indeed prefer to retain a degree of independence in this respect. Even in committed and enduring relationships, they do not expect their partners to be 'breadwinners.' In evaluating their continued involvement with baby-fathers, they are more likely to consider whether the baby-father will 'be there' for them and their children, and to value support in the form of child care and shared financial responsibility. Mothers who have ended their relationship with the baby-father also value support in the form of babysitting, but view token financial support in the absence of real responsibility for the child as a potential threat to their parental independence.

Motherhood as a Path to Maturity

Independence also arose as a theme in relation to motherhood as a pathway to maturity. For teen mothers who lived at home, the issue of independence arose in the context of the relationships they had with their own mothers, particularly around the work of mothering. For teen mothers from disrupted homes, the issue of independence focused instead on the opportunities that motherhood offered for moral reform (Jacobs 1994; McMahon 1995).

Even though the pregnancy and motherhood of a teenage daughter may create considerable upset for their families, the parents of teen mothers still living at home usually rally to support their daughters both emotionally and practically in helping to care for their grandchildren (Geronimus 1992; Forste and Tienda 1992). For example, in describing how her pregnancy had brought her closer to her mother, Monica said: 'She kept by me and then I began to feel like I could trust her and everything and I got closer to her. And day by day as the time flew I became closer to her.' As teen mothers became increasingly involved with mothering, however, they came to experience this support, particularly around mothering itself, as interference with their own responsibilities and claimed their independence, usually by moving out. Jacobs has similarly noted the tensions that can arise as young mothers seek to 'establish their independence within the framework of motherhood' (1994: 456).

Despite her closeness to her mother, Monica, for example, now prefers living on her own. She says: 'I'd rather be living on my own because it's easier for me to care for my son alone. Like my mom, she's way old-fashioned ... I try to explain to her this is like 1995, they're raising children differently. And like she's always nagging me and like she's totally nervous ... I found it more relaxing [now] ... I can give him a bath, feed him, raise him how I want ... Especially I find it's easier for me and for my son to get a closer bond [without] my mom always nagging ... Because he needs his mother the most. And my problem is it's always my mother or my sister and it's like it's my right for [the children] to come to me when they feel lousy.'

Alice also decided to move out, despite the added expense, in order to claim her independence as a mother from her mother. She talks about the tensions that developed between her and her mother: 'She was playing more mother than I was and I felt the worrying. I needed to be on my own and to experience me being on my own. To be a mother to my son.'

Claiming one's independence as a mother from one's own mother is by no means unique to teen mothers. In her analysis of how women experience motherhood, Martha McMahon (1995) suggests that working-class women, who tend to be younger when they have their first child, experience themselves as acquiring maturity through mothering. She contrasts this with middle-class women who feel they must achieve maturity before having a child: 'the middle-class women indicated they felt they had to achieve maturity before having a child, but working-class women's accounts suggest that many saw themselves as achieving maturity through having a child' (p. 110). In this sense, the process of having a child, leaving home, and claiming responsibility for mothering from their own mothers is, for the teen mothers we have just described, a path to maturity and independence. This theme, which sees motherhood as the route to achieving recognized adult status, is echoed in the literature (Jacobs 1994; Pearce 1993). The fact that young mothers in our study place more importance on their independence than on child-care support suggests that they experience motherhood as a way of growing up.

Among the teen mothers we interviewed, this experience of claiming independence by moving out can be contrasted with the rather different experience of getting thrown out. After years of separation from her drug-involved mother, Lucy and her sister had rejoined the household before Lucy got pregnant. Expecting support from her mother, she had scarcely returned from the hospital when her mother announced that she had to leave.

Thrown out on her own, Lucy was terrified about living alone, about supporting herself (she found out about welfare from friends), and about taking care of her child. She recalls her experiences: 'I felt really secure when I was living at my mom's house, because there was somebody there every night with me. When I moved out, like for two months, [it] was just me and the baby, and I was really scared because I didn't know the neighbourhood that well. There was a lot of break-ins, a lot of rapes in the area, and then I just came to the decision I can't take it anymore and I asked [the man who would become] my husband to move in with me and I felt a lot better ... but there was still a lot of stress when the baby got sick and she cried all night and she was teething – it was hell.' Lucy's reaction suggests that the experience of independence has to be claimed not imposed and that teen mothers are more likely to claim independence once they have become comfortable with the tasks of motherhood.

Like Lucy, several teen mothers we interviewed also came from problem homes and had been 'on their own,' sometimes as 'system kids,' for some time before getting pregnant. For them, the experience of motherhood provided a different pathway to maturity by serving as a powerful motive for reforming their lives. Jacobs describes how choosing to become a mother can be positive for teenagers living in difficult situations. She refers to motherhood as 'a choice to save one's self' (1994: 453). Our data suggest that the experience of reform begins with pregnancy, which calls for the revision of bad habits for the developing baby's sake, but then extends to motherhood and hopes for becoming better parents than their own mothers had been. Lucy, for example, says that the birth of her daughter 'changed my life because, from after I had her, I stopped drinking, I stopped doing drugs, I stopped going to all these parties, I stopped associating with the people I did so I wouldn't be involved with that anymore.' She also clearly connects these changes with the inadequacy of her own upbringing and her desire to do better for her own child. She comments, 'I would never abandon her to go and do like my mother did to me, so it was like a really strong point in my life where it's like you've got to change, you don't need all of this shit ... I didn't want anything from my mother to reflect on me and my child ... Every time I see something that my mother did, or what I heard that my mother used to do, I tried to change my life so it doesn't have to be like hers.'

For Jane, another 'system kid' who now at the age of eighteen is the mother of three, the decision to have her first child led her to quit using drugs, to end her relationship with an unsuitable baby-father, and to change her friends. She says, 'So when I found out I was pregnant I was scared because I was doing drugs ... So I went to Linden Place and I spoke to a nurse there and I said listen, you know ... I really want to have this baby ... At that time I didn't really want to party... Most of my friends were involved into drugs and their party was drugs, or alcohol and I wasn't really involved into drugs or alcohol at that time. All I was focusing on was my child and my life, trying to get myself back on my feet because, you know, Social Services was becoming involved ... I wanted to prove to myself, and also prove to my son, that I didn't need other people to help me.'

For Jane, too, the experience of motherhood is framed by her abusive background; through motherhood she has become more understanding of her parents but at the same time all the more firmly convinced to treat her own children differently: '[Being a mother] made me realize really what my mum and dad were going through, and even to this day, I mean, when I'm alone and I sit and say, "wow it's really hard raising children in this world today," and now I know what my mom and dad went through ... [But] I don't scream [at my kids] because that's what my parents did ... I don't do what my parents did to me. I listen to my children, you know, because I never got listened to as a child myself.'

For teen mothers from disrupted homes, pregnancy and motherhood thus served as a pathway to maturity through what McMahon (1995) calls 'moral reform.' She contrasts middle-class and working-class experiences of motherhood and contends that working-class women experience motherhood as 'moral reform' – that is, as an opportunity to become a better person through taking on the responsibilities of motherhood.

Perhaps more than working-class women in general, teen mothers from disrupted homes have a special attraction to redemption through motherhood: they have experienced the costs of disorderly family lives, and sometimes as a result they have been leading disorderly lives themselves. Pregnancy and motherhood thus provide a strong incentive for change.

The independence concerns and discourse of teen mothers thus arose in two rather different ways around the issue of motherhood as a pathway to maturity. For teen mothers living at home, motherhood became the context in which they claimed their independent adult status as mothers by moving out. For teen mothers from disrupted homes, motherhood became the context for moral reform.

Welfare

Since the birth of their children all of the mothers and their children, except for one, have been supported by welfare. Only one was already on welfare prior to the birth of her child.

The path from pregnancy to welfare was particularly striking because half of all the women we interviewed, including four teen mothers, were in fact self-supporting prior to the birth of their first child. For them, having a child meant that they had to stop working, often with no alternative means of support other than welfare. Pam, who had been supporting herself for a year before getting pregnant, continued to work until she was seven months pregnant. She talks about her experiences in the workplace: 'First, I was working in a factory where they used to make women's clothes. It was pretty hard, actually, and then I got a job at the Eaton Center as a cashier in one of the little restaurants ... I used to start at 10 o'clock in the morning and I used to finish at 9 o'clock at night, and even that wasn't enough. I was working six, seven days a week, and it wasn't enough really to support me because you don't make that much. You know, at minimum wage you don't make enough money to live on comfortably.' Sally, another teen mother, also continued working into her eighth month of pregnancy, quitting only when her boss told her that welfare programs existed.

The four teen mothers who were still living at home when they got pregnant are also supported by welfare. This includes Alice and Thelma who were in high school, and Lucy and Monica who had dropped out of school. For two of them, who were thrown out of their homes, welfare made survival possible. For the other two, welfare made it possible to choose to leave home. Although welfare recipients in the Province of Quebec are docked $100 a month for sharing a residence with anyone else, teen mothers usually could save more living at home because of the support their families provided. Their decision to move out thus involved some financial sacrifice.

New to motherhood and welfare, all of the teen mothers had to learn how to manage on very little. For some, this was a more dramatic experience than for others. Despite the difficulties they had managing on welfare, even the teen mothers who had worked felt they could not afford to go back to work after the baby was born given the new costs and risks of working. As Pam, who had supported herself as a factory worker and cashier, observed: 'The way I see it, I could go to work right now, but I wouldn't really make it, because I would be making about $600 a month and that's not even enough – already with the money that you get from welfare, you don't get enough for the month. And imagine: if I go to work, I'm going to have to pay the babysitter, the bus pass, this and that, so it wouldn't really work ... Some people might imagine that it's fun for us to get pregnant because we get out of working, and we get out of going to school or whatever, but it's not. It's pretty hard, you know.'

These young women worried not just about the extra expenses that going back to work would involve, but also about the unreliability of the kinds of jobs they could get. Lucy, for example, describes her concerns: 'I filled out an application and then after I sent it back [there was] a delay. So it was like, "Oh my God, am I still going to get this job?" And then I was surprised when they actually called me. And then I have the worries of working there, because they just laid off a lot of people. Oh my God, am I going to take the chance, take the job, get off of welfare, and then get laid off? I'm really worried about that because then I'll be in the unemployment line.'

The young women's concerns about the unreliable nature of the job market are similarly reflected in research studies on women's work. For example, McKinnon and Ahola-Sidaway (1994) point out that 'nonstandard' forms of work (part-time, short-term, temporary help, self-employment, at-home work) are becoming more frequent and with them wages and basic employee power are declining. Thus, there is a strong likelihood that many young women (especially those who leave school with high school graduation or less) will find themselves in jobs within women-dominated niches, doing work that pays little, has few benefits, and offers minimal job security.

Of the teen mothers that we interviewed, only Sally had returned to work, largely out of discomfort with being on welfare. Despite her commitment to working, her experience expresses and bears out the same concerns other teen mothers had about the costs and risks of working. She says:

After a year I went back to work ... What I get from work is not a lot. If I work full-time, usually 48 hours [a week], I get about $600 a month, and that's nothing because my rent is about $500 ... I told welfare that I got a job, they cut my cheque a week after. It's been five months I've been working, and it's been five months since they haven't helped ... I get this feeling that because I'm working, that's it, I don't get a dime ... After a year, for someone to have a baby, it's really hard just to go back to work. Okay, it's not a lot of parents that go back to work ... Now, where I work, it's like a weekly thing, I go to my boss [and say], 'Are you gonna fire me? ... [Because] if you're gonna fire me, please give me two weeks because I have a kid now ... I can't starve her for two weeks because you fire me.'

The teen mothers, like the other young mothers we interviewed, thus weighed the kinds of jobs they could get against the costs and risks of working and, with one exception, chose welfare over work as the more responsible course of action at this time. They did, however, see the welfare option as temporary. They viewed it an appropriate choice given their responsibilities for young children and the lack of access to day care and other support services.

Conclusion

Our interviews suggest that teen mothers are making decisions about having children, about their relationships with baby-fathers, about leaving home, and about staying on welfare rather than looking for work, for their own reasons. These often have to do with claiming their adult responsibilities as mothers while preserving a degree of independence in relation to their baby-fathers and their own mothers.

A community resource like Linden Place supports the young mothers in assuming their parental responsibilities despite their limited financial and family resources. It provides concrete assistance in the form of clothing and furniture exchange and a drop-in centre to meet and talk with other mothers while their children attend a supervised play group.

Insofar as the experiences described by the teen mothers that we interviewed are common, recent proposals put forward in the United States, for example, to make teen mothers live at home would seem counter-productive. Such policies would prevent some teen mothers from claiming the independence their motherhood leads them to feel ready for, and would place other teen mothers back into the disrupted homes that they have managed to escape, while also disrupting the process of moral reform that motherhood has generated.

Our interviews suggest that we need to find ways to support teen mothers in the process of becoming independent. In relation to the baby-fathers, this means supporting their choices around the extent to which they chose to be involved or not involved – emotionally and financially – with the fathers. It means supporting these women in their efforts to secure adequate housing and child care.

In relation to their mothers, it means recognizing and supporting young mothers in their development as adults and mothers. It means accepting their choices around parenting and promoting the development of an expanded notion of 'family' to include broader community networks than simply the teen mother's immediate family.

In relation to welfare, it means providing sufficient resources for teen mothers to have a decent income rather than restricting them to a survival allowance. It means working with young women to develop services that respond to their needs for education, health, housing, and child care.

Some might suggest that these conclusions are 'unrealistic' or unworkable given the current economic climate of cutbacks to social services. However, given the efforts of teen mothers such as the ones we interviewed to assume their responsibilities and claim their independent adult status, we urge policy makers and service providers to work towards policies and resources that will contribute to continued self-sufficiency for young mothers.

Acknowledgment

This work was supported by the Social Sciences and Humanities Research Council of Canada, Strategic Grants Program, Women and Change. The opinions expressed in this chapter do not necessarily reflect those of the council.

References

Adams, G., Pittman, K., and O'Brien, R. (1993). 'Adolescent and Young Adult Fathers: Problems and Solutions.' In A. Lawson and D. Rhode, eds., *The Politics of Pregnancy*, pp. 189–215. New Haven: Yale University Press.

Forste, R., and Tienda, M. (1992). 'Race and Ethnic Variation in the Schooling Consequences of Female Adolescent Sexual Activity.' *Social Science Quarterly* 73(1): 12–30.

Geronimus, A. (1992). 'Clashes of Common Sense: On the Previous Child Care Experience of Teenage Mothers-to-Be.' *Human Organization* 51(4): 318–29.

Griffin, L. (1993). *Representations of Youth*. Cambridge: Polity Press.

Jacobs, J. (1994). 'Gender, Race, Class and the Trend Toward Early Motherhood.' *Journal of Contemporary Ethnography* 22(4): 442–62.

Kelly, D. (1996). 'Stigma Stories: Four Discourses about Teen Mothers, Welfare, and Poverty.' *Youth and Society* 27(4): 421–49.

Lawson, A., and Rhode, D., eds. (1993). *The Politics of Pregnancy*. New Haven: Yale University Press.

Lesko, N. (1995). 'The "Leaky Needs" of School-Aged Mothers: An Examination of U.S. Programs and Policies.' *Curriculum Inquiry*. 25(2): 177–205.

Macintyre, S., and Cunningham-Burley, S. (1993). 'Teenage Pregnancy as a Social Problem: A Perspective from the United Kingdom.' In Lawson and Rhode, eds., pp. 59–73.

McKinnon, M., and Ahola-Sidaway, J. (1994). 'Office Workers, Factory Workers, Cashiers or Cooks: A North American Perspective on Vocational Education Reform at the Secondary School Level.' *Vocational Aspect of Education* 46(1): 41–60.

McMahon, M. (1995). *Engendering Motherhood*. New York: Guilford.

Pearce, D. (1993). '"Children Having Children": Teenage Pregnancy and Public Policy from the Woman's Perspective.' In Lawson and Rhode, eds.

Phoenix, A. (1991a). *Young Mothers?* Cambridge: Polity Press.

– (1991b). 'Mothers under Twenty: Outsider and Insider Views.' In A. Phoenix, A. Woollett, and E. Lloyd, eds., *Motherhood Meanings, Practice and Ideologies*, pp. 46–57, 86–102. London: Sage.

Thompson, S. (1995). *Going All the Way*. New York: Hill and Wang.

5

A Critical Feminist Perspective on Teen Pregnancy and Parenthood

DEIRDRE M. KELLY

Public opinion polls in Canada tell us that our adults are every bit as concerned about teen pregnancy as our neighbours to the south. One survey found that 90 per cent of those polled believe 'unwanted teenage pregnancies in Canada is a serious problem' (Bozinoff and Turcotte 1992). The pollsters phrased their question vaguely enough to elicit concern across the ideological spectrum, from those worried about access to contraception and abortion or sympathizing with a 'girl in trouble' to those perceiving a threat to taxpayers and the traditional family. In any event, pregnant teens, especially those who become mothers,[1] can be seen as magnets for the anxieties, frustrations, and anger of many different groups in society; as such, teen mothers 'serve to condense and transform a range of discontents and also to build political coalitions' (Edelman 1988: 80).

The image of the teen mother is pregnant with meaning; as a 'condensation symbol,' the image 'draws its intensity from the associations it represses' (Edelman 1988: 73). For people concerned about changing family structures, gender relations, and sexual 'permissiveness,' teen mothers represent adolescent female sexuality out of control. For those worried about the breakdown of traditional lines of authority, teen mothers represent rebellion against parents and other adults. For those anxious about global economic restructuring, teen mothers represent 'dropouts' who refuse to compete yet expect the welfare system to support their 'poor choices.' For those distressed about poverty and child abuse, teen mothers represent both the cause and consequence. Unstated assumptions about 'the good mother,' 'the good student,' and 'the good citizen' – shaped by inequalities based on age, gender, sexuality, class, and race – often form the backdrop to the ongoing morality play about teen mothers (see Kelly, in press).

To the extent that these assumptions and repressed associations can be identified, explicated, and viewed in a fuller social context, the easier it will be for those who feel teen mothers are being unfairly scapegoated to challenge the political uses to which they are being put and to present alternative views. I undertake part of this work here by focusing on how teen mothers have come to signal expansion of the welfare state in a period when Canadians across party lines are evincing fiscally conservative attitudes (Peters, this volume). Specifically, I summarize scholarship that calls into question a number of widely held assumptions about teen mothers, welfare, and poverty. I then present a critical feminist perspective on adolescent sexuality, pregnancy, and childbearing. In an attempt to gauge the relevance to Canada of the American experience and research, I begin by briefly comparing the two contexts of the policy debate on teen pregnancy and motherhood.

Debating Teen Pregnancy and Motherhood in the Liberal Welfare State: A Comparison of Canada and the United States

In March of 1995 national Reform Party leader Preston Manning travelled to Washington, DC to meet with the speaker of the U.S. House of Representatives, Republican Newt Gingrich. The two men spoke of their common political agendas. Both oppose 'big government,' support market economics, and espouse 'traditional values' (both were raised as Baptists). In what *Maclean's* described as a 'political love-in on Gingrich's weekly cable-TV show,' the Republican leader credited Manning and Reform's 1993 campaign as a model and inspiration for the GOP's successful electoral program (*Maclean's* 1995).

For his part, Manning basked in Gingrich's endorsement but, for the benefit of Canadians watching at home, he also attempted to portray himself as more moderate than his American ally. When introduced as 'a real revolutionary in our midst,' Manning replied, 'A revolutionary should neither look like one nor act like one to get ahead in our country' (*Maclean's* 1995). At a press conference, Manning took pains to state that he did not agree with some of the harshest measures proposed in the Republican agenda, specifically the denial of welfare to teenage mothers (Canadian Press 1995).

The meeting between Manning and Gingrich points to some of the similarities as well as some of differences in the political cultures of the two men and their countries. In addition, it shows how the political debates cross the border – in both directions. First to the differences. In an effort to gain wider credibility, Manning did not want to be perceived by his fellow Canadians as 'revolutionary,' whereas this label harks back to a proud beginning for many Americans. Nor does Manning want to be seen as intent on destroying social programs – an important way that many Canadians distinguish their national identity from that of Americans. And it is true that Canada's social safety net produced markedly lower poverty rates than did the U.S. social programs in the mid-1980s (Blank and Hanratty 1993). In addition, Canada has a more equitable way of funding its public schools and a universal health insurance system.

Indeed, the difference between the two countries' health systems provides one explanation for the fact that the American teen pregnancy rate is more than twice as high as Canada's. Canada's system provides coverage for virtually all of its citizens, including reproductive and contraceptive services.[2] In the United States, 'government-sponsored health programs cover primarily individuals aged 65 and older and people with disabilities (Medicare) and those with very low incomes (Medicaid). Most health care coverage in the United States is provided through private, employment-based health plans with varying levels of coverage. But about 15% of the U.S. population is uninsured' (Delbanco et al. 1997: 70). U.S. plans provide limited, if any, coverage of reproductive and contraceptive services. Such services, furthermore, are provided by relatively inaccessible specialists, whereas in Canada these services are provided through primary care providers, such as general practitioners (ibid.).

Canada's universal health system represents a nod towards a social democratic welfare state model, and, historically, Canada has had more generous and universal social programs than in the United States. But over the past twenty-five years, there has been a 'dramatic reversal' (Cohen 1993: 266). Taken overall, Canada is, like the United States, an archetypal liberal welfare state. Both countries, for example, have stigmatizing, means-tested welfare programs that provide only modest benefits. In both countries, the middle classes are 'institutionally wedded to the market' rather than the welfare state (Esping-Andersen 1990: 32); they rely, for example, on private pensions and child care arrangements.[3] Without having forged 'middle-class loyalties' to the welfare state, both countries thus are vulnerable to periodic welfare-state backlash movements and tax revolts (ibid.: 33). Although Gingrich is no doubt the most famous political leader to have pandered to middle-class anger at the welfare state by invoking negative images of teen mothers, politicians throughout both countries have done likewise.

In addition, both Canada and the United States have similar antimodern, 'pro-life,' 'pro-family' movements to which politicians like Manning and Gingrich appeal for support. In fact, the two movements have made alliances across national boundaries (e.g., the influential Christian Coalition, led by Pat Robertson in the United States). Leaders have spearheaded attacks on reproductive rights, creating barriers to access to abortion and contraception (e.g., British Columbia Task Force 1994). 'Pro-life' supporters in British Columbia, for example, have, in the recent past, gained control of regional hospital boards and brought abortions to a halt. More recently, they have formed the majority on school boards and insisted on an abstinence-only approach to sexuality education.

Many Canadians, like many Americans, continue to take a moralistic stance towards teen sexuality and contraception. Neither government has played an active role in providing public information about reproductive health. Sex education programs vary by province or state and by school district. It is not surprising that Canada's teen pregnancy, birth, and abortion rates are higher than in countries like the Netherlands, which combines a major sex education program (which extends beyond the schools to the mass media) with a very liberal, non-moralistic contraception policy (Ketting and Visser 1994).

Unlike with issues such as sex education and abortion, conservative politicians seem in teen motherhood (and single-parent families generally) to have hit upon an issue that resonates beyond social conservatives in North America. Direct or veiled attacks on teen mothers seem to promise savings to taxpayers in two ways: by reducing the amount spent on them directly, and by discouraging others from becoming teen mothers who feel entitled to make a claim on the state's resources. In this political climate, centrist leaders like Prime Minister Jean Chrétien and President Bill Clinton have presided over decentralization and reduced funding of social programs to the provinces and states, where punitive measures have been taken against teen mothers as supposed examples of the 'undeserving' poor.

In sum, Canada's teen pregnancy and birth rates are lower than those in the United States. However, for reasons shared with the United States – the class character of its liberal welfare state, its Puritanical roots, and the ascendancy of conservative populism in its present political culture – an increasing number of Canada's citizens seem predisposed to seeing teen mothers as icons of welfare dependency. Indeed, the *Globe and Mail* asserted recently that for 'many' Canadians, teen pregnancy 'is a proxy for the state of the nation's moral health' (Mitchell 1998: A6). As Gingrich's admiration for Reform Party strategy suggests, it is not just that conservative attitudes are drifting across the border into Canada; the animus towards the welfare state is also home grown.

A Feminist Interpretation of Research on Teen Mothers, Welfare, and Poverty

My admittedly partial view is that teen mothers provide a convenient scapegoat for, among others, those who would ignore the structural causes of poverty. As a critical feminist, I participate in an oppositional discourse about teen mothers. Before laying out that stance and exploring its implications for policy, it is important to summarize feminist and other scholarly research in this area that calls into question assumptions commonly made about teen mothers, welfare, and poverty.

Poverty is not a straightforward cause of early motherhood. There appear to be many other precipitating factors. Phoenix (1991: 90) reviewed the research in North America and England and concluded: 'While many young people experience poverty and do not have "proper jobs," most young women who lack money do not become mothers. Poverty is thus the context within which the overwhelming majority of instances of motherhood under 20 occur, rather than a causative factor.'

That said, low-income women's reproductive choices may be severely constrained, given the social and material circumstances of their lives. Researchers in North America have found consistently that social class shapes the various 'choices' that culminate in teen parenthood. Young women from higher socioeconomic status backgrounds are less likely to become sexually active at an early age, are more likely to use contraception, particularly at first intercourse, and if they do get pregnant, they are more likely to obtain abortions (British Columbia Task Force 1994; Miller and Moore 1990; Nathanson 1991: 161–2; Orton, this volume). The relatively few young women who do place their children for adoption 'are more affluent, have higher aspirations for themselves, and are performing better in school' (Luker 1996: 162).

Teen motherhood does not necessarily cause poverty. To examine the long-term economic outcomes associated with female adolescent marriage and childbearing, Grindstaff (1988) looked at women who were thirty years old in the 1981 Canadian census. As expected, he found that women who became mothers when young obtained less formal schooling, but in terms of income, the early childbearing women did not have substantially less than the women who became mothers later. The timing of marriage and childbearing was 'secondary to the overriding issue of whether the woman has a child' (Grindstaff 1988: 54). In other words, today's economy does not easily accommodate women of any age who combine childrearing and paid work. The data also showed that at least some teen mothers eventually do quite well economically. Grindstaff concluded that 'ways must be found that will permit women with children to participate fully in the economic life of the society' (ibid.: 56).

Welfare payments do not entice women to become pregnant. Most of the research in this area has been done in the United States. Wilson and Neckerman (1987, cited in Phoenix 1991: 87) reviewed U.S. studies that explored the connection between welfare policies, levels of welfare benefits, and the incidence of teen motherhood and single motherhood; they found no relationship between welfare provision and low-income women's childbearing.

In Canada, a few provincial governments have investigated the claim that availability of welfare benefits encourages teen pregnancy and found it to be without merit (on Alberta, see 'Study' 1989; on Nova Scotia, see Clark et al. 1991). In fact, an international study found that countries with some of the highest welfare benefits, such as Sweden, have the lowest teen pregnancy rates (Jones et al. 1986).

Researchers have not established that teen motherhood is a prime cause of welfare dependency. To show such a causal link, one would need to design longitudinal studies, which are expensive, difficult, and comparatively rare. More often, researchers conduct statistical analyses of large extant data bases; these studies have found strong correlations between teen motherhood, school dropout, reduced earnings, and welfare status. Yet new research suggests that these earlier cross-sectional studies may have overstated the negative socioeconomic consequences of teen childbearing (Geronimus and Korenman 1992).

The few longitudinal studies that exist tend to paint a much less bleak portrait of teen mothers and their children. Pozsonyi (1973) did a longitudinal study of unmarried, first-time mothers who kept their children and who were clients of a family and children's services agency in Ontario, checking back with the mothers at six-month intervals for the first eighteen months after the baby's birth. At the last face-to-face interview, only 30 per cent were receiving welfare and 26 per cent had married. Pozsonyi concluded: 'The majority of unmarried mothers and their children were found to fare well in the community' (1973: 59; see also Clark, this volume).

Studies in the United States have followed women who became teen mothers over decades; they have refuted the stereotype of teen mothers as chronic welfare recipients (Furstenberg, Brooks-Gunn, and Morgan 1987; Harris 1997). Over time, many of the women in these studies obtained paid work, achieved more education, and increased their levels of employment. The lack of affordable child care services, however, often hindered them (Harris 1997).

Fewer teen mothers would not mean a big cut in welfare spending. According to Statistics Canada, single-parent families (male-led and female-led) made up only 13 per cent of all families in 1991, and only 6.4 per cent of families led by female lone parents were led by young women (aged fifteen to twenty-four) (Mitchell 1993). Further, if the ranks of teen mothers somehow thinned significantly, this alone would not result in commensurate savings to taxpayers. Luker (1991: 80) summarizes the findings of U.S. policy analysts Richard Wertheimer and Kristin Moore, who 'have estimated that if by some miracle we could cut the teen birth rate in half, welfare costs would be reduced by 20 percent, rather than 50 percent, because many of these young women would still need welfare for children born to them when they were no longer teens.'

This conclusion is underscored by a group of U.S. studies that have used innovative ways to assess whether young women already disadvantaged by having grown up in poverty and so forth (i.e., those most likely to become teen mothers) are further disadvantaged by teen motherhood in and of itself. Geronimus and Korenman (1992) compared a national sample of sisters and found no correlation between teen childbearing and high school graduation or subsequent family income. Corcoran and Kunz found 'teen mothers to be no more likely to be welfare recipients after age 25 than their sisters who became mothers at older ages. So too, Joseph Hotz et al. comparing teens who gave birth to those who miscarried in recent data from the National Longitudinal Survey of Youth concluded that a teen mother is no more likely to participate in welfare programs, to have her labor market earnings reduced, or to experience significant losses in spousal earnings, than the same woman would have experienced if she had delayed childbearing' (Geronimus 1997: 5).

To be sure, a subset of women spend extended periods of time receiving government assistance. They tend to be those who have had troubled childhoods, left school before getting pregnant, and face multiple and severe barriers to paid employment – beyond those that result from teen motherhood. As sociologist Frank Furstenberg has written in the U.S. context, 'State government can remove them from the welfare rolls but it will not help them make the transition into the labor force without intensive and extensive assistance that certainly costs more than the modest funding provided by AFDC [welfare], as we presently know it' (1997: x–xi).

In summary, many of the problems facing teen mothers are problems for all women with children, and teenagers cope as well or as poorly as others in the same situation. Further, women who grow up in poverty, as many teen mothers have, face long odds of doing well later in life whether or not they become pregnant early in life. Obtaining further schooling is no guarantee of access to meaningful, well-paid work and affordable child care.[4]

Towards a Critical Feminist Stance on Teen Pregnancy and Motherhood

There are a number of feminist lenses through which to view the subordination of women; there is no unified feminist perspective. But a feminist stance typically indicates, at a minimum, a focus on gender – an oppressive, ideological structure that is socially produced through unequal relations of power – and a political commitment to 'changing unequal power relations between men and women in society' (Weedon 1988: 1). In synthesizing and extending feminist thinking on the issue of teen pregnancy and motherhood, I have found the work of multicultural and critical (poststructuralist, socialist, and materialist) feminists most useful and persuasive. As a way to signal the importance of a deep restructuring of the existing political economy to the creation of a more just society, I refer to the stance I outline below as *critical feminist*.

Only recently have those with such critical views – feminist scholars and practitioners, for example – begun to articulate a position on teen pregnancy and childbearing (e.g., Lawson and Rhode 1993). This inattention can be partially attributed to the fact that feminists, too, have been caught up in what I have called elsewhere the 'good choices' discourse (Kelly, in press). In seeking to explain the paucity of feminist analysis in this area, Nathanson (1991) notes that, on the one hand, 'empowering women to make their *own* choices' has been a goal of feminism. On the other hand, though, feminists (particularly white, middle-class ones) have found it difficult to view positively young (particularly working-class and ethnic minority) women's choices to have sex and to become mothers: 'To "choose" motherhood is to be suspected by modern feminists either of being victimized or of copping out. In neither circumstance is the choice ideologically acceptable' (1991: 222).

As Nathanson points out, feminists have a different conception of the good society 'and the place of women in it' (1991: 222). It is worth trying to articulate a critical feminist stance towards adolescent sexuality, pregnancy, and childbearing in the hopes that it might gain more political force and thus influence policy. In the remainder of this chapter, I attempt to sketch such a stance. In the process, I will critique the dominant discourse – including such ideologically loaded terms as *personal responsibility* and *welfare dependency* – arguing that it frames the problems facing teen mothers as solely individual rather than also structural. That is, conventional wisdom does not acknowledge that becoming a teen mother might, under certain circumstances, be a 'good choice,' given the ways in which the current economic and political order restricts other choices for young people.

Reproductive Rights for All Women, Regardless of Age, Class, and Race

Feminists have long supported a woman's right to choose when, where, how, and with whom to give birth. Among mainstream feminists, the struggle for reproductive rights has focused on making contraception and abortion services more widely available, safer, and less stigmatized. Feminists have also stressed the need not only to increase access to sexuality education but to improve it, guided by an invitation to 'adolescents to explore what feels good and bad, desirable and undesirable, grounded in experiences, needs, and limits' (Fine 1988: 33).

Feminists employing a multicultural framework have tended to recognize more often than others that reproductive rights must extend beyond prevention issues and abstract talk of rights to the concrete needs of socially disadvantaged women and the ability to bear children and raise them in a healthy, supportive environment. Multicultural feminists, among others, recognize that low-income women, disabled women,

women of colour, and young women have, historically, been more vulnerable to coercive sterilization and birth control policies, supported by people who erroneously believe or imply that social problems are caused by disadvantaged groups of women bearing children (Luker 1996; McLaren 1990; Roberts 1997).

First Nations parents, for example, must cope with the legacy of colonialism (including forced residential schooling), institutional racism, and poverty. As a spokesperson from the Indian Homemakers' Association of British Columbia put it: 'The courts are racist towards native women. They don't want to hear the voices of native mothers. We must have a beautiful two-bedroom house with new paint, wall-to-wall carpeting and wonderful curtains. When we don't, they take away our children' (quoted in Bolan 1993: A1).

Mindful of this history, I believe society should respect and support the right of young women to bear and raise their own children. To do otherwise compromises the reproductive rights agenda as a whole. Nearly two-thirds of births to teenagers are to women who are eighteen or nineteen years old (Wadhera and Millar 1997: 13); they are legal adults, entitled to vote as citizens. As mentioned earlier, the available research suggests that were they to postpone childbearing into their twenties, most would still be poor. Few people would want to deny their fellow citizens the right to have children on the basis of income level. In this light, restrictive policies, although ostensibly aimed at teen mothers, can be seen ultimately to threaten the full reproductive rights of all but the most privileged.

Respect and support for teen mothers means providing a variety of resources without judgment and surveillance. One model for this is Jessie's Centre for Teenagers in Toronto, which is run as a feminist collective. Founder June Callwood describes Jessie's philosophy: 'The feminist approach of respect for teenage women and encouragement to enable them to achieve self-worth and independence happens also to be the most effective way of helping their babies to thrive ... It provides what young moms, what *all* moms, need: friendship, information, relief' (1982: 38).

Suggestions by policy makers, both conservative and liberal, to 'restigmatize' teen pregnancy and motherhood are misguided. To start with, teen mothers, as I have argued elsewhere (Kelly 1996, 1998; see also Kaufman, this volume), still face considerable stigma, albeit within updated constructs. Were it not so, I would not in the course of my research be hearing stories from young women who desperately denied their pregnancies for as long as they could. To the extent that mores about childbearing outside of marriage have become less rigid over the past twenty-five years, calling for 'the return of shame' (to quote a *Newsweek* cover title) is impractical and unlikely to succeed (Luker 1996). Although a dubious means of lowering teen pregnancy and birth rates, efforts to increase stigma and shame may produce more denial. 'A shame-ridden subject lacks a sense of entitlement, she settles for less than she deserves; she is more easily dominated' (Bartkey 1996: 225).

Nurturing Agency, Promoting Social Responsibility

Rather than seeking to create more shame-ridden subjects, we should be nurturing agency in young people, partly by taking collective action to change the context that currently so limits their sexual and reproductive choices, and partly by supporting them as they attempt to 'do the right thing' under difficult circumstances. A critical feminist perspective helps to locate the various choices that culminate in teen motherhood in historical and social context. It illuminates, among other things: that unequal power relations between men and women complicate the negotiation of contraceptive use; that in the classroom and beyond, pregnancy options are weighted unequally; that material and cultural conditions (e.g., barriers to access to contraception and abortion services, mixed messages about sexuality, and the pervasiveness of poverty and unemployment, child abuse, racism, heterosexism, and sexism) constrict the choices available.

The prevailing policy discourse condemns teen mothers, particularly those on welfare, as lacking in 'personal responsibility.' A critical feminist discourse would highlight instead how our major institutions have failed young people. In addition to pursuing a reinvigorated campaign for reproductive rights, for example, we need to tackle high youth unemployment. In short, we need to create more and better choices for young people 'so that having a baby is not the only or most attractive one on the horizon' (Luker 1996: 183). This strategy could be summarized as the promotion of social responsibility.

In addition to trying to broaden and improve the options open to young people, particularly those growing up in poverty, we need to provide second chances. By helping those in need, we model a particular type of responsibility, not one of duty enforced through punishment and reward, but one of empathy, nurtured 'through being cared for and respected, and through caring for others': 'Children develop best through their positive relationships to others, through their contribution to their community, and through the ways in which they realize their potential and find joy in life' (Lakoff 1996: 108).

Based on interviews and fieldwork with teen mothers enrolled in school full time, I am convinced that, for the most part, they desired to take responsibility, and with support they found a renewed sense of themselves and joy at demonstrating their competence as parents (see also Davies, McKinnon, and Rains, this volume; Kaufman, this volume). Such successes should be built upon and encouraged, not only through the provision of material support, but ideologically as well. Critical feminists need to develop their own policy rationales rather than relying on conventional wisdom that stigmatizes teen mothers and considers their needs in isolation from other women facing similar or related difficulties.

Challenging the Dependence–Independence Dichotomy

Conservatives tend to oppose government-funded support for teen mothers (e.g., day-care subsidies) because they believe it encourages 'welfare dependency' (construed as a moral failing) and discourages 'personal responsibility' on the part of teen parents and their families. Liberals reason that some government support now prevents long-term, intergenerational welfare dependency as well as child abuse and neglect. Critical feminists, in contrast, avoid and oppose talk about welfare dependency altogether. This discourse blames the poor for poverty and its consequences and perpetuates a false dichotomy between dependence (read: unpaid care-givers) and independence (read: paid workers).

The discourse about dependency also contains at least two major tensions. First, 'when the subject under consideration is teenage pregnancy, these mothers are cast as children; when the subject is welfare, they become adults who should be self-supporting' (Fraser and Gordon 1994: 329). Second, when teen mothers gain a measure of personal autonomy through state aid, this is considered 'bad' dependency; when these young women are forced to rely on individual men for material support (whether the men are abusive or present by dint of the proverbial shotgun or not), this is considered 'good' dependency.

Given segmented labour markets and unequal pay, benefits, and access to on-the-job training, women – particularly members of ethnic minorities and those with working-class or poverty backgrounds – do not have the same choices as middle-class, white men regarding how to combine family and paid work lives. Furthermore, a woman with a partner earning a middle-class salary chooses to be an 'at-home parent' with much different consequences than a single mother receiving social assistance.

In contrast to divisive talk about dependence and independence, critical feminists stress *interdependence* and the need to respect and support the diversity of family types. Toni Morrison, for example, has said, 'You need a whole community – everybody – to raise a child': 'The notion that the head is the one who brings in the most money is a patriarchal notion, that a woman ... is somehow lesser than a male head. Or that I am incomplete without the male. That is not true ... [The nuclear family] isolates people into little units – people need a larger unit' (in Angelo 1989: 122).

Although the current welfare system provides material support to low-income people and some autonomy to women, feminists argue that it is seriously flawed. It treats recipients in stigmatizing ways, as clients of public charity. Socialist feminists, in particular, have joined with anti-poverty and anti-racism activists to describe the system as 'public (capitalist) patriarchy' and 'welfare colonialism.' End Legislated Poverty in Vancouver, for example, places an emphasis 'on how the state and its institutions not only keep people poor, but actually make them poor. The state makes people poor when it institutes policies that accept high levels of unemployment as inevitable: if some people are not allowed to work, they certainly cannot provide for themselves. The states makes people poor when it permits employers to pay some workers less than a living wage. The state makes people poor when it perpetuates an under-valuation of some forms of labour, particularly the labour involved in caring for and raising children' (Cohen 1993: 270).

Feminists disagree in their analysis of the welfare state and what reforms would best serve women. Some argue, for example, that higher welfare payments or more effort to create employment for women would not constitute serious reform. Because women are discriminated against in the home as well as the wage workplace, goes the argument, a wholesale attack on gender inequality, including within-family roles, is necessary to deal truly with what makes female poverty unique (Gordon 1990: 7).

Diana Pearce argues that, in any such reform, 'an essential element is the establishment of rights and entitlements for poor women and their families, such as the right to shelter, income support, equal pay, and quality child care' (1990: 275). Further, the dichotomy independent–

dependent must be challenged as the current premise of the welfare system. Otherwise, '[the single mother] must choose between limiting her paid employment to devote more time to her children or limiting her time with her children in order to take more time for paid employment. Either choice perpetuates her poverty, both of income and of life' (ibid.). Single fathers, who are much less likely to live in poverty, do not face such harsh trade-offs; one out of ten single fathers in Canada lives in poverty compared with almost half of single mothers, a fact that cannot be explained by differences in education (Evans 1991: 162).

Translating the Critical Feminist Stance into Policy

How might the critical feminist stance that I have just sketched translate into policy? One reform being tried throughout British Columbia and elsewhere in Canada is the provision of government-subsidized, school-based day-care centres for the children of teen parents. Critical feminists would support this initiative but would reject as its guiding rationale the prevention of 'welfare dependency.' Instead, critical feminists might justify the full integration of teen parents and their children by arguing that the school itself is a public place and part of the larger community. They would reject as ideological any sharp distinction between public and private. Issues related to sexuality, procreation, and childrearing are deeply *political*. Categorizing them instead as only *private* or *personal* de-legitimizes struggles to change practices in these areas (Jaggar and Rothenberg 1993: 121).

What might this mean in practice? Official and unofficial rules and structures that operate to exclude student-parents would need to be rethought. For example, critical feminists would support a flexible attendance policy for teen parents, particularly with regard to absences related to caring for sick children. If schools and workplaces introduced more flexible hours, then men and women, students and staff, would be better able to perform school, work, and family duties. Enhancing 'flexibility for all [students and] workers offers an alternative that acknowledges pregnancy and child care as a human, not just a woman's, problem' (Minow 1990: 89). Ultimately, as lawyer Patricia Blockson has argued in a different context: 'There needs to be a shift from thinking about parenthood as a personal choice to thinking that society as a whole should bear part of the burden for bringing up children ... The current reality is that women bear most child-rearing responsibilities and need accommodation now' (quoted in Cox 1993: A2).

Such a critical feminist stance obviously challenges prevailing values and assumptions; its discourse is not easily heard. The prospects for mobilizing around it may seem dim in the current conservative climate. Blackmore (1995) has argued persuasively that when developing gender equity policy, reformers need to be 'strategic rather than idealistic ... depending upon the level of commitment and opposition which exists in specific contexts' (1995: 310). Yet it is also worth articulating what is desirable, what might define the good society – a society that would not deny women the right to raise children and maintain their self-worth simply because they are young and live in poverty.

In articulating this definition of the good society, critical feminist policy analysts, scholars, practitioners, and activists would be expanding and challenging the individualistic discourse of 'good choices' and 'personal responsibility.' They would be voicing a rationale for why those *in power* must make 'good' choices that respond to the realities of those who, pushed to the margins by present policies, find their personal choices constricted.

Acknowledgments

This work was supported by a grant from the Social Sciences and Humanities Research Council of Canada. Thanks to Sheila Martineau and Jim Wong for comments on an earlier draft. Earlier versions of parts of this chapter appeared in 'Stigma Stories: Four Discourses about Teen Mothers, Welfare, and Poverty,' *Youth and Society* 27(4) (1996): 421–9, and in 'Teacher Discourses about a Young Parents' Program: The Many Meanings of "Good Choices,"' *Education and Urban Society*, 30(2) (1998): 204–21.

Notes

1 In Canada in 1994, among women aged 15 to 19, there were 46,800 pregnancies; just over half (51%) ended in a live birth (Wadhera and Millar 1997).
2 Access to contraception and abortion services in Canada is far from barrier-free. For example, only two provinces pay the full costs of abortion, four pay partial costs, and four pay no costs. 'Access to abortion still varies considerably across Canada, and there is significant financial hardship involved for women in many settings, particularly in remote northern areas and in PEI, Newfoundland, and Saskatchewan (the three most rural provinces)' (Barrett et al. 1997: 308).

3 In Canada, the primary means-tested assistance program is Social Assistance (SA). Low-income individuals are not excluded from this program based on their family composition as they are in the United States. However, 'most nonworking households with an employable family member will receive UI [unemployment insurance] rather than SA,' which means that so-called welfare (i.e., SA) recipients tend to be single women with young children or families with long-term employment problems (Blank and Hanratty 1993: 197). Thus, despite a difference in program rules, in reality Canada's social-welfare system, like the American system, 'is currently divided into two gender-linked [and unequal] subsystems: an implicitly "masculine" social insurance subsystem tied to "primary" labor force participation and geared to (white male) "breadwinners"; and an implicitly "feminine" relief subsystem tied to household income and geared to homemaker-mothers and their "defective" (i.e., female-headed) families' (Fraser 1989: 9).

4 See Paquette (1995) for an in-depth analysis of Canadian census data that calls into question the widely assumed causal links between schooling and future earnings. Those who completed a secondary diploma did earn more than early school leavers, and the advantage 'was much greater for females than for males, although the average real-dollar employment-income levels of females in these educational attainment groups is only about half that of their male counterparts' (1995: 42). On a bleaker note, there were declines in real-dollar earning power for workers of both genders at all educational attainment levels, especially for the young. Unless young people expect to complete university, their economic prospects appear gloomy; the traditionally male-dominated manufacturing and resource-based jobs that paid well without requiring a lot of schooling are disappearing (1995: 40–3).

References

Angelo, B. (1989, May 22). 'Interview with Toni Morrison: The Pain of Being Black.' *Time* (pp. 120–2).

Barrett, M., King, A., Levy, J., Maticka-Tyndale, E., and McKay, A. (1997). 'Canada.' In R.T. Francoeur, eds., *The International Encyclopedia of Sexuality*, vol. 1, *Argentina to Greece*, pp. 221–343. New York: Continuum.

Bartkey, S.L. (1996). 'The Pedagogy of Shame.' In C. Luke, ed., *Feminisms and Pedagogies of Everyday Life*, pp. 225–41. Albany: State University of New York Press.

Blackmore, J. (1995). 'Policy as Dialogue: Feminist Administrators Working for Educational Change.' *Gender and Society* 7(2): 293–313.

Blank, R.M., and Hanratty, M.J. (1993). 'Responding to Need: A Comparison of Social Safety Nets in Canada and the United States.' In D. Card and R.B. Freeman, eds., *Small Differences That Matter: Labor Markets and Income Maintenance in Canada and the United States*, pp. 191–231. Chicago: University of Chicago Press.

Bolan, K. (1993, Aug. 21). 'Native Leaders Label Custody Ruling Racist.' *Vancouver Sun*, p. A1.

Bozinoff, L., and Turcotte, A. (1992, Sept. 21). 'Canadians Worried about Unwanted Teenage Pregnancies.' *The Gallup Report*. Toronto: Gallup Canada, Inc.

British Columbia Task Force on Access to Contraception and Abortion Services. (1994). *Realizing Choices*. Victoria, BC: Queen's Printer for British Columbia.

Calgary Herald (1989, March 18). 'Study Contradicts Osterman Comments,' p. B2.

Callwood, J. (1982). 'Jessie's: Young Moms and Thriving Babies.' *Canadian Woman Studies* 4(1): 37–9.

Canadian Press. (1995, Mar. 14). 'Manning in U.S.: Republican Plans to Slice Welfare Labelled Too Harsh.' *Vancouver Sun*, p. A10.

Clark, S., Dechman, M., French, F., and MacCallum, B. (1991). *Mothers and Children: One Decade Later*. Halifax, NS: Nova Scotia Department of Community Services.

Cohen, M.G. (1993). 'Social Policy and Social Services.' In R.R. Pierson, M.G. Cohen, P. Bourne, and P. Masters, eds., *Canadian Women's Issues*: vol. 1, *Strong Voices*, pp. 264–84. Toronto: James Lorimer.

Cox, B. (1993, Aug. 26) 'Stirs Controversy at Bar Meeting.' *Vancouver Sun*, p. A2.

Delbanco, S., Lundy, J., Hoff, T., Parker, M., and Smith, M.D. (1997). 'Public Knowledge and Perceptions about Unplanned Pregnancy and Contraception in Three Countries.' *Family Planning Perspectives* 29(2): 70–5.

Edelman, M. (1988). *Constructing the Political Spectacle*. Chicago: University of Chicago Press.

Esping-Andersen, G. (1990). *The Three Worlds of Welfare Capitalism*. Princeton: Princeton University Press.

Evans, P. (1996). 'Single Mothers and Ontario's Welfare Policy: Restructuring the Debate.' In J. Brodie, ed., *Women and Canadian Public Policy*, pp. 151–71). Toronto: Harcourt Brace.

Fine, M. (1988). 'Sexuality, Schooling, and Adolescent Females: The Missing Discourse of Desire.' *Harvard Educational Review*, 58(1): 29–53.

Fraser, N. (1989). *Unruly Practices: Power, Discourse and Gender in Contemporary Social Theory*. Minneapolis: University of Minnesota Press.

Fraser, N., and Gordon, L. (1994). 'A Genealogy of Dependency: Tracing a Keyword in the U.S. Welfare State.' *Signs* 19(2): 309–36.

Furstenberg, F.F., Jr., Brooks-Gunn, J., and Morgan, S.P. (1987). *Adolescent Mothers in Later Life*. Cambridge: Cambridge University Press.

Furstenberg, F.F., Jr. (1997). 'Foreword.' In K.M. Harris, *Teen Mothers and the Revolving Welfare Door*, pp. i–xi. Philadelphia: Temple University Press.

Geronimus, A.T. (1997, Fall). 'Teenage Childbearing and Personal Responsibility: An Alternative View. *Political Science Quarterly*, 112: 1–15. Available online: http://epn.org/psq/geronimus.html

Geronimus, A.T., and Korenman, S. (1992, Nov.). 'The Socioeconomic Consequences of Teen Childbearing Reconsidered.' *Quarterly Journal of Economics* 107: 1187–1214.

Gordon, L. (1990). 'Introduction.' In L. Gordon, ed., *Women, the State, and Welfare*, pp. 3–8. Madison: University of Wisconsin Press.

Grindstaff, C.F. (1988). Adolescent Marriage and Childbearing: The Long-term Economic Outcome, Canada in the 1980s.' *Adolescence* 23(89): 45–58.

Harris, K.M. (1997). *Teen Mothers and the Revolving Welfare Door*. Philadelphia: Temple University Press.

Jaggar, A.M., and Rothenberg, P.S., eds. (1993). *Feminist Frameworks: Alternative Theoretical Accounts of the Relations between Women and Men*, 3rd ed. New York: McGraw-Hill.

Jones, E.F., Forrest, J.D., Goldman, N., Henshaw, S., Lincoln, R., Rosoff, J.I., Westoff, C.F., and Wulf, D. (1986). *Teenage Pregnancy in Industrialized Countries*. New Haven: Yale University Press.

Kelly, D.M. (1996). 'Stigma Stories: Four Discourses about Teen Mothers, Welfare, and Poverty.' *Youth and Society* 27(4): 421–49.

– (1998). 'Teacher Discourses about a Young Parents' Program: The Many Meanings of "Good Choices."' *Education and Urban Society* 30(2): 224–41.

– (in press). *Pregnant with Meaning: Teen Mothers and the Politics of Inclusive Schooling*. New York: Peter Lang.

Ketting, E., and Visser, A.P. (1994). 'Contraception in the Netherlands: The Low Abortion Rate Explained.' *Patient Education and Counseling* 23(3): 161–71.

Lakoff, G. (1996). *Moral Politics*. Chicago: University of Chicago Press.

Lawson, A., and Rhode, D.L., eds. (1993). *The Politics of Pregnancy: Adolescent Sexuality and Public Policy*. New Haven: Yale University Press.

Luker, K. (1991, Spring). 'Dubious Conceptions: The Controversy over Teen Pregnancy.' *American Prospect* 5: 73–83.

– (1996). *Dubious Conceptions: The Politics of Teenage Pregnancy*. Cambridge: Harvard University Press.

McLaren, A. (1990). *Our Own Master Race: Eugenics in Canada, 1885–1945*. Toronto: McClelland and Stewart.

Maclean's. (1995, Mar. 27). 'Newt's Axis: Preston Manning Gets a Warm Welcome from Conservatives in the American Capital,' pp. 30–1.

Miller, B.C., and Moore, K.A. (1990, Nov.). 'Adolescent Sexual Behavior, Pregnancy, and Parenting: Research through the 1980s.' *Journal of Marriage and the Family*, 52: 1025–44.

Minow, M. (1990). *Making All the Difference: Inclusion, Exclusion, and American Law*. Ithaca: Cornell University Press.

Mitchell, A. (1993, Nov. 9). 'Family Thriving, Study Finds.' *Globe and Mail*, pp. A1, A7.

– (1998, Jan. 17). 'Teen-age Pregnancy on the Rise Again.' *Globe and Mail*, pp. A1, A6.

Nathanson, C.A. (1991). *Dangerous Passage: The Social Control of Sexuality in Women's Adolescence*. Philadelphia: Temple University Press.

Paquette, J. (1995). 'Universal Education: Meanings, Challenges, and Options into the Third Millennium.' *Curriculum Inquiry* 25(1): 23–56.

Pearce, D. (1990). 'Welfare Is Not *for* Women: Why the War on Poverty Cannot Conquer the Feminization of Poverty.' In L. Gordon, ed., *Women, the State, and Welfare*, pp. 265–79. Madison: University of Wisconsin Press.

Phoenix, A. (1991). *Young Mothers?* Cambridge: Polity Press.

Pozsonyi, J. (1973). *A Longitudinal Study of Unmarried Mothers Who Kept Their Firstborn Children*. London, Ont.: Family and Children's Services of London and Middlesex.

Roberts, D. (1997). *Killing the Black Body: Race, Reproduction, and the Meaning of Liberty*. New York: Pantheon Books.

Wadhera, S., and Millar, W.J. (1997). 'Teenage Pregnancies, 1974 to 1994.' *Health Reports* 9(3): 9–17.

Weedon, C. (1988). *Feminist Practice and Poststructuralist Theory*. New York: Basil Blackwell.

6

Teenage Pregnancy: Social Construction?

IAN HACKING

Participants in this conference, and the authors in this volume, have taught us a lot about young unmarried mothers. From time to time social construction has cropped up, and has often seemed to lie at the edge of discussions, so I should like to examine it directly. Would it make sense, and be useful, to say that teenage pregnancy is a social construction? What would it mean? We hear so much talk about social construction nowadays that I would like to step back from the fray for a few minutes to examine these questions. I am not asking whether teenage pregnancy is a social construct or construction. I am asking about the meaning and use of the idea of social construction.

Many different kinds of things are said to be socially constructed. The very first 'social construction' book title was *The Social Construction of Reality* (Berger and Luckmann 1966). Among other titles you will find the social construction of postmodernism, emotion, the feeble mind, the 1980s, and quarks. You read statements such as 'the experiences of being female or of having a disability are socially constructed' (Asche and Fine 1988: 5). It has been said that each of us is a social construction.

Social construction is then a kettle of many very different kinds of fish. Postmodernism, quarks, deafness, experiences, and reality are, in turn, a movement, style, or epoch; the conjectured fundamental particles of recent physics; a condition or disability; what individuals experience; individual human beings; everything that exists. That is only the beginning of a list of disparate items. James Wong argues that the 'discourse of "teenage pregnancy" is a social construction' (Wong 1997). Discourse is what people say, or the system of talk in which they say it – another type of fish to add to the stew. If we took the word 'construction' fairly literally, as building or assembling from parts, we would have to think that very different types of construction must be involved in building such disparate items.

The situation is even worse than that. Allow me first to express the difficulty abstractly, and then to give an example. It might be nice if, for any particular X (e.g., deafness), 'the social construction of X' referred to exactly one X, be it experiences, discourse, or a disability. Usually, however, this is not the case. Constructionists intend to use one name, X, to refer simultaneously to several different types of item. Moreover, when they discuss the social construction of X, the most important part of their work may be a description of how the different types of X interact.

It is very important, in getting clear about a concept, not to focus so hard on a single example that one cannot see it clearly. I should like to take our minds off teenage pregnancy for a moment. I chose another example at random from titles in a library catalogue. I took X = literacy: *The Social Construction of Literacy* (Cook-Gomperz 1986). This is in fact an anthology about how children in disadvantaged Californian homes learn to read. But let us imagine a more ambitious project. Of course you or I or a poor child in California acquired the ability to read in a social setting, in a school, religious foundation, at home, or in the street. Our ability to read and write was not 'constructed,' it was learned, and it would be silly to call this process the social construction of literacy. But we could argue that the very *idea* of literacy was socially constructed. We can be more specific than that. In the context of social constructionism, 'literacy,' may refer or allude to many different types of thing, including:

1 X = A minimal ability to read or write, whatever the name for it. Long ago English had the word 'lettered,' which the *Oxford English Dictionary* traces back to 1303.
2 X = The word 'literacy' itself. The *Oxford English Dictionary* gives 1883 for its first printed usage. It was formed as an opposite to 'illiteracy.' The *American Heritage Dictionary* notes that 'for most of its long history in English, *literate* has meant only "familiar with literature" or more generally "well educated, learned"; it is only during the last hundred years that it has also come to refer to the basic ability to read and write.'
3 X = The historical connotations. The word 'illiterate' was invented for a family of reasons. These include British rules for voting (the literate mark ballots in one way, the illiterate with a cross; only the

latter may be helped with how to vote). After the American civil war, literacy became a criterion for voting intended to exclude blacks. More universally, the new public education systems took the 3 Rs as their mandate. Two of the Rs constitute literacy. It is no accident that the first traced use of the word 'literacy' is to the *New England Journal of Education*.

4   X = The socioeconomic connotations. Formerly, 'literate' meant learned. A lettered priest was merely one who knew his letters; it was the scholar or humanist who was literate. Literacy picked up the connotations of social class; illiterates were the underclass, a status confirmed as literacy became customary for the prosperous, and (not the same thing at all) more and more jobs required an ability to read and write.

5   X = Qualitative measures of literacy, at first simplest tests for the voting booth, with special meanings for race in the American South.

6   X = Quantitative measures of literacy (the ability to read and write) using approved methods of psychological testing.

7   X = Grades of literacy, as 'functionally illiterate.'

8   X = Metaphorical extensions of the idea, such as computer literacy, geographic literacy (*American Heritage*), and physical literacy, referring to girls' knowledge of how to move their bodies gracefully! (*OED*). Literacy now denotes minimal mastery of a skill deemed to be essential, but which must be acquired by education, including physical education.

9   X = The experiences of literacy and illiteracy. Superiority, and confidence on the one hand, felt chiefly by those who have struggled to learn to read and write. On the other hand inferiority, social contempt or condescension, increasing difficulty at finding work, the skills of deception, acting as if one could read, pain, resistance, shame, perhaps violence as compensation.

10 X = A social problem, though here the problem is illiteracy, the necessary companion to literacy.

11 X = Expert knowledge. A host of pedagogues and reformers instruct on how to teach literacy, or the causes of permanent functional illiteracy. Studies, studies, studies. Even 'Studies in Interactional Sociolinguistics' (the series in which *The Social Construction of Literacy* was published). Chairs of educational psychology are endowed, perhaps a chair of interactional sociolinguistics.

12 X = Institutions. Literacy Access Network. Literacy Ontario Coalition.

13 X = Political bravura. Cries of horror and demand for change when we learn that 37 per cent of adult Canadian citizens whose first language is English are functionally illiterate. Talk-shows. Politicians orate. Pollsters investigate. Editors inveigh. Royal commissions. Throne speeches. The international marketplace! How will Canada compete? What is wrong with our schools?
14 X = The discourse of literacy and illiteracy, the ways in which consumers, providers, experts, and activists talk about it. What it is possible to say; what it is not possible to say.
And so on.

These items are *half* the story; I shall turn to the other half presently. Thirteen of these fourteen distinct kinds of item are called to mind when we hear about social construction. Perhaps the only thing *not* referred to in the 'social construction of literacy' is (1) literacy itself, the minimal ability to read and write.

The thirteen types of item (2)–(14) interact. The choice of a new word (2) has a lot to do with a new type of focus, associated with historical events such as universal suffrage and education (3). The new word cements what had hitherto been only loosely interlaced ideas. As the ideas become a solid block, the word 'literacy' appears to name a single well-understood skill. So we tend unreflectively to take for granted that the idea of literacy is a perfectly clear one. Numbers (1) and (3) reinforce each other. The social implications (4) of literacy and illiteracy are taken for granted, as natural; they in turn make the literate secure in their condescension towards the illiterate.

The measures (5) and (6) make the idea of literacy 'objective,' even though we recall that a first purpose of measuring was totally political: to exclude blacks from voting. As tests become mandatory in schools, the experiences (of illiteracy) become more acute (9). The illiterate person, once simply a member of the broad mass of the unlettered, becomes a *distinct kind of person*, a kind of person about whom sociologists, pedagogues, and psychologists are acquiring expert knowledge (11). And once we have a distinct kind of person, a person can decide to change, or deny, or resist. Whole new courses of action become open. In our present culture of victimization, self-help, and resistance, you might think that a number of any kind of person X can form into an X support group. But although we have learning-to-read support groups, it seems unthinkable that the illiterate could band together to form an illiteracy support group, with the full intention of remaining illiterate, and proud of it. Illiteracy is a negative condition, held in contempt or condescension by proper society. Homosexuality was far more negative than that, but homosexuals banded together to create pride. In the study of the social construction of homosexual culture (Kinsman 1983), we undoubtedly have another X in addition to my fourteen already listed:

15 X = Identity, self-ascription, and self-pride. Independent decisions by those who are X. Rejection of external expertise. Changes in evaluation of X (or not-X). There is no (15) for illiteracy.

I have now told what I called *half* the story. What is the other half? The entire point of talking about social construction. Before emphasizing the point of the enterprise, let us first take the phrase apart, *social + construction*. Everything in my list (2) to (15) is social. Each alludes to events or circumstances of which there is a social or cultural history. The word 'social' seems positively redundant! On the other hand, if we ask about construction, and think literally, in terms of building up or assembling out of parts, it is hard to see much 'construction' in (1) to (14). There is a historical process, yes, but not much step-by-step construction. There is something more like 'construction' in (15) than in all the preceding fourteen put together. That is to say, there is something of a step-by-step process by which homosexuals took control of knowledge about themselves, became public, and generated the self-conscious idea of specifically homosexual culture.

Why not talk simply of the historical constitution, formation, or production of the idea and institutions of literacy? Why the much vaunted phrase 'social construction'? Because social construction has become a slogan. It reflects an antiestablishment, essentially political attitude. This is clearest in connection with the social construction of gender. Feminists of many different allegiances have argued that present and past gender distinctions need not be the way they are, have been harmful to women, and that all people, especially women and children, would be much better off without our present gendered social arrangements. I shall call this *radical* social constructionism. X need not have existed or be like it is; X is quite bad; and we would be much better without X, or with a very different version of X. Off with your X! Not all social constructionist theses have such a firmly radical political stance. Nevertheless, they all urge that some X need not have been the way it is. X, in its present form, is not inevitable but contingent. The intent is to deflate X, to make it seem less important because less inevitable. I shall call this *sceptical* social constructionism.

For example, literacy seems like an altogether obvious concept. After all, a person can either read and write, or cannot. That is as simple as could be, a plain distinction, everyone understands it, and it is natural – in our world, inevitable – to divide people into literate and illiterate, with a continuum of abilities between the two. We need not have had reading and writing, and those skills need not have become paramount in Western civilization – that much is contingent. But given the invention and dissemination of printing, the concept of literacy seems as inevitable as apple pie – and just as beyond question for intrinsic value. The sceptical social constructionist urges, in contrast, that the notion of literacy, with its historical and present connotations, is not in the least inevitable.

There is another element of both sceptical and radical social constructionism that I have not yet mentioned. Taking a word from Karl Mannheim's translator, I call it 'unmasking' (Mannheim 1925/1952: 140). Mannheim was one of the great founders of the sociology of knowledge. Unmasking is a type of criticism that does not strive to refute an idea, but to reveal what Mannheim calls the 'extratheoretical function' served by the idea. Unmasking may try to 'disintegrate' an idea, but not by showing that it is mistaken. Rather one argues that the idea has at least its present contours in response to some social function not visible to those who take the idea for granted. Thus, not only is X contingent, but it has its place as serving some underlying ideology.

Until recent times, social constructionism about X, radical or sceptical, has gone out of its way to put down X. But it may have a more positive aim. Try first to show how contingent an idea is, argue that it is the way it is because of the way that it has been produced in a cultural setting. Then try to use that investigation to change X, to improve it, to recognize that in our present state we cannot abolish X, but we can make it much better if we are aware of how it was formed. We may call this *critical* social constructionism.

Talk of social construction of any of my three types is not purely descriptive. It is not mere cultural history. It has a sceptical, critical, or possibly radical aim. The very phrase 'social construction' conjures up an alliance of shared attitudes and interests. One speaks somewhat from the left, or from a segment of the left. One need not be insisting that some X is literally constructed. One need not make a big discovery that

Teenage Pregnancy: Social Construction? 77

the construction, if we call it that, was social, for in most cases – think of (2) to (15) above – how could it be anything else? Rather the phrase serves to declare allegiances.

I spoke of two halves of social constructionism, and have been describing the second half. The first half is in the details, the working out of the historical and material conditions under which (2) to (15) took place. Now let us see how these two halves look in the case of teenage pregnancy. I shall use the same numbers to refer to the same types of item as above.

I take for granted that the primary meaning of 'teenage pregnancy' is the pregnancy of a woman in our society of no more than eighteen years of age who is neither married, nor about to be married to the father of the child. Conception has been caused by more or less consensual sex; perhaps we should add that the woman is not about to undergo an abortion.

I do not know of an essay or study titled 'The Social Construction of Teenage Pregnancy,' but we do have a subtitle, 'The Invention of Teenage Pregnancy' (Arney and Bergen 1984), and a title, 'The "Making" of Teenage Pregnancy' (Wong 1997). Now one thing that we know the authors do *not* mean by their titles is (1) the invention of teen-age pregnancy by whatever name, for that has been with us always, and needs no invention (what needs invention, or at any rate social constraints, is teenage non-pregnancy).

Instead Arney and Bergen point out that the very name (2) 'teenage pregnancy' (like the word 'literacy') comes into being at a quite specific time and place, namely, middle-class America about 1970. This is not only a change in word from the pair 'unwed mother' and 'illegitimate child,' but also a change in connotation of the fact of teenage pregnancy. Before then, middle-class young unmarried pregnant women were a secret. They were sent away to relatives or had their children in sanctuaries, or else there were illegal abortions. The phrase 'teenage pregnancy' went together with coming out. The social connotations (3) changed. Notice that in the early days discussions of teenage pregnancy, although directed at all parts of society, was a focus of attention because it affected middle-class life. Of late, especially in the United States, the socioeconomic venue (4) has changed to the ghetto and to race, also, perhaps, a threat to the middle classes, but now a threat from without rather than within. In 1970 the central social problem (10) was pregnancy in the suburb; now it is pregnancy in the ghetto. We certainly have expert knowledge (11), witness this very conference. Institutions abound, both governmental and non-governmental. There has been plenty of political bravura (14). It takes different forms as the focal social problem devolves from the middle classes to the poor. An intricate pattern of discourse, or discourses (14), has been created.

More interesting than any of the items mentioned so far is the way in which, for lack of a better word, the experiences (9) of unmarried adolescent mothers have dramatically changed in the past thirty years. No longer is there automatic secrecy, shame, and withdrawal. We have heard throughout this meeting how so many of these mothers experience themselves as having 'grown up,' matured, become responsible, as their babies have come to term and been infants in their arms. Of course, talk of growing up and maturing is itself the adoption of a set of values derived from, even imposed by, middle-aged middle-class culture. I expect that many of us at this conference felt cheered by accounts of what happens to the single mothers. We could become suspicious of our own feeling of relief that everything is going to be all right (that our comfortable norms will not be challenged after all).

There are plenty of help and self-help institutions for young single mothers. But we have something more, proud self-ascription and independence of choice derived from self-pride in being X (15). The most impressive feature here is the change in attitude to adoption. In the 1960s it was the norm to put the child out for adoption, and there was an elaborate infrastructure of institutions and physical plant dedicated to just that. Where once Ontario was full of clinics, homes, wards, and private hospitals dedicated to adoption, now there are virtually none. Apparently without any formal structure, the pregnant young women have declared as with one voice that if they give birth, they will do their best to keep their babies. I am absolutely certain that nearly all 'proper' persons would prefer that most teenage mothers gave up their infants for adoption (incidentally solving the difficulties of all those childless middle-class parents who cannot get white babies to adopt). But these mothers themselves have resisted. By some process that should fascinate sociologists, they now find adoption to be unthinkable (Luker 1996; Cavigan, this volume; Round-Table Discussion, this volume).

What I called *half* the social constructionist story, namely, (2) to (15), is very much the same for teenage pregnancy as for literacy, except that I add (15) and delete questions of measurement, (5) to (7). The other half is there too. First, we are reminded by authors from Arney and Bergen to several in this volume that the very idea of teenage pregnancy is not inevitable. Of course teenage + pregnant is about as natural a class as there is, but that we should treat this as a significant or salient class, worthy of its own label, is a fact of thoroughly contingent social history. Thus far, we have a sceptical social constructionist thesis. We do find something a little stronger. A revised nomenclature has been coming into fashion, and has been adopted for the present volume: early parenting. There is a subtext here. The locale is the American black inner city. It is proposed that in African American culture, perhaps going back into West African roots, it has been the cultural norm for young women to begin to conceive not long after puberty, and by no means consistently with a permanent let alone lifetime partner. Thus, 'early' parenting is deviant relative to a European American setting; it is or could be conceived of as the norm in other milieux. The theme of this revision is not 'Off with your X.' This is not radical constructionism. It is a rethinking of the cultural implications and assumptions of teenage pregnancy, a modest example of what I have called critical, as opposed to sceptical, constructionism.

The final element in social constructionism is what I have called unmasking. There is a certain amount of that in connection with teenage pregnancy, of drawing attention to the ways in which the proper middle-class adult world has generated a concept to keep order among the young and the poor. Notice incidentally that talk of social construction usually has an overtone of oppression, of something being fostered from above. Yet if we were even-handed, and being merely descriptive, perhaps the most exciting thing to call 'socially constructed,' in connection with teens, is the new consensus from below that adopting is unthinkable. But then the slightly self-righteous tone of social construction would disappear. Here, it seems, the underclass is deciding for itself, in the face of, and utterly against the expectations of, propriety.

Perhaps we who have ceased to be teenagers could do with some more unmasking. The people assembled for this conference are primarily from the welfare or knowledge industries. Some of us might begin sceptically to ask, what are we really doing? Those providing services, advice, and welfare are serving the interests of those who need help – or are they? Someone who began to ask these questions would begin to seek out the allegiances expressed by the slogan 'social construction,' because that challenge would require both courage and allies.

Failing that, it does not seem to me helpful to speak of the social construction of teenage pregnancy. The trouble is that, except as a political slogan, the very phrase 'social construction' is tired, imprecise, pretentious, and self-righteous. When it is not fired with political rhetoric we are better off without it. There are so many more interesting, informative, thought-provoking things to say about that remarkable cultural phenomenon, teenage pregnancy as a social problem, as a field of expertise, as a domain of discourse, and above all, as the experience of young women and their children.

I began with three questions. Would it make sense, and be useful, to say that teenage pregnancy is a social construction? What would it mean? Here are my answers. It makes sense, but it is not very useful. What it means is that the very idea of teenage pregnancy is one that came into being, in certain historical circumstances, and the practices, institutions, and experiences are the product of those circumstances. It means that the idea of teenage pregnancy is not an inevitable one, a mere description of the state of certain young women, but rather a label used both to identify, advise, and control, and also, at a later time, to work internally to create pride and self-control. But there are much better ways of saying that, than by talking about social construction.

References

Asche, A., and Fine, M. (1988). 'Introduction: Beyond Pedestals.' In A. Asche and M. Fine, eds., *Women with Disabilities*. Philadelphia: Temple University Press.

Arney, W.R., and Bergen, B.J. (1984). 'Power and Visibility: The Invention of Teenage Pregnancy.' *Social Sciences and Medicine* 18: 11–19.

Berger, P.L., and Luckmann, T. (1966). *The Social Construction of Reality: A Treatise in the Sociology of Knowledge*. New York: Doubleday.

Cook-Gomperz, J., ed. (1986). *The Social Construction of Literacy*. Cambridge: Cambridge University Press.

Kinsman, G.W. (1983). 'The Social Construction of Homosexual Culture.' Master thesis, University of Toronto.

Luker, K. (1996) *Dubious Conceptions: The Politics of Teenage Pregnancy*. Cambridge, Mass: Harvard University Press.

Mannheim, K. (1925/1952). 'The Problem in the Sociology of Knowledge.' In *Essays of the Sociology of Knowledge*. London: Routledge and Kegan Paul.

Wong, J. (1997). 'The "Making" of Teenage Pregnancy.' *International Studies in the Philosophy of Science*. 11(3): 273–88.

7

How Should We Live? Some Reflections on Procreation

KATHRYN PYNE ADDELSON

Teen pregnancy is currently defined as a public problem that begs for a solution. Given the pressing need, it may seem like philosophical foolishness to waste time pondering the large and perhaps unanswerable question of how we should live. Yet teen childbearing is an important part of more general questions about procreation, questions that are central to issues of how we should live.

Procreation includes the responsibility of individuals, families, communities, and societies to raise a new generation that is as healthy and wise as can be. This is a responsibility to the future. Responsibilities of procreation are our joy but also our moral spur, because they force us to look at how we do live and so too the question of how we should live.

Childbearing among very young women has been integrated into ways that people lived since the ancient beginnings of human life on earth. In many communities, it has usually been treated as a private problem, with a young woman labelled promiscuous, or deserving of pity, and often, if a private solution was not found, a tragedy of major proportions might have followed. The private solutions included legitimating the pregnancy by post hoc marriage, eliminating the birth by abortion, or concealing it by disappearing for a visit a distant relative or a stay at a maternity home. These personal solutions solved the private problem by erasing the young woman's 'misstep' so that the good name of the family, and the young woman, were saved.

Since the late 1970s in the United States – and more recently in Canada – youthful childbearing has become a public problem. Some of the solutions have themselves become problematic – for example, offering welfare assistance to the young mothers or, for that matter, offering sex education and contraceptives to 'sexually active adolescents.' The current definitions of the problem arose out of long historical passages during which pregnancy and childbearing moved from a private to a public problem, one in which the authorities on procreation changed from the traditional moral or religious to the scientific and professional – and the conceptions and solutions of problems altered accordingly. Sex and childbearing became matters of choice even for the very young. The claim was that education and birth control technology would insure rational choice and eliminate 'unwanted pregnancies.' The change was something that former U.S. President Ronald Reagan (or his speech writers) saw with great clarity: 'Girls termed "sexually active" – that has replaced the word "promiscuous" – are given [birth control drugs and devices by federally subsidized clinics] in order to prevent illegitimate birth or abortion ... no one seems to mention morality as playing a part in the subject of sex. Is all of Judeo-Christian tradition wrong? Are we to believe that something so sacred can be looked upon as a purely physical thing with no potential for emotional and psychological harm? And isn't it the parents' right to give counsel and advice to keep their children from making mistakes that may affect their entire lives' (*New York Times*, 9 Mar. 1983, p. I1).

This observation is correct on the transformation that has taken place. The implication that we should jettison the 'birth control' solution and return to the moralizing approach is of course seriously flawed. In fact, it represents a kind of polarizing move that I want to argue against in this chapter, not only when social conservatives like President Reagan make it but when modern professionals make it as well. Caught up in the daily struggles to ease the tragedies and sufferings within fiscal constraints, it is difficult to step back and ask about alternatives to the polarized solutions that dominate the policy scene. But stepping back is required for responsibility – the responsibility of professionals and ordinary citizens for the outcome of public policy, not just responsibility of the young women, narrowly defined as the responsibility not to get pregnant. In the end, it is the issue of collective responsibility that I want to raise, responsibility for the larger outcome of how we define the problem of teen pregnancy and how we try to solve it. This concerns responsibility for framing and answering the question of how we should live.

I will begin in a suitably philosophical way, by talking about Plato.

Goodness, Truth, and Beauty

The question of how we should live is a complex one, for it concerns questions of knowledge of goodness, truth, and beauty (as Plato insisted), as well as knowledge of practice and possibility, given the social and material resources. Who is it that has the knowledge we need to guide our practice?

Plato addressed this question of knowledge throughout his life's work. In *The Symposium*, he wrote of how an individual might move from love of the beauty and goodness in another person, to love of good and beautiful institutions, to the full knowledge of goodness, truth, and beauty. With that knowledge, a person would know how he or she should live and the rational part of the soul would govern the spirited and appetite parts of the soul. A meritocracy of the person was suggested, with the part of the soul suited for governance giving the orders – knowledge in the pilot's seat.

In *The Republic*, Plato wrote of an ideal society, a utopian recipe for how we should live. Like the soul, the republic has three functional parts. People settled in the productive part provide the food and labour necessary to give material sustenance to the republic. Those who are auxiliaries form the spirited part and protect the republic, doing both wartime and peacetime duty. The guardians are those in the pilot's seat, recruited according to their merits from the auxiliaries' group. In *The Republic*, Plato takes procreation seriously. Traditional ways of the family and household operate in the productive class (guided, of course, by the guardians). However, because of their special role, procreation among auxiliaries and guardians is organized differently.

This ideal republic is a meritocracy in a fairly strict sense, and, in fact, among guardians and auxiliaries breeding is organized to suit eugenic goals, to insure that the best and the brightest govern. Individuals are selected according to their inborn capacity for achieving knowledge – and women are selected as well as men. They live communally, sharing austere, disciplined lives under a lifelong training process that will lead some of them towards knowledge of the good and the ability to know how the peoples of the republic should live. The story to be told in the republic is that 'golden' children may be born into the 'bronze' productive class and raised up to become auxiliaries or even guardians, according to their inborn merit.

The outcome of everyone doing their part in the republic is supposed to be a just society that embodies goodness and truth as much as is possible in an imperfect world. The republic is an outcome of the collective work and life. Everyone participates in that outcome, and everyone shares responsibility for the outcome. However, the productive class shares responsibility by following its members' traditional ways of life under the guidance of the guardians, with a prod from the auxiliaries when they go astray. Because the guardians make policy, they must understand their responsibility for the outcome more explicitly. By 'outcome' here I do not mean consequences of their actions, or predictable effects, or measurable or testable results. The emphasis on prediction and measurement came with modern science. Plato believed the world was too imperfect for measurement. Rather, to understand outcome is to have a moral grasp of what will come of instituting such and such a policy, or of allowing things to go on as they are. Understanding outcome is more like having a sense of history, but towards the future rather than the past. It requires wisdom and experience, and it must be one reason that Plato insisted that the guardians have knowledge of goodness, truth, and beauty.

Wisdom and experience are needed to set and apply policy, for policy requires understanding both history and future outcome. Of course, setting policy requires more than designating some group of people as the guardians who make decisions for the collectivity. Plato wrote *The Republic* out of his disgust with the excesses of democracy. Athens, the city state, was a direct democracy, not a representative democracy like the modern ones, and citizens met together to decide issues. Rhetoric was a high skill, stirring up citizens to vote by emotion and self-interest rather than their reason and their understanding of the good of the whole. More important to Plato, perhaps, it left decisions on how we should live to the ignorant and unworthy. In *The Republic* he offered a solution – a rule by those with knowledge, in a society designed to give proper training to those who would rule. However, *The Republic* tells a utopian story. Plato offered no strategy for getting from the problem to the solution.

In any society or community, setting policy also requires political know-how. Knowing how we should live requires knowing how we do live and how we might practically move on from there. Whose knowledge are we to rely on to answer these important questions? The moral and practical knowledge of ordinary people in a democracy? The special knowledge of people with expertise who might function as our guardians? As modern, industrialized nations emerged in the West, the knowledge that gave the answers to how we should live began to shift from the first to the second.

Moralizing Procreation

'How should we live?' is a moral question – though also a political and economic one. I will talk about some different ways that 'problems' in procreation have been handled, using – because of my training and knowledge – cases out of United States history, particularly in the mainly white, dominant classes. Slaves, native peoples, the poor, immigrants, and people in the wilds of the frontier followed different ways.

In the United States, from colonial times to about 1970, problems of procreation among unmarried, younger women were taken to be 'private' in certain senses. The young woman might be labelled as a deviant – 'promiscuous' (as President Reagan said) or worse. If she bore the child alone, it would be an illegitimate birth, with the child labelled a bastard, even on its birth certificate. The woman's expectations of making a good marriage would, in many social circles, be gone. She would bring shame on her family. In some cases, the family itself might be socially shunned – cut socially, in a world where social connections were everything. In some cases, the woman would find prostitution the only way to support herself and the child. It would be a tragedy, but a private tragedy.

On the other hand, there were ways to keep all this hidden and so escape the deviance label and its consequences. The responsible man might be induced to marry the young woman. Or if not, she might be seen as an innocent who was seduced and abandoned, and a kindly and sympathetic physician or midwife might provide an abortion, or a knowledgeable woman in her family might obtain herbs to serve as abortifacients (see Mohr 1978). On the other hand, she might be sent out of town to visit a discrete relative and have the baby outside the prying view of neighbours at home, then give it up for adoption or place it with a relative's family.

By the second half of the nineteenth century, there were maternity homes in the United States which offered Christian charity to these girls who made a 'misstep,' sheltering them in the later months of pregnancy and placing their babies for adoption. These homes persisted in the United States until the early 1970s (see Rains 1971; Nathanson 1991).

The idea of a 'misstep' was something new, suited to changes in the modernizing world. The idea of innocents seduced and abandoned was no longer quite plausible. On the other hand, the young women were worthy of what Prudence Rains dubbed 'moral rescue' (1971). Thus, the homes for unwed mothers came into being. But like the earlier efforts, these homes treated the problem as a private one suffered by the young woman and her family. The solutions were aimed at hiding the problem. They set the young woman (and her family) back on the proper route that 'everyone knew' was the way we should live, and that every upstanding person claimed to be the way they did live. Upholding norms is a complicated business of maintaining a public face and hiding what would mar or undermine that appearance. Figure 1 shows the 'generally accepted norm.'

Figure 2 shows some of the complex efforts at hiding variations that go into maintaining the appearance of general acceptance, when procreation is moralized in the ways I have described. The various hidden solutions to the private problems offer 'elevators' back to the proper course that a good girl is said to follow, the normal way of procreation.

These methods were differentially available – if a young woman came from the lower classes, she would be much less likely to be classified as a good girl who made a mistake than as a promiscuous or lustful girl ('you know those poor, they breed like rabbits'). The risk was much greater if she was poor and belonged to a race or ethnicity that was labelled. Even today, she might not have resources to spend an extended time far away visiting a relative. She might or might not have good access to marriage as a solution – which might or might not be a tragedy. She might or might not have neighbourhood support. The higher, better established classes have always had greater possibilities for hiding missteps of every sort and so they can offer a more substantial appearance of moral uprightness and reliability. Their lives appear to be proper and orderly, and so they could appear to embody the way we should live – in contrast to the 'disorderly' lives of the poor.

So much for effort at dealing with the private problem. There were also efforts to define early childbearing and pregnancy as public problems by 'moralizing' them in rather different ways. During the 1830s in the United States, there were many groups made up of good Christian people who believed that the Millennium might be made to come soon by perfecting people's lives and making society virtuous in the present (see McLoughlin 1978). The New York Female Moral Reform Society (founded in 1834) was associated with an important part of this movement, for this was a time when women were considered guardians of morality and repositories of knowledge on how we should live (see Smith-Rosenberg 1971). Members of the society took up the private problem of 'illegitimate pregnancy' and redefined it as a public problem in need of a public solution. Their definition was that women were innocent victims – they rejected the good girl–promiscuous girl dichotomy to the extreme degree that they opened shelters for prostitutes and offered them training for 'honest work.' Women were trusting innocents. Some men were licentious deviants – they used the label,

Figure 1
Good-Girl Life Plan

Education Dating Work Courtship Marriage Sex Family Grandchildren

Figure 2
Career of an Unwed Mother

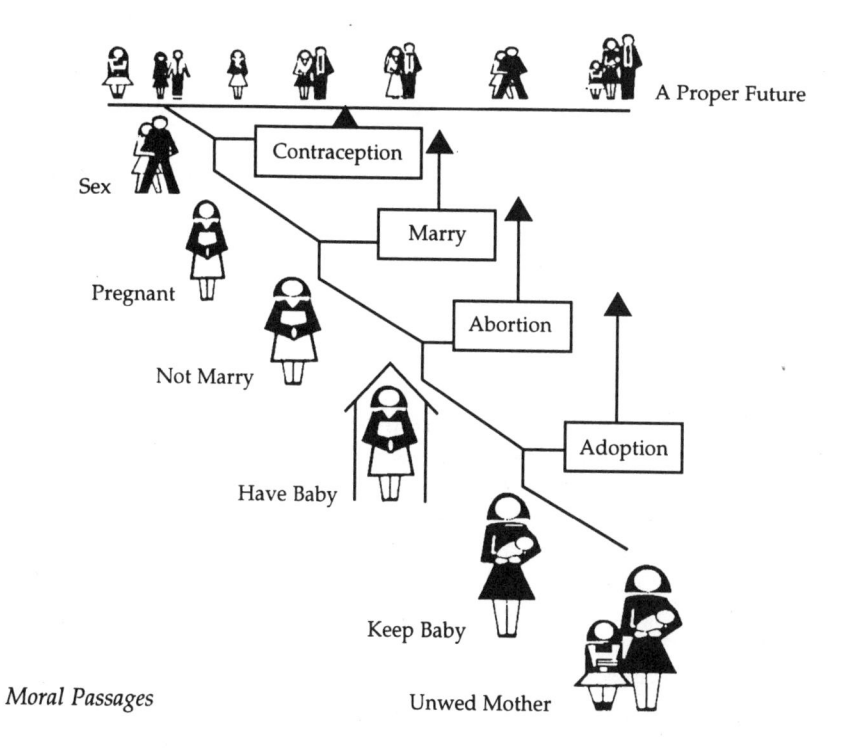

A Proper Future

Sex

Contraception

Pregnant

Marry

Not Marry

Abortion

Have Baby

Adoption

Keep Baby

Moral Passages

Unwed Mother

'the destroyer.' These men initiated adultery and fornication and were the source of America's immorality.

Early on, this group of people moved against prostitution, not by jailing or labelling the prostitutes but by hiring agents to stand outside known houses of prostitution and write down the names of the 'respectable' men who entered. The 'respectable men' (some of whom held very powerful social, political, and business positions) naturally enough fought back, and the effort failed. The strategy had been to shame these men by making their sinful behaviour public. This would allow the society to label the men, not the women, morally deviant and cut out the cancer of corruption that infected even the highest levels of society. The effort was squelched so that the men's behaviour could remain hidden.

The society's more effective campaign came through a strategy that used its very successful newspaper, the *Advocate of Moral Reform* (at its peak, it had a circulation of about 15,000). The newspaper played the major theme that corrupt men were the source of suffering and immorality. Their solution was a national union of women who could control male behaviour. The strategy included publishing the names of men who were known to be seducers of women in their local communities. Small town and rural readers sent in the names of such men, and the newspaper published them, along with accounts of the methods of seduction used by these men and the tragedies they had visited on innocent women. Readers gave advice that all women should avoid the men they named and refuse to include them in the social life of the towns. This was intended to be social death to the destroyer, not to the innocent seduced.

The Female Moral Reform Society took what had been treated as a private problem, much to the detriment of women, and transformed it into a public problem by redefining it. They defined a problem of 'the destroyer,' or the seduction of women, they saw a solution (ostracizing the seducers), and they made it a public problem with the effective *strategy* of using women's social power, organized through their newspaper. They relied on ordinary, Christian women's knowledge of social fact and moral value.

The problem of the destroyer was not discovered because of a sudden increase in seductions. Rather, a new force had gathered to define a public problem (compare this with the problem of 'spousal abuse' today). The definition of the problem was dependent on the available knowledge, solutions, and strategies. Through its work with prostitutes, the society could learn the stories of seduction and how women's lives were destroyed, as well as of the culpability of many 'respectable' men. From their own experience, readers of the newspaper knew stories of seduction and could send them in to be published. The newspaper and the society were able to organize women into a force that reached down into the rural towns. Their knowledge integrated facts and values in the definition of the public problem, but, most important, the society had a power base and an effective strategy.

It may seem that these women were not addressing the problem of teen pregnancy at all. And of course they were not – teen pregnancy is a public problem defined in our own times, with solutions and strategies suited to our institutions, organizations, and movements, and relying on the knowledge of those we take to be guardians. I could say that the members of the society were dealing with a different problem and drop the subject. On the other hand, there is a great deal to be gained by looking at different ways that public problems of procreation come to be defined and resolved. Solutions and strategies arise out of political efforts and resources in existing institutions, organizations, or movements. This is as true today, in the problem of teen pregnancy, as it was in the nineteenth-century problem of 'the destroyer.'

Demoralizing Procreation

In the latter part of the nineteenth and throughout the twentieth century in the United States, there was a continuous, expanding movement of change in the knowledge of how we should live. This movement was fed by problems in the democracy of the United States. The nation was industrializing, and it was faced with massive problems of immigration and urbanization. More directly, there were massive problems from the explosion of wealth and power of 'robber barons' and corporate giants, complemented by massive problems of 'labour unrest.' For a century, the democratic government had suited a mainly rural, relatively homogeneous nation in which elected officials and the respectable classes might govern out of some sort of consensus on how we should live. The industrializing nation held problems that required expert and specialized knowledge (see Freidson 1986; Oleson and Voss 1979). Today, some analysts of the plight of the nation propose what they call a 'communitarian' solution, which sometimes seems not much more than a wish to return to the nineteenth-century ideal of a nation guided by Protestant values and consensus (see particularly Bellah et al. (1985, 1991).

'Science' became the watchword, not only in scientific medicine (said to be the basis of the new health professions) but in the institutionalization of natural and social sciences in the new universities, including the new sciences of home economics, and even scientific management for business and industry. The scientizing was accomplished through the development of professions and disciplines, each with its own body of knowledge and training and certification procedures. By the 1920s, the 'charity' work that had been done by ordinary church folk or brotherhoods was in the process of being transformed into professional social work. During the Roosevelt years of the 1930s, the federal government began to take a place in setting and solving problems of how we should live through its bureaus and agencies and through support of nongovernmental agencies.

This new national order was a meritocracy of knowledge, but of rather a different sort from the one in Plato's *Republic*. Those who had knowledge of how we should live were the professionals, and their knowledge was based in science and their disciplinary training. In *The Republic*, the guardians were both the ones with knowledge of goodness, truth, and beauty, and the ones who governed and made policy. In this modernizing nation, the professionals were said to have knowledge only of truth. Goodness was left to those who governed in the name of the electorate, though the governors were to be guided by the knowledge and advice of the professionals. Scientific knowledge was said to be knowledge of fact, not value (a distinction Plato did not make).

These new knowledgeable professionals began to separate sex from procreation. They came to understand it as a natural, biological need that should be satisfied. This new understanding of procreation began early in the century. Here is a quote from a book published in 1910 by Havelock Ellis, one of the first, great sex researchers.

Sexual union, for a woman as much as for a man, is a physiological fact; it may also be a spiritual fact; but it is not a social act. It is, on the contrary, an act which, beyond all other acts, demands retirement and mystery for its accomplishment ... It is not until a child is born or conceived that the community has any right to interest itself in the sexual acts of its members. The sexual act is of no more concern to the community than any other private physiological act. It is an impertinence, if not an outrage, to seek to inquire into it. But the birth of a child is a social act. Not what goes into the womb, but what comes out of it, concerns society. The community is invited to receive a new citizen. It is entitled to demand that citizen shall be worthy of a place in its midst and that he shall be properly introduced by a responsible father and a responsible mother. The whole of sexual morality ... revolves around the child. (Ellis 1910: 417)

The movement away from the suffocating, Victorian moralizing was liberating in many ways, but it has had complex outcomes for the good of the whole that should not be overlooked in the joys of free choice.

The separation of sex from procreation does not, strictly speaking, move sex out of the sphere of ethics altogether. Rather it puts sex under a different sort of ethics – one of individual choice and individual value. 'Responsible sex' eventually came to mean sex with contraceptive 'protection,' unless the couple (married) was planning to have a child – provided they could afford one. A planning motif went hand in hand with this individualist ethics. An early poster from the Planned Parenthood Federation of America (PPFA) shows three children of step-stair heights with the ditty:

Three little maids from school are we,
Healthy and happy as we can be,
Because our parents planned carefully,
For three little maids from school.

The organization that became the PPFA was founded in 1938, after 'obscenity' laws restricting importing and distributing contraceptives and contraceptive information were struck down in the United States. It did not become an organization of major national importance until the 1960s. During the 1960s, the federation did focus on a public problem – a problem in which poverty, ignorance, and overpopulation were linked. Their solution was birth control, construed as a technology suited for private choice by individual couples. Diaphragms or the newly developed birth control pill were the preferred technologies. The definition of birth control as a technology has been so well integrated into modern thinking that it is difficult to see birth control in a larger sense, as meaning not a technology but as a way of life. In fact, defining birth control as a technology open to individual (or couple) choice was forced by the political context, and it requires the individualist ethics that I mention in this section of the chapter. For a contrast, consider Margaret

Sanger's original use of the term 'birth control' (coined by a group of her friends) as a way for women to transform society by acting together to share knowledge, to fight an unjust government, and to decide together, in community, the good of the whole society on the basis of their shared knowledge. The politics here are absolutely different from those of PPFA, and Sanger herself disliked the name of 'Planned Parenthood' (see Addelson 1994; Kennedy 1970).

The PPFA's strategy was integrated with the federal declaration of a 'war on poverty' (poverty had been discovered as a social problem, and the population bomb had been named). The PPFA's contribution was education and the delivery of services by professionals and trained para-professionals. This strategy was supported by biomedical and sociological research, and it used a new, interconnected set of concepts: unwanted pregnancy, a wanted child ('every child a wanted child'), a life plan, family planning, and eventually (by the 1970s), a woman's choice – the 'pro choice' language of the abortion movement in the United States owes a great deal to the PPFA. There was emphasis on the nuclear family rather than on extended families or communities (Nathanson 1991; Fried 1988). 'Unwanted pregnancies' were (ambiguously) pregnancies not intended in a family life plan, or pregnancies not in accord with an 'ideal' life plan and so 'unwanted' by society and the taxpayer. The latter became a dominant meaning where teenagers and the poor were concerned. The advice on how we all should live was based on the way 'middle-class' Americans were supposed to live.

In the late 1950s, the PPFA commissioned a study of poor people's attitudes and practices concerning sex and procreation. Eventually Lee Rainwater published a book out of the study, entitled, *And the Poor Get Children*. In it, he writes:

The ideas of family planning and planned parenthood embody a particular world view, a particular way of looking at the world and oneself. Planning to become a parent implies that the planner is an adult member of a society who makes a choice and who accepts the responsibility which that choice entails. This kind of planning suggests continuous thought and intention ...

Planning means that one looks ahead, orients himself toward the future, and commits himself and others to some course of action. Middle class people are used to doing this, and the ramified consequences of looking ahead and making commitments characterize the middle class way of life in connection not only with the family but also with the worlds of work, education, voluntary association, and the like. Middle class people live in a matrix of commitments toward the future, in terms of personal goals, and to other people in terms of reasonably clear-cut obligations. Planning thus involves a picture of the way things will be in the future and of the way one will be and act then. (Rainwater 1960: 50)

Rainwater is quite clear that the planning ethic is a middle-class ethic that requires stability in work life and home life. It carries a picture of the world that does not hold for poor people – and does not hold now, in the 1990s, even for professionals and 'middle-class' people who find themselves 'downsized,' or forced to 'retool' and change career direction with no guarantee that their income will not shrivel. There is no guarantee that the picture of the way things will be in the future is the way they will actually be.

Teen pregnancy did not begin to be named a public problem in the United States until the mid-1970s, and again, the Planned Parenthood Federation of America was in the forefront of naming it. The Alan Guttmacher Institute, though independent of the PPFA, has acted as its research arm. In 1977, the institute published a pamphlet, *11 Million Teenagers*, which raised the spectre of rampant adolescent sex and pregnancy. It had considerable impact on the U.S. Congress, and it transformed the 'unwanted pregnancy' problem from one belonging to the poor and black to one that was beginning to infect the young and white. Even the daughters of Congressmen and their neighbours were not immune. Nor was this problem named because of a sudden increase in teen pregnancy (see Nathanson 1991).

In the early years of the problem, the aim was to eliminate 'unwanted pregnancies' among very young women through contraceptive education and services. Again, 'unwanted' here seems to mean unwanted by 'society' or unplanned according to the 'good girl' life plan which located childbearing after school and marriage. It did not really mean 'unwanted by the young woman,' for after the initial surprise, at least some of them wanted their babies. It meant rather what they ought not to want. This, of course, was a moral judgment on the part of the PPFA professionals, but it was a judgment that vocal people on the political right, left, and centre agreed upon, and so it was not publicly attacked. The solution of sex education and contraception was attacked, of course.

Sex education in the schools had been promoted by some professionals for a generation or more, and this problem of teen pregnancy (not childbirth, note) gave impetus to the effort. Contraceptive education may be a solution to a problem of teen pregnancy among sexually active girls. It is not a solution to a problem of sexual promiscuity among adolescents (the problem President Reagan was distressed about), nor is it a solution to teen childbearing, as adoption or community support would be. It is a solution suited to what organizations like the PPFA and the U.S. Congress could supply.

Defining the problem as one of teen pregnancy, to be solved by contraceptive technology and education, placed authority with existing health, social service, and education professionals rather than with parents and religious leaders or with some other source, like neighbourhood wise women or political activists working to change the nation. Not that religion and morality, wisdom, or activism were denied. Rather they were explained under the secular ethics of individual choice of values. One chose the values and should be allowed to live by them – though not to impose those values on others. On this view, the secular ethics itself was not seen to be an imposition of values (or it was seen as the 'official morality of the United States'), and the professionals were supposed to refrain from imposing their own religious or moral values on their clients and patients. This is a division in what counts as morality that, once again, was unacceptable to conservatives like Ronald Reagan and many others besides.

The upshot of the 'de-moralization' of procreation was a political polarization that made it very difficult for those struggling to resolve the problem to find ways to consider viable alternatives. The battle lines were drawn, and the political parties soon appropriated the issues for their own purposes, leaving wisdom by the wayside.

Recently, there has been something of a return to moralizing procreation, particularly by politicians courting the more socially conservative voters. In the United States, this return has been given support by attacks on the welfare system. For example, the breakdown of the nuclear family (rather than the breakdown of the community) is considered to be a cause of crime and welfare dependency. Crime is not considered a proper avenue for getting off welfare, though in many cases it is very successful. Massachusetts Governor William Weld recently declared that 'mothers too young or too stoned or too beaten down to do a decent job of raising their kids' were a root cause of poverty and moral decline (cited in Kaminer 1996).

Know Thyself

Plato's meritocracy in *The Republic* was structured so that those who had knowledge to guide the group were also those who had responsibility for the outcome of their collective activities and for the outcome of public policy (to use a the modern terms). The responsibility for outcome that I am speaking of is not the same as accountability in a task that is defined to have certain measurable results, for example, getting a certain number of young women off welfare and into jobs of some sort, or improving mortality and morbidity statistics for infants and mothers. That sort of accountability has its place, and it is essential in that place. But it does not take the place of responsibility for outcome as I mean it (and perhaps as Plato meant it). Accountability *presupposes* that the task is properly defined, and it measures consequences only in terms of that definition. It defines responsibility narrowly and in terms of job descriptions and task assignments. It overlooks social 'side effects' of the cure for a problem that has been narrowly defined for political reasons. Iatrogenic illnesses brought on by scientific or biomedical cures have been noticed and deplored – particularly those that have had an overall outcome detrimental to the environment or people's health. Are there iatrogenic social illnesses that are long-term outcomes of the cures that have been applied as solutions to social problems? Are iatrogenic ills endemic in the modern strategies that give over authority to interest groups, politicians, and professionals? I do not know the answer to those questions in general, because the answer must be given with wisdom, and that requires full practical knowledge in the local circumstances. But I do know that the responsibility for overall outcomes is not part of the day-to-day thinking in most professional millieux. Nor is it part of the day-to-day thinking of ordinary citizens or politicians. Nor, for the most part, of political interest groups. The emphasis is on today's battle in today's terms, when the most urgent need is to examine those terms.

In this chapter, I have tried to approach the public problem of teen pregnancy in a way that will aid thinking about overall responsibility for considering the question of how we should live. Answers to that question are contained in the ways we define public problems and the strategies we use to solve them. Definitions and strategies must often be acted upon because the problems seem to require some immediate action. The suffering requires mitigation, the children require protection, the community must not be bankrupted, the election must be won, the agency must be saved, the career must be secured. At the same time, it is important to avoid being trapped in the definitions, and particularly, to avoid being trapped in polarized thinking – 'the demoralized, modern solution has created problems, we must go back to moralizing procreation.' That is fallacious reasoning. It is fallacious to suppose, for example, that reintegrating sex and procreation means swallowing the view of the Roman Catholic hierarchy on contraceptives and abortion, or the view of some Protestants that sexually active girls are promiscuous, or the view of some 'fundamentalist' Muslims that women must be severely guarded and controlled by men of the family, or by social and religious segregation. Nor does criticizing the demoralized definition leave us with nothing but utopian solutions. In many communities, people live with wisdom, and there is much to be learned from understanding their ways. There is wisdom to be gained from understanding our own ways, for that matter, rather than staying with the slogans and rules promoted by some ideology.

Part of what being responsible involves is understanding that the definitions we are working under are not the only possible ones, and they are not the only ones being tried out at present. That is, it requires something that Plato's teacher Socrates thought was of central importance – the responsibility to 'know thyself.' The responsibility to know ourselves and the way we live and the way we might come to live requires pondering long-term outcomes of our collective action today.

It is difficult to ponder the outcome of our collective work when we are brought, by circumstances, to be preoccupied with fighting for a little space in which to do the work – whether it is a struggle with funding, with public policy and legislation, or with people who are difficult to work with or to serve. We are, at the same time, of necessity, concerned about our own livelihoods and careers, and our own futures, our own children, our own families. It is difficult given how we *do* live now. But considering overall outcomes of our collective work is not an additional task to add to our exhausting load. It is more a way of thinking about the work and the way we live. It does not take more time, it takes a different approach and a different way of hearing others, so that it becomes possible to begin to know oneself, even from the words and actions of political opponents.

Even more, it is possible to think of how we might live by looking at the world around us to see strategies, definitions, and solutions that might offer alternatives to those that find centre-stage in the national debate. There are, for example, community groups who work at problems of procreation in their own ways. In the United States, they exist both among people who would be labelled conservative and among people who would be labelled feminist. They exist in spaces of tension between the official agencies, bureaucracies, and legislatures that rely on professional knowledge and the community locations in which they work. All of us here know of such work, and many of us do it. In this sort of effort, the understanding of responsibility for the outcome of the work is different from the procedures of established agencies and bureaucracies. Often the understanding of how we should live is different. It is different, but well worth looking at for new ideas on how we should live, and for knowing ourselves and the possibilities of the future.

Acknowledgments

Some of the arguments in this chapter were developed from Addelson (1994), as were the 'good girl' charts. I thank the editors of this volume for their helpful suggestions for revision. My thinking was also much improved by discussions at the conference.

References

Addelson, K.P. (1994). *Moral Passages*. New York: Routledge.
Bellah, R., Madsen, R., Sullivan, W., Swidler, A. and Tipton, S.M. (1985). *Habits of the Heart: Individuals and Commitment in American Life*. Berkeley: University of California Press.
– (1991). *The Good Society*. New York: Alfred A Knopf.
Ellis, H. (1910). *Sex in Relation to Society*. Studies in the Psychology of Sex, vol. 6. Philadelphia: F.A. Davis.
Freidson, E. (1986). *Professional Powers: A Study of the Institutionalization of Formal Knowledge*. Chicago: University of Chicago Press.
Fried, A. (1988). 'Abortion Politics as Symbolic Politics: An Investigation into Belief Systems.' *Social Science Quarterly* 69(Mar): 137–54.
Furstenberg, F.F., Brooks-Gunn, J., and Morgan, S.P. (1987). *Adolescent Mothers in Later Life*. Cambridge and New York: Cambridge University Press.
Kaminer, W. (1996). 'Thank Heaven for Little Girls.' *Otherwise*, 18 Apr.– 1 May.
Kennedy, D.M. (1970). *Birth Control: America – The Career of Margaret Sanger*. New Haven: Yale University Press.
McLoughlin, W.G. (1978). *Revivals, Awakenings, and Reform: An Essay on Religion and Social Change in America, 1607–1977*. Chicago: University of Chicago Press.
Mohr, J.C. (1978). *Abortion in America: The Origins and Evolution of National Policy 1800–1900*. New York: Oxford University Press.

Nathanson, C. (1991). *Dangerous Passage: The Social Control of Sexuality in Women's Adolescence*. Philadelphia: Temple University Press.

Oleson, A., and Voss, J. (1979). *The Organization of Knowledge in Modern America*. Baltimore: Johns Hopkins University Press.

Rains, P.M. (1971). *Becoming an Unwed Mother: A Sociological Account*. Chicago: Aldine-Atherton.

Rainwater, L. (1960). *And the Poor Get Children*. Chicago: Quadrangle Books.

Reed, J. (1978). *From Private Vice to Public Virtue: The Birth Control Movement in American Society since 1830*. New York: Basic Books.

Schneider, J., and Conrad, P. (1980). 'The Medical Control of Deviance.' In Julius Roth, ed., *Research in the Sociology of Health Care*, vol. 1, pp. 1–53. Greenwich Conn: JAI Press.

Smith-Rosenberg, C. (1971). 'Beauty and the Beast and Militant Women: A Case Study in Sex Roles and Social Stress in Jacksonian America.' *American Quarterly* 23(4): 563–84.

Solinger, R. (1992). *Wake Up Little Susie: Single Pregnancy and Race before Roe vs Wade*. New York: Routledge.

Wattleton, F. (1990). 'Teenage Pregnancy: A Case for National Action.' In Evelyn C. White, ed., *The Black Women's Health Book*. Seattle: Seal Press.

8

The Construction of Teen Parenting and the Decline of Adoption

LEA CARAGATA

Once, long ago, I was a foster parent to a child given up for adoption but never adopted. Later as a policy analyst, I worked on developing a provincial foster care policy which, among other things, tried to take account of the fact that many of the children given up for adoption would not be white or perfect or ever adopted. Now, as an academic, I struggle to understand why, when, and how we allocate our social resources.

In 1985 over a million teenage girls became pregnant in the United States; 46 per cent of these pregnancies resulted in live births, 40 per cent were 'terminated,' and 13 per cent were stillborn or miscarried (Henshaw and Van Vort 1989, as cited in Powell 1991). On the basis of this and other data, Powell et al. conclude that 'most adolescent women who become pregnant, carry their pregnancies to term and keep their children' (1991). In one year we are talking about almost 500,000 babies born to American teenage women.

To inquire about who is raising half a million children and in what circumstances seems a matter of legitimate social interest. In Canada, teen pregnancy rates are lower than in the United States – in 1994 there were 48.8 pregnancies per thousand teen women, compared with 106.1 per thousand south of the border. Since 1993 a majority (by a small margin) of pregnancies in teens under 18 have ended in abortion in Canada (Mitchell 1998: A7). Careful inquiry into the significance and causes of such numbers, and any trends they manifest, is needed. But such care has been overtaken by a discourse about a 'crisis' of teen pregnancy and parenting – a discourse more pronounced in the United States than in Canada, but perceptibly 'flowing northward' (see Kelly, this volume). The identification of teenage women having (and keeping) babies as a 'crisis' derives, of course, from attitudes towards appropriate behaviour for young women, child rearing, economic independence or self-sufficiency, welfare state spending, and race.

Recently, a new discourse has emerged countering the rhetoric of 'crisis.' This alternative discourse, reflects, as Ian Hacking (this volume) suggests, 'an anti-establishment, essentially political attitude.' In the case of the 'social construction of teenage pregnancy' one expects to find – and finds – a literature that contests what have been presented as the 'facts of the case,' as well as the conclusions drawn from these. Literature on the social construction of teen pregnancy and parenting generally seeks to expose the values and prejudices of those choosing to inquire about 'this set of facts,' and the way in which the presentation of selected facts can misrepresent an issue.

While I agree with Hacking that one function of the phrase 'social construction' is to suggest or declare allegiances, unlike him (apparently) I believe that this use has continued value. In the same way that there are slogans and phrases from other political agendas (e.g., the neo-liberal) which have slipped unnoticed into our everyday language, a label that symbolizes an alternative discourse can be a useful, politically unifying tool. Some of the symbols which constitute our culture must 'belong' to others besides those who manufacture sports clothing and hamburgers. 'Social construction' has thus become such a symbol. Although functioning as a symbol and declaring allegiances, a 'constructionist' perspective can also be 'critical' and oriented to 'unmasking' – Hacking's terms distinguishing more thoughtful social constructionist literature from that which is *merely* political. (In this area his analysis is very useful.) If social constructionism is to be more than a political slogan – or, I would suggest, *effective* as a political slogan – then it must be precise and critical rather than merely oppositional.

A literature has arisen that seeks to understand and explain the decline of adoption as a 'pregnancy outcome' for teenage women (Powell et al. 1991; Sobol and Daly 1992; Aitken 1995). This literature also explores adoption itself and its structuring as a state and public policy option (Aitken 1995; Sobol and Daly 1992). A further literature comments on how public views of teenage pregnancy have been and are being 'reconstructed' (Murcott 1980; Jencks and Edin 1994; Luker 1996).

Changing Views of Teen Pregnancy

We must begin by examining the phrase 'teenage pregnancy' – how and when it is used in describing, that is, constructing, a social issue. There are a number of terms that are used seemingly interchangeably to invoke the same general cluster of topics. However, what is invoked by all of these is not, I would suggest, the same distinct 'set.' 'Teenage pregnancy' as a classificatory concept is equally inclusive of a married 18-year-old with a newborn, a 14-year-old waiting for an abortion, and a 19-year-old with three preschoolers (in our mind's eye, likely single, black, native, or a member of some other minority group). We use such a phrase almost unthinkingly, and it becomes what Blanco (1994) calls a metaphor for certain meanings. That is, no matter what those using the term really intend on an occasion, through broad and sometimes polemical usage the meaning becomes less precise. Over time a framework of associations, images, and attitudes cluster around the term and reinforce its ideological reproduction. 'Teenage pregnancy' comes to mean more than the literal meanings of the words. In using it we refer to and evoke, fully intentionally or not, the 'gestalt' of teen pregnancy (the political and social context, the 'social problem'). Through such implicit linkages (sometimes purposeful), 'teenage pregnancy' and 'teen parenting' come to appear as self-evidently noteworthy categories. This process, together with its resultant conceptions, is one thing that is meant here by the term 'social construction.' Because a term comes to have a varying and often pejorative subtext, the term 'deconstruction' has come to signal a 'delayering' or unmasking of these 'other' meanings.

Blanco (1994) describes the difficulty in genuinely responding to social problems that have been 'constructed' by and *as* metaphor. I suggest this has happened in the case of teenage pregnancy, a fact which accounts for much of the trouble in thinking through and enacting adequate policy responses. Social problems as metaphors are implicit analogies and as such 'rely on a person's implicit recognition of the pattern inherent in the familiar situation' (Blanco 1994). The relational mapping of the elements that constitute the 'problem' is not explicit, and it is therefore more difficult to evaluate or criticize, or even 'get at,' assumptions about causes and current policy successes and failures. What 'is often needed is a fresh examination of causal structures, functional and temporal relations, and natural tendencies. Instead, when a metaphor [such as 'teenage pregnancy'] is introduced ... the goal and strategies for action are quickly accepted, often by-passing a comparison of causal structures, functional, temporal and other aspects of the situations' (Blanco 1994: 185).

Once the issue is so identified, the construction continues to support hidden meanings. In reporting incidence data on teen pregnancy there are many categories or 'cases' of 'teenage pregnancy' that might imbue the data with different meanings. Whether pregnancy occurs in a context of being married (or in a stable relationship) or not; wanted or not; whether there is capacity to care or not; and whether the pregnant teenager is 14 or 19 should surely be important as indicators of 'problematicity.' So too are the broader social context and various norms such as average age of marriage, onset of puberty, being sexually active. To be meaningful, incidence data must be considered in these contexts. Luker (1996) provides data not usually referred to that illustrate this: births among teens have been remarkably consistent *across this century*, including remaining relatively stable in the face of a doubling, between 1960 and 1990, of the number of sexually active teen women. Her data also demonstrate that out-of-wedlock births to teens *are actually decreasing* as a percentage of out-of-wedlock births. These statistics evoke no air of crisis.

To summarize: construction of a 'social problem' hides the meaning by casting into shadow issues in need of examination. Yet the basis of our concern is important to the direction of our response. The nature of policy responses in many jurisdictions suggests that public concern has been 'manufactured' by the construction of 'teenage pregnancy' to focus on the 'crisis' of teenagers who have babies in order to sustain themselves on welfare. This is largely an American tale (Clark 1991; Kelly, this volume) which does, however, influence the Canadian view of the issue, subsequent discourse, and sometimes policy.

A Subculture of Pregnant Teens?

Fischer (1974) suggests that one of the results of urbanism is sufficient population mass to effect and sustain subcultures. In the United States, some subcultures have been further reinforced by poverty and economic isolation. As Castells (1977) suggests, many U.S. inner cities have become urban 'reservations' – the exclusive enclave of an economic and social underclass whose separation from others is also reinforced by race.

This theme of subculture is important to understanding the construction of teen pregnancy as a social problem. Henslin and Reynolds (as cited in Davis 1989: 19) define a social problem as a 'condition of society that has negative effects on a relatively large number of people.' The emphasis here is the breadth of impact. A more common formulation of a social 'problem' is: 'a large number of people expressing or "having" some condition or behaviour which is viewed as undesirable' (ibid.: 19). In this latter sense, teenage pregnancy is clearly a social problem. In the former it is doubtful that teenage pregnancy has a negative impact – even through welfare spending – on a large number of people.

The Construction of Teen Parenting and the Decline of Adoption

One of the factors that lies behind the 'crisis' of teenage pregnancy is a belief that welfare fosters a deviant subculture. Seeking a qualification for welfare, 'causes' teen women to seek out pregnancy and parenting. Hidden by this concern are further assumptions about the life prospects of these young women were they not to become teen parents, that they could otherwise get jobs and be economically self-sufficient. As Jencks and Edin (1995) argue, whether employment and educational opportunities existed for these young women *before pregnancy*, is completely obscured by the nature of the discourse. Unless one examines whether these opportunities are available, the significance and even the rationality of a decision to become a teen parent cannot be assessed.

Relatedly, Davis refers to an assumption that a 'subculture of permissiveness' (Davis 1989; Brown 1985) has taken hold. In the literature there are also references to attitudinal differences (Chilman 1980): one further subculture theme is that black teenage girls are seen to have a different attitude to pregnancy than their white counterparts – or is it that *we assume* that black teenage girls have such different attitudes (Powell et al. 1991)? The subculture notion is threatening to predominant normative assumptions about young women, sexuality and marriage, and work. Fischer notes that one of the features of subcultures in large urban centres is that they express and sustain values and beliefs that often counter those of the 'established' society and are thus seen as a threat to moral order. Teenage pregnancy 'fits' with this subculture theory – as a 'social problem' it can be seen to involve a number of subcultures, each of which expresses values contrary to those of the dominant culture.

A frequent consequence of a phenomenon being problematized is that we assume individual deviance on the part of those involved. This is the case with teenage pregnancy, as we employ social workers and mental health professionals to engage with pregnant teens, to help them cope with their situation, but also to support appropriate pregnancy outcomes. Underlying much of this aid there appears to be a message of deviance and dysfunction. At the very least, the pregnant teen is seen as a 'casualty.' There is no clear distinction made in current social attitudes to, and tolerance for, adolescent sexual activity versus that for pregnancy. Rather they are generally lumped together in the construction of the 'problem of teenage pregnancy' (see, e.g., Mitchell 1998). In this context, the differences in American and European data must be noted. In Europe and North America adolescent sexual behaviour is similar (according to age of becoming sexually active and frequency of sexual activity). However, European teens 'are much less likely to seek abortions or get pregnant in the first place' (Luker 1996: 9). In the pathologized American view, teen pregnancy and illegitimacy are seen to result from underlying emotional problems (as does 'promiscuity' – which is often seen to lead to the 'problem') (Murcott 1980). Is this the explanation for the differences in American and European teen pregnancy rates? Does the behaviour of American teens express emotional problems, while the sexual activity of European teens does not? It seems unlikely that such a widespread and complex phenomenon can be explained by the individual pathology of more than one million American teenagers. More likely, the rates of pregnancy can be attributed to a wide variety of differences – among them, perhaps, better information to European teens about birth control, and the absence of an economic underclass which sees few life options.

Among blacks, the 'problem' is generally seen to derive from widespread social dysfunction, whereas in white girls a psychological perspective is applied (Johnson 1974; Solinger 1992; Addelson 1994). This latter psychological dysfunction has been addressed by the pattern of the white girl having the baby, giving it up for adoption, returning to school, and preparing for marriage and legitimate children. Solinger describes white, unwed mothers as having been viewed as socially productive breeders whose babies, while conceived out of wedlock, could still most usefully be given up to offer infertile couples good quality stock for families (Solinger 1992).

It was not long ago that pregnant women were viewed as in a 'delicate condition,' and pregnancy was *almost* effectively reconstructed as illness. Murcott locates teen pregnancy at the *'intersection* of ideologies of reproduction ... and ideologies of childhood' (1980: 2). Indeed, the reproduction of our social structure is based quite literally on the reproduction of children, including their social reproduction.

Research on children has tended to focus on children in the process of being socialized as adults. The dominant ideology of childhood appears different from that of any other stage in the life cycle. Adults, parents, the 'older adult,' seniors, and the 'aged' are all regarded, analysed, and ideologized as legitimate stages of life, with particular and legitimate expressions. These stages are not viewed *only as transitory*, as stages prior to emergence in some other 'real' form. Childhood is seen as a special state, qualitatively different, lacking in citizenship, and the *basis* for being accorded the rights of citizens. 'The equivalence of children to servants persists' (Murcott 1980: 7). An ideological perspective of childhood obtains in which childhood is viewed as privative, and children viewed as deficient adults (McKay 1973).

Situating teenage pregnancy in this context of a sharp divide between child and adult is revealing of our response to a pregnant teenage girl. Teenage pregnancy signifies a breach in this divide and, hence, a moral affront or a category mistake. It signifies sex and the loss of innocence, a value strongly associated with childhood. Parenting at such a time is not only 'early,' but 'premature.'

We must look briefly at the other end of Murcott's child–adult divide. Although teenage pregnancy challenges our notions about childhood innocence and feminine innocence, it is also an affront to social values about women. Our society formally acknowledges the equality of women, even while innumerable structures and social roles reinforce male dominance and control. The values and gender identities of teenage women are forged in this context. Teenagers are affected by the way women are portrayed in advertising, by the expectation that women will be more romantically and sexually passive, and by expectations that they will both attract men with their bodies and remain 'pure.'[1] In short, we see 'the persistence of a sexual ideology and social reality that persuades women that the only true measure of their worth existence is a romantic attachment to a man' (Petcheskey 1985: 218).

A number of studies point to these issues in explaining teenage use of contraception. It is socially 'wrong' for a teenage woman to look 'prepared' (signified by contraception use). 'If she is frankly expecting to have sex ... she need not be courted on the same terms as a woman whose sexual availability is more ambiguous. For many women the loss of this bargaining position outweighs all the benefits of contraception' (as cited in Petcheskey 1985: 218).

A second factor influencing teen pregnancy is the desire, reinforced by the sexual and gendered nature of the culture, to *test the relationship*. Studies of women seeking abortion (as cited in Petcheskey 1985) found two primary circumstances where this occurred. The first identified women who were in stable monogamous relationships where the non-use of contraception grew out of a desire to test the love and commitment of the man, sometimes arising out of an expectation of marriage. The second group of women were teenagers who 'maintained a conviction of the inappropriateness of contraceptive preparedness' (Newman, as cited in Petcheskey 1985). Understanding the incidence of teenage pregnancy and why the (U.S.) numbers are disproportionately high requires an examination of the cultural context in which teen sexual activity occurs: 'Patriarchal societies have traditionally served up a double mystification of women – mother and temptress, virgin and whore. Like its more traditional counterparts, the current commercial image of preteen sexuality is not one of female self-assertion or sexual autonomy but one of availability to fantasized male desire' (Petcheskey 1985: 220).

Seen against a social context where personal autonomy, responsibility, and rationality are conceived in terms of 'a matrix of commitments toward the future' (Rainwater, quoted in Addelson 1994: 106) requiring skills in, and attitudes appropriate to, 'life planning' (Addelson 1994: 106), such mystification is almost guaranteed to manifest itself in attitudes that will appear irrational and, therefore, pathological, immature, or otherwise defective (e.g., those just mentioned towards contraceptive preparedness).

Teen pregnancy may or may not be a social problem. It is, however, clearly *associated* with other phenomena that are social problems and might be considered a unifying subculture from among those constituted by race and class. In the United States, 25 per cent of all black babies are born to teenagers. Along with an increased use of social assistance by young blacks, this means that a lot of black American children will be raised in poverty. Poverty correlates negatively with further life chances. Thus, teen parenting and teen pregnancy have become associated with a reliance on welfare,[2] with other 'problems' in a predominantly black subculture, and, ultimately, in the 'public mind' with being a significant contributor to the social, educational, and economic disadvantage already faced by blacks. In the previous sentence, 'associated' could mean 'statistically correlated' in its first use – 'associated with a reliance on welfare' – but certainly by the third use – 'associated in the public mind with being a significant contributor to social, educational, and economic disadvantage' – 'associated' has come to describe something far stronger and exemplary of what I have been calling 'the social construction of the problem.'

The way in which teen pregnancy has been constructed fuels the fire of those who are ideologically opposed to welfare state spending. 'At least part of the new found concern about black teenage pregnancy is due to the desire (on the part of certain conservatives) to destroy welfare' (Jacobs, as cited in Davis 1989: 25). More recently, in a Canadian context, similar implications have been drawn – that accessible welfare induces young women, if not to become pregnant, then certainly to be less concerned about pregnancy as a consequence of sexual activity. And, related to the psycho-social value associated with having a baby it is often argued that an accessible welfare system actually *contributes* to the incidence of teen pregnancy and/or parenting.

Teen pregnancy moves from being a real life issue for the teen parent and her child and his or her reduction in life chances to being conflated with what are perceived to be the 'problems' of race, sexual permissiveness or promiscuity, dependency, and the welfare state. For these reasons, teen pregnancy is then seen to be undesirable and, ideally, to be prevented.

In the United States, 'the old bedfellows of race and sexuality were combined again to bolster fraying systems of domination and control' (Solinger 1992: 11). Although the Canadian data and issues around teen pregnancy are somewhat different, the problematization of teen age pregnancy and the consequences of it being so constructed are similar. We are moving to a less liberal welfare state, and the issues of domination and control to which Solinger refers are readily apparent in the changes made to welfare eligibility and benefits in Ontario since the election of the Harris Conservatives.

While arguing that much is bound (unfairly and uncritically) into our construction of teenage pregnancy, I do not wish to imply that there are not issues associated with teen pregnancy or early parenting that have enormous implications for teen parents and their children. Scott (1983) reports, not surprisingly, that about 80 per cent of teen pregnancies are unplanned. Although pregnancy, birth, and parenting may appear 'romantic' and desirable at the time of intercourse or when pregnancy is acknowledged, and having a child is strongly associated with meeting psycho-social needs, teen parenting is in a quite another sense 'problematic.' Teen pregnancy is of concern because of how it effects those directly involved: 'Teenagers are often unprepared socially (e.g., high unemployment, lack of education) and physically to start families. Consequently, they are far more likely than adults to bring a child into a poverty level situation and to be forced to raise the child on welfare' (as cited in Davis 1989: 23).

Jencks and Edin (1995), however, argue that delaying pregnancy and parenting would have little economic benefit to those who are engaging in early parenting in America. It may be true that '40 per cent of current welfare recipients had their first child before their nineteenth birthday' (as cited in Jencks and Edin 1995: 1); it does not, however, follow that the relationship between the two states is straightforward: 'When a teenager comes from a troubled family, has learned little in school, and has left school without graduating, she is unlikely to be economically self-sufficient no matter how long she delays motherhood' (Jencks and Edin 1995: 2). These same authors also argue that even if high school graduation is achieved and becomes the new norm, the 'sheepskin effect' will disappear because teenagers will find themselves competing against so many other high school graduates. Jencks and Edin make a well-grounded economic argument that there are not sufficient adequately paying jobs to support these new families. The young women who become pregnant and choose to be parents *do so in the absence* of other opportunities. Contrary to the implicit story in the mainstream construction of the problem, these young women are not foreclosing opportunity and reducing their (and their babies') life chances. For many teenage women in the United States, early parenting might be seen to be the creation of a new opportunity in the seeming absence of any others.

Formerly, divisions in the structuring of teen pregnancy broke down by race in the United States and, to a lesser extent, by pregnancy outcome. Blacks were more likely to be teen parents, and blacks were more likely both to carry a pregnancy to term and to keep their babies. Current data postulate an end to divisions along these lines, instead raising the 'problem' of the reproductive practices of the new underclass. In the United States, the incidence of pregnancy among white teens is increasing. 'At the very moment when we have become most concerned about black teenage pregnancy, it has started to decline. But equally telling is the fact that it is declining at the very time when white rates are rising' (Davis 1989: 22). 'It is male unemployment, not AFDC (Aid to Families with Dependent Children), that spurs the rise in female-headed households' (Anderson, as cited in Davis 1989: 25). While Anderson was referring to unemployment in the black community, the issue can be seen more broadly. In both Canada and the United States, though long-term 'dependency' rates differ, there is a consistent and significant underclass who grow up on welfare and will raise their children on welfare. Many of these children are being raised by their single teenage mothers. But blaming the problem on welfare dependence is akin to blaming air pollution on air. The economic prospects of those who are on welfare, *and 'have' other issues associated with being on welfare*, such as 'family dysfunction,' poor school achievement, poor schools, poor housing, less good health and health care, are simply, grim. There are fewer jobs and those that are being created require higher levels of skill, or do not pay enough to move probably anyone and certainly not a family, out of what has been significantly referenced as the 'welfare trap' (Jencks and Eden 1995).

The Construction of Teen Parenting and the Decline of Adoption 109

That young teenagers, faced with an unplanned pregnancy decide to parent almost certainly has more to do with the lack of there being anything else meaningful to do, rather than the prospect of an easy life on welfare. Further, as Luker argues, decreasing welfare rates have not been associated with curtailing teen parenting, and generous welfare rates are not associated with increased rates of teen pregnancy. 'The United States provides less support for single mothers than any other industrialized country, yet it has one of the highest proportions of teenage mothers, married and unmarried' (Luker 1996: 126). Well over half of all women who give birth as teenagers come from profoundly poor families (Luker 1996: 107). 'Typically a young person ends up as a teenage parent only after going through a series of steps, and at each step the successful and affluent are screened out' (Luker 1996: 114).

The previous comment provides an effective summary of the issue of teenage pregnancy. The 'problem' is not so much one of teenage pregnancy as it is of poverty and lack of opportunity. The consequence of enduring poverty has been the development of a subculture composed of teenage girls who see little in the way of life chances and opportunities. In these circumstances, the traditional story of marriage and co-parenting, of economic security and improved economic circumstances is mythical. What is being experienced in the United States, and may be starting to happen in Canada, is truly the creation of a subculture that has little reason to embrace the norms of the dominant culture.

Structuring Possible Pregnancy Outcomes

It is important to keep in mind that most of the pregnancies in question remain largely 'unplanned' or 'unintended.' There is some additional evidence that suggests that while a pregnancy may be unplanned, it is not necessarily unwanted, and having a baby may well satisfy a need for some young women who then choose to parent. In such a context, parenting provides meaning, and the extent to which it limits the *real* life chances available to the young women in question is at least debatable. For the pregnant teen described by this circumstance, neither abortion or adoption are likely to be chosen options.

For some young women, however, early parenting likely results not so much from the factors explored above, but from being unwilling or unable to access an abortion. The third option, adoption, is not well understood (including misinformation about what is involved). Moreover, there is at least some social censure at the idea of 'abandoning' one's baby. Recent data suggest that only 3 per cent of unmarried mothers elect to place their baby for adoption (as cited in Sobol and Daly 1992).

I wish to explore how the elements of a 'pregnancy outcome' are conceived and structured. The literature identifies three outcomes: abortion, adoption, raising the child (Aitkin 1995; Daly 1994; Powell et al. 1991). There is an extensive literature and survey data that report on how these choices are played out (Resnick 1984, 1990; Powell et al. 1991; Sobol and Daly 1992).

Daly (1994) explores adoption in two circumstances – a teen's view of it for herself, and its suitability as an option for others. While only 6 per cent of respondents indicated that they would place a baby for adoption if they or their partner were to become pregnant, when asked what a friend should do if she were pregnant, nearly half said the baby *should* be placed for adoption. This coincided with highly positive views of adoptive relationships. '[These] data suggest that there is a sharp discrepancy in respondent's thinking about adoption as an option for themselves and thinking about adoption as an option for others ... When thinking about friends ... moral rhetoric about what teenagers should do to be 'responsible' appears to take over' (Daly 1994: 340).

Powell et al. (1991) identify a number of issues related to physicians counselling on pregnancy outcomes. General practitioners differed from specialists including pediatricians, obstetrician–gynaecologists, and those specializing in family practice on 'outcome' preferences. GPs were significantly more likely to recommend abortion over adoption. General practitioners ranked the desirability of outcome options as 1, *abortion*; 2, *adoption*; and 3, *raising the child*; specialist practitioners, however, ranked the choices as 1, *adoption*; 2, *abortion*; and 3, *raising the child*. Neither of these ordinal rankings reflect the outcome choices made by pregnant teens.

A U.S. general population study done by Rinck et al. (1983) found significant differences between black and white respondents with respect to choices for pregnancy outcome. Of black respondents 69 per cent chose first that the girl should raise the child, whereas whites most often chose adoption. Whites were also much more supportive of abortion as an outcome, choosing it 19 per cent of the time compared with only 5 per cent of black respondents (as a first option). The reasoning behind these preferences is largely unexplored.

A number of studies investigated the differences between those who choose to parent and those who place their baby for adoption, reporting significant differences between the two groups. Parenting teens tend to be less educated, no longer in school, and come from non-intact homes (Grow 1979; Festinger 1971). Grow (1979), however, found no evidence of differences in emotional health between the two groups. Resnick (1984) reports data that correlate adoption 'placers' with higher psychological functioning. Decisions to place a baby for adoption are likely made with more parental influence, and 'placers' reported parental relationships that satisfied more needs than the parental relationships of those who chose to keep their babies (Resnick 1984). Perhaps we no longer *encourage* adoption for fear that we will influence pregnancy outcome choices such that 'the wrong kind of girls' will give their babies up for adoption. 'Previous studies have shown that there is more reason to be concerned about the adolescent mother who keeps her baby than the one who chooses adoption' (Leynes, as cited in Resnick 1984).

A number of research studies indicate that the decision-making process of the teenager who is pregnant is often not well informed and judicious. How informed are the choices made by pregnant teenagers? As part of any reconsideration of the 'problem,' it would seem a prerequisite to good choices that good information be available (see Orton, this volume). Other perceived constraints can also influence either the quality or voluntariness of a choice. These are after all, *teens*. Although I do not wish to minimize or denigrate their decision-making ability, I do wish to contextualize it. The discovery of pregnancy occurs in an environment where the teen is simultaneously a minor, a child (likely with some mix of being both fearful and defiant about 'telling mum and dad'), sexually active (whether this is acknowledged or not), perhaps viewed as immoral or 'bad,' and generally without independent economic or social resources. While socially, today's teenagers are grown up and 'worldly' in many ways, their status is still that of 'child,' confirmed by social norms of increased length of school attendance and bleak economic prospects for their age group. The 'shotgun' wedding and the 'work your way up the ladder job' for the new husband are no longer social or economic options. Against such a backdrop, the extent to which pregnant adolescents make informed choices or appreciate the long-term consequences of their choices is certainly questionable.

A significant literature explores what influences the teenager's outcome considerations during her pregnancy. The presence of family support is a consistent theme for young women who chose to raise their babies (Grow 1980; Furstenberg 1980; but compare Resnick 1984). The teen's mother appears as the person most likely to influence outcome decisions (Furstenberg 1980; McLaughlin, as cited in Cervera 1993); nevertheless, other research demonstrates that teens who receive counselling during their pregnancy 'are better able to weigh their alternatives, rehearse their roles with the baby and examine their motivation and beliefs about parenting or relinquishing the child' (Cervera 1993: 358). Some data suggest that teens associated with counselling agencies which help the pregnant teen weigh the burdens and benefits associated with placing or rearing her child in fact have a higher number of babies placed for adoption (McLaughlin 1989; Mech, as cited in Cervera 1993).

I began this section talking of the three choices available to the pregnant teenager. Viewed differently, there are only two pregnancy outcomes – birth of a child or not-birth. I suggest that this different conceptualization may be useful in understanding how we value the possibility of adoption. Certainly it suggests a simplified and hierarchical view of the decision-making process of the pregnant adolescent. The notion that there are two levels of choice, organizes the decision process as follows: (a) first choice: abortion or birth; (b) subsequent choice, parenting or adoption. Such a structure might change and improve how adoption is considered as an outcome alternative.

Clearly, the choices the pregnant teenager must make are complex. Their implications are life-defining in important ways. In suggesting this different way of viewing the decision-making hierarchy, I wish to make it very clear that, in practice, it would be unacceptable to organize the provision of information to a pregnant teen in any which obscured *any* of the options and their implications. My point is not that these choices are independent, rather, the point (with the previous qualification in mind) is that the pregnant young woman might more fully consider adoption if the outcome choices were phrased as suggested. The current circumstance may inadvertently encourage abortion for those who are clear about not wanting to raise their baby and parenting for those whose values or circumstance do not permit abortion.

While we may or may not wish to encourage adoption, it should be sufficiently understood as a possible outcome by the pregnant adolescent as well as professionals, family members, and peers who surround the pregnant teen with advice. Some researchers strongly suggest that decisions to parent often result from a poorly informed teenager who lacks appropriate opportunity to consider *all* of the pregnancy outcome choices (Cervera 1993). Furthermore, agencies and caseworker's are often reluctant to even raise the issue of adoption (ibid.). As was noted in

The Construction of Teen Parenting and the Decline of Adoption

the previous paragraph, counselling with pregnant teens that focuses their attention on *what it would be like* to parent or to place a child for adoption is exactly what this type of hierarchical approach might enable. For those teens choosing to carry their baby to term, counselling of this type could give them both time and an appropriate environment in which to consider their choices.

Some studies confirm that adoption is not fully understood and thus not fully or appropriately considered (Daly 1994; Cervera 1993; Voss 1985). Daly (1994) inquires about peer support for adoption, and her data suggest that adoption is seen or might be seen as 'abandoning the baby' and is therefore associated (whether correctly or not) with being judged badly by one's peers. Other data found that adolescents' hypothetical discussions about pregnancy outcomes for teenagers infrequently considered adoption (Daly 1994). Adoption as an option for the pregnant adolescent has fallen from view. We cannot assume this is a considered rejection of the least desirable option.

In order for adoption to be considered fully – as a 'real' choice – it must be reconstructed. I do not yet make the argument that adoption is a choice to be consciously promoted by professionals or in policy. Rather, I am noting its association with a negative view and with poorly available information. If we desire informed and considered choices this is a problem.

The literature on abortion also suggests that there might be value in helping the pregnant teenager reflect differently on the choices before her. Many pregnant teens feel that they 'should' abort – absolute and immediate resolution suggests it as the 'preferred' option. In spite of this, many young women continue to find the idea involves significant moral difficulty. Although they wish abortion to be an option – in fact, a *solution* – they 'feel' that it is not. Reconstructing pregnancy outcomes as I have suggested, encourages women to explore their feelings about the issue of pregnancy and whether there are overwhelming reasons why their pregnancy *should or should not* be carried to term. Then, the subsequent question can be posed, 'If I have the baby, who should raise him or her?'

There are ethical limitations in the creation of a hierarchy of choice that suggest that it must only be proposed in a context that recognizes the interrelatedness of all of the choices, and the need for young pregnant women to be served in a holistic fashion. Thus, using such a hierarchical postulate in counselling must be carefully considered; however, there does appear to be value in broadening teens' understanding of real pregnancy outcomes. While in the short run, raising a baby may promise and deliver many rewards, the emotional, social, and economic costs can appear later. Abortion is not, for many women, easily psychologically endured. Adoption, as it is currently structured, involves guilt about 'giving up' the baby and further emotional distress related to the uncertainty of the outcome and the child's well-being. Although there is no pregnancy outcome without difficult and enduring consequences, there are suggestions that adoption might be reconsidered and restructured to reduce the sense of loss to the birth mother and the uncertainty and confusion faced by some adopted children.

Issues That Help to Render Adoption 'the Third Option'

Before we can consider further whether there are important implications from considering the choice(s) facing pregnant teens differently, we must review the current literature about adoption as a chosen pregnancy outcome. Sobol and Daly (1992) report on how an adoption decision affects the birth mother. Their findings hardly recommend it: even when 'best,' it is not an easy option. Further, these findings must be contextualized in considering how adoption takes place. The birth mother signs away all rights to her child. She is urged 'to proceed with her life as if pregnancy, birth and legal separation never occurred' (Sobol and Daly 1992: 150).

While the data available are often obtained through samples that are either self-selecting (referrals to counselling following adoption placement), or very small, they do point to an enduring sense of loss and guilt felt by the birth mother (Rynearson 1982; Millen and Roll 1985). The very presence of groups of birth parents and adopted children organizing search services demonstrate the power of the feelings involved. There has been little by way of effort directed at structural changes to adoption processes to alleviate some of these emotional costs inspite of their being well documented over an extended period of time.

Compare the circumstances of adoption to those of abortion. Abortion, which involves a shorter state of pregnancy and lacks the very powerful experience of giving birth, is well acknowledged to have significant psychological impact. Counselling is generally provided, and women who have had abortions often report continued therapy for ongoing and unresolved feelings. Adoption as it is currently structured and practised in Canada, must invoke as many feelings as abortion –

including the biological and physiological effects of birth that are associated with maternal bonding. These are effectively denied by a policy and practice which, as effectively as if the baby had been aborted, declares it dead as far as the needs and interests of the birth mother are concerned.

These policies have not arisen from insensitivity or cruelty but from a consideration of the needs of the adoptive parents and a consideration of the best interests of the child *at the time they were formulated*. They may require re-examination in light of the many changes that have transformed familial and social relations in the several decades since these policies were formulated.

Aitken (1995) raises the issue of post-adoption contact, or what is known as 'open adoption.' She also suggests that care be taken in using the phrase 'open adoption' as it is presently used to describe different things. It is generally contrasted with 'confidential' adoption in which the birth mother or family of origin are given no information about the adoptive parents and have no way of establishing any future contact. Similarly, the adoptive parents receive general background information about the birth mother (or parents), but are given no identifying information. The birth mother (or parents) may, from time to time, through the adoption agency receive reports about the child's well-being. Such adoption practices are the established Canadian norms which have evolved out of beliefs about the importance of the pregnant or birthing teenager 'getting on with her life,' perhaps overly simplistic notions about the best interests of the child, *and the desire to protect the adoptive parents*. This latter point requires emphasis because, as social values have changed, it remains the only party in the 'adoptive triangle' that would seem to be clearly advantaged by confidential adoption. Current practice fits with the notion that the child is truly 'theirs' and permits them full control over if, when, and how much information about the birth mother or parents is to be given to the child. This perspective is supported by Berry (1991), whose research suggests that the biological mother or parents have the most to gain from an open process and that the resistance of adoptive parents is related to their lack of control over contact in any such system.

In considering the possibilities of open adoption, we must have regard for the age of the child. For children who are older and have established relations with their birth family, although there may be reason to control access, it is hard to imagine the justification (unless perhaps desired by the child) for terminating all contact. The interests and issues with regard to infant adoption are slightly different. In this case, a 'confidential' adoption appears to be hardest on the birth mother and may be a factor in the number of young women who choose instead to raise their babies. The idea that one will know nothing about the fate of one's child may encourage fears that 'anything could happen' and, with this, a sense that 'surrendering' for adoption is irresponsible. Thus, the issue of requiring 'confidential' infant adoption is not just a matter of the harm it may cause birth mothers. Rather, we must be concerned to the extent that the cost of losing contact with the infant effects a rejection of adoption as a pregnancy outcome.

Aitken (1995) importantly notes that the social context has changed so as to make open adoption less at odds with contemporary social norms. Single parenting, reconstituted families, and what she describes as 'altered family structures' encompass significant variety. The idea that a child should have two mothers is no longer a social oddity.

In considering the pragmatics of open adoption, Bernstein et al. (1992) identify levels of contact and suggest that these be resolved in detail and stipulated in a signed affidavit which would then be filed with the court. These authors argue that this would protect the interests of adoptive parents and make them secure about their rights. This in turn would help to secure their abiding by the terms of the agreement. Finally, the limits to the contract are those necessary to ensure that the child has an appropriate opportunity to bond with his or her adoptive parents.

Overall, adoption has an image problem. While it is seen by teens and their peers as the responsible choice, it is more personally viewed as abandoning one's baby. Teens appear particularly concerned that their peers will not be supportive of a decision to give a baby up for adoption. Teenagers almost never talk hypothetically about adoption: Daly reports that only 13 per cent of her respondents stated that they felt they knew how to go about placing a baby for adoption. Almost two-thirds of her sample thought it to be a complicated process. Teens in her sample were also unclear about the legality of adoption (Daly 1994).

Daly (1994) reports that the teens she surveyed had strong perceptions about adoption services. In Ontario, the Children's Aid Society (CAS) was characterized as 'pushy,' 'bureaucratic,' and 'slow,' and private agencies as 'underhanded,' 'profit-hungry,' and 'expensive.' Daly's findings suggest that there are two classes of adoption services in the minds of youth: a 'public' one associated with an underclass, bureaucratized and judgmental, stigmatizing but legal; and a 'private' adoption alternative associated with less stigma and better service but expensive and of questionable legality.

Conclusions and Implications

Murcott suggested that the current view of teen pregnancy creates the potential for 'moral panic,' and while this has not occurred, a pejorative and moral view has certainly been strengthened. Jencks and Edin (1995), Murcott (1980), and many others make a significant contribution to separating 'the facts of the case' from what Blanco (1994) refers to as the metaphor of a social problem. More such critical analyses are required, as is an expanded public discourse about the real nature of teenage pregnancy. Most teen pregnancies are unplanned, birth control usage or lack thereof is related to a sexual identity forged in patriarchy, and those young women who choose to parent in order to receive welfare do so, not because welfare is too available, but because often there are no other opportunities or 'life chances' awaiting them.

Related to the need for an expanded public discourse on teenage pregnancy, the same is required with respect to adoption. It is just not talked about. This is reflected in how much young women know about adoption and reflected in how readily they consider it. Adoption must join abortion and teen parenting as a possible outcome when teenagers talk with their peers, sexual partner, and family about 'What they would do if ...'

It appears that policies prohibiting open adoption are outdated. As suggested by Bernstein et al., open adoption need not be without structure. The level of 'openness' can, in principle, be individually defined so as to be appropriate in each circumstance. For pregnant teens, knowing that they will have some level of access to their child, and/or to information about their child, might make adoption significantly less painful to contemplate. As many young women who choose to place their baby change their minds following the birth, factors such as having met with the adoptive parents could affect these decisions.

Confidential adoption arose out of the social norms of the time of its formulation. There were also many more babies available, so more care perhaps was required to insure an adequate number of adoptive parents. These trends have now been reversed, and while I do not suggest policy changes that would be knowingly prejudicial to adoptive parents, I think that it is time for a more equitable balancing of interests for all of the parties to the adoption triangle. Open adoption appears to be a move in this direction.

To conclude: First, teenage pregnancy and parenting is not so much a social problem as an economic one. To convince young women to take not getting pregnant seriously, there must be compelling alternatives. Available data indicate that for many of these young women there are none. Second, there must be a public discourse about adoption if it is to be more than a residual third option. Restructuring how pregnancy outcomes are postulated may support young women in better exercising and developing their autonomous decision-making skills. It might also lead them to recognize adoption as a real option. However, that seems only advisable if the policies which govern adoption are substantially reconsidered and revised. Our society is filled with the most complex of human relations – separated and reconstituted families, single parents, biological parents, and gay and lesbian parents. The notion of a young woman remaining in touch with her offspring now parented by others seems well within contemporary norms.

References

Aitken, G. (1995). 'Changing Adoption Policy and Practice to Deal with Children in Limbo.' *Child Welfare* 74: 679–93.
Bernstein, M., Caldwell, D., Clark, G.B., and Zisman, R. (1992). 'Adoption with Access or Open Adoption.' *Canadian Family Law Quarterly* 8: 283–300.
Berry, M. (1991). 'The Effects of Open Adoption on Biological and Adoptive Parents and the Children: The Arguments and the Evidence.' *Child Welfare* 70: 637–51.
Blanco, H. (1994). *How to Think about Social Problems*. Westport, Conn: Greenwood Press.
Castells, M. (1977). *The Urban Question*. London: Edward Arnold.
Chilman, C. (1980). *Adolescent Sexuality in a Changing American Society – Social and Psychological Perspectives*. Bethesda, MD: National Institutes of Health.
Daly, K.J. (1994). 'Adolescent Perceptions of Adoption.' *Youth and Society* 24(3): 330–50.
Davis, R.A. (1989). 'Teenage Pregnancy: A Theoretical Analysis of a Social Problem.' *Adolescence* 24(93): 19–28.
Festinger, T. (1971). 'Unwed Mothers and Their Decisions to Keep or Surrender Their Children.' *Child Welfare* 50: 253–63.

Fischer, C. (1974) 'Toward a Subcultural Theory of Urbanism.' Working Paper No. 211.

Furstenberg, F. (1980). 'Burdens and Benefits: The Impact of Early Childrearing on the Family.' *Journal of Social Issues* 1: 64–87.

Grow, L.J. (1980.) 'Follow-up Study of Early Childrearing.' *Child Welfare* 59: 311–13.

– (1979). 'Today's Unmarried Mothers: The Choices Have Changed.' *Child Welfare* 58: 363–71.

Jencks, C. and Edin, K. (1994). 'Do Poor Women Have a Right to Bear Children?' *American Prospect*, no. 20 (Winter): 43–52.

Johnson, (1974). 'Adolescent Pregnancy: Intervention into the Poverty Cycle.' *Adolescence* 9(35): 391–406.

LaClau, E., and Mouffe, C. (1987). 'Post-Marxism without Apologies.' *New Left Review* 166: 79–106.

– (1985). *Hegemony and Social Strategy: Towards a Radical Democratic Politics*. London: Verso.

Leynes, C. (1980). 'Keep or Adopt.' *Child Psychiatry and Human Development* 11: 105–12.

Luker, K. (1996). *Dubious Conceptions*. Cambridge, Mass: Harvard University Press.

Millen, L., and Roll, S. (1985). 'Solomon's Mothers: A Special Case of Pathological Bereavement.' *American Journal of Orthopsychiatry* 55: 411–18.

Murcott, J. (1980). 'The Social Construction of Teenage Pregnancy: A Problem in the Ideologies of Childhood and Reproduction.' *Sociology of Health and Illness* 2(1): 1–23.

Powell, V., et al. (1991). 'Physician's Preferences for Adoption, Abortion, and Keeping a Child among Adolescents.' *Research in the Sociology of Health* 9: 33–47.

Resnick, M.D. (1984). 'Studying Adolescent Mothers' Decision Making about Adoption and Parenting.' *Social Work*, Jan.–Feb.: 5–10.

Rynearson, E.K. (1982). 'Relinquishment and Its Maternal Complications: A Preliminary Study.' *American Journal of Psychiatry* 139: 338–40.

Scott, J.W. (1983). 'The Sentiments of Love and Aspirations of Marriage and Their Association with Teenage Sexual Activity and Pregnancy.' *Adolescence* 18(72): 889–97.

Sobol, M., and Daly, K. (1992). 'The Adoption Alternative for Pregnant Adolescents: Decision Making, Consequences and Policy Implications.' *Journal of Social Issues* 48(3): 143–61.

Solinger, R. (1992). *Wake Up Little Suzie*. New York: Routledge.

Strinati, D. (1995). *An Introduction to Theories of Popular Culture*. London: Routledge.

Voss, R. (1985). 'A Sociological Analysis and Theoretical Reflection on Adoption Services in Catholic Charities Agencies.' *Social Thought* 11: 32–43.

9

Changing High-Risk Policies and Programs to Reduce High-Risk Sexual Behaviours

MAUREEN JESSOP ORTON

Young people 'growing up sexual' today experience sharply divergent and conflicted values concerning individual and collective rights and responsibilities. This leaves them often ill-prepared for personal relationships as well as their role as citizens, in a time of volatile social, political, and economic change. Personal and public values are intertwined. To strengthen each we must also strengthen the other, and the mutually reinforcing links between them, in working towards a more democratic, just society. The only potentially universal links are public policies and programs to support people's basic needs, thereby enabling them to avoid problems. Our experience in the promotion of sexual health and prevention of adolescent pregnancy demonstrates the policy conflicts we must resolve and the potential gains for all of us.

Although Canadian adolescents have brief or no access to even limited sexuality education in schools, all have full exposure to seamlessly blended advertiser-media which use narcissistic illusion to manipulate potential consumers. Sexual images, violent images, and frequent depiction of casual sex without consequences are used to catch viewers' attention.

Meanwhile poverty has been increasing since 1980 among Canadian children (National Council of Welfare 1998: Table 3). The percentage of children living in poverty has risen sharply since 1989: 14.5 per cent rising to 21 per cent in 1995. In that six-year period the number of children living in poverty increased by 58 per cent. This rise in numbers was steepest in Ontario (99 per cent) and British Columbia (85 per cent) (Campaign 2000, 1997). One in five Canadian children is now living, not just on the edge of poverty, but far below adequate levels. For an excellent discussion of the dimensions of child poverty, Canada's record to date of family support, and a proposed policy based on a life cycle response, see Novick and Shillington (1996).

Clearly, federal and provincial policies greatly affect trends in child poverty. Business interests and the mainstream media they influence have pressured governments and the public to focus on the 'real world' of global market competition. Since the mid-1970s Canadian federal and provincial governments have reduced corporate taxes. Rising public deficits and debt levels have been blamed on program spending rather than, more accurately, on federal monetary policies (high interest rates escalating government debt charges) and federal tax cuts and rising unemployment (both reducing revenues). Federal policies as well as increasing automation have contributed to rising unemployment. The Bank of Canada's high interest rates reduced capital investment and job creation within Canada, simultaneously as federal Free Trade Agreements with the United States and Mexico accelerated corporate export of jobs to low-wage countries.

Rather than pursuing strategies to increase employment and revenues, governments are downsizing the state's role and reducing their program expenditures. Two provinces (Alberta and Ontario) have further reduced revenues by cutting personal income taxes, by a flat percentage that also gives greatest benefit to the affluent. Governments are drastically cutting public service jobs and funding for programs of education, health, housing, child care, and environmental protection that are the foundation of an equitable, healthy, creative, and productive society. Income support benefits (unemployment insurance and welfare) have been cut back severely, even as the incidence and depth of family poverty have been increasing and the unemployment and underemployment rates remain high (Schellenberg and Ross 1997).

These particular federal and provincial policies give priority to corporate gains for the benefit of the already affluent. They manifest government indifference to the needs and rights of all citizens. They contradict and undermine our public health policy to promote responsible personal values among young people, to protect each other from sexual coercion, unplanned pregnancy, sexually transmitted diseases, and AIDS. Why should they care about each other when we adults don't? The stress of family deprivation impedes their academic achievement and their perception of life opportunities. Deprived of long-term prospects they (like adults) are more likely to seek immediate indulgence via a range of high-risk behaviours, including alcohol, drugs, casual unprotected sexual intercourse, delinquency, and crime.

Today we are struggling amidst a tidal wave of nineteenth-century market values flooding back primitive notions of individualism (competitive, exploitative self-interest) and of a limited government role to protect and promote the public good (severe cutbacks in program funds and standards and further loss of standards and universality by looming privatization of programs for basic human needs). Everything we have learned about communities that work and prevention of social problems tells us this is immensely destructive. We have to create a new tide of values and goals for social development in which economic development is only a means to that end. In a comparison of Western industrialized countries, Novick and Shillington conclude that 'national values, and the political will to act on these values ... not the level of national wealth ... appear to be significant determinants of levels of public support for the well-being of families' (1996: 15). The following discussion of research findings on adolescent pregnancy is set within broad goals and values. It emerges within professional social work's goal of social equity and its ethical standard of client self-determination. Both are essential to all human services in a democracy. Otherwise human services, implicitly or explicitly, reinforce conformity to the power status quo. Social equity and individual self-determination reinforce each other, if we recognize the implications of each for the other. Recently two Canadians have contributed important ideas towards such an integrated conception.

Charles Taylor (1991) responds to critics who view the struggle over the last two decades for individual rights and pursuit of self-knowledge and growth as simply narcissism. He mentions several such critics, including Christopher Lasch, author of *The Culture of Narcissism* and *The Minimal Self*. Taylor offers a tentative definition of individual authenticity in today's world. He includes 'creativity,' the 'originality' of each individual, and 'frequently opposition to the rules of society.' Of equal importance he also includes 'openness to horizons of significance' (i.e., awareness that not all choices are equally good) and 'self-definition in dialogue' with others (ibid.: 66).

John Ralston Saul (1995) argues against 'revisionist' claims that democracy and individualism emerged from economics and, in particular, from our Western Industrial Revolution. This is a frequent claim since the collapse of communism, implying that deregulated capitalism for global trade is not a threat to democracy here at home and will spread democracy around the world. Saul traces the historical linkage of democracy with individualism back to classical Greece.

In a democracy the individual as participating citizen is of central importance and 'the source of legitimacy' for government's role to promote and safeguard the public good based on disinterest. Without that government role, the individual is powerless. Saul contrasts this concept of democracy in which 'the citizen is the government,' with the recent nineteenth-century concept of corporatism wherein group rights override individual rights and government is simply the sum of group interests. The most effective way to 'formalize' individual rights in a democracy, he recommends, is via the daily participation of individual citizens in the process of the public good.

It should be noted that the possibility of thinking or acting with absolute disinterest or objectivity is very much in dispute these days. In recent years the social sciences have been identifying steps throughout research processes to reduce the potential for biases (of gender, race, ethnicity, sexual orientation, etc.) in the development of our knowledge. Similarly, some democratic governments have initiated policies to reduce bias and achieve greater inclusivity in governing processes, public institutions, and programs. We also have to find ways to make governments more accountable to represent the interests of all. Of course, at election time we have to pressure political parties to clearly state their policy objectives both positive and negative (what they will *not* do, e.g., increase poverty).

To integrate these ideas, I suggest the following working goal: A society that aims to be democratic and just supports and encourages self-development towards authenticity in all individuals because their active participation as citizens and their creative contributions to the well-being of others are essential to building a democratic, just society. Individuals who are denied the opportunity to so develop, are treated unjustly.

This goal encompasses recent emphasis on health promotion and its important concept of healthy public policy, that is, that all policies should take account of their effects upon people's health. However, as I intend it, this goal goes far beyond health promotion. It emphasizes that all public policies must take account of their effects upon individuals as potentially participating citizens building a democratic, just society. We have to nourish values, knowledge, and skills for participation, especially among young people. This broadens our public priorities to promote social equity and has important implications for education and the public media.

Within any framework it is important to identify both positive objectives (what we want to achieve in specific fields) and negative objectives (problems we want to avoid). By keeping both types of objectives clearly in mind, we are more likely to achieve both. Positive objectives (e.g., to promote sexual health within the overall goal of social equity) tend to be general, and we need the specificity of problem definition (e.g., unintended pregnancy in adolescence, sexually transmitted diseases, child sexual abuse, sexual harassment) to help us identify the most effective combination of possible strategies.

This chapter's focus on prevention offers a reality check precisely for that sector of public opinion that easily absolves collective responsibility by blaming the individual. We move beyond the current group of young parents to the total youth population and look at trends over time. Most of the data presented here pertain to adolescents (under age twenty). I want to highlight the following: (a) what we have achieved by sexual health policies (formerly called family planning), using Ontario as a case study; (b) what we have *not yet* achieved; (c) some ethical issues in program content, in the public policy process, and in the social consequences for young people that are especially urgent today amidst increasing family poverty.

Parenthood in adolescence has long been the tip of the iceberg of unintended pregnancy. Historically, unintended pregnancy among single adolescents was usually hidden by a quick marriage, when illegal abortion or adoption were the only alternatives. A 1992 study of young mothers in Metropolitan Toronto (most under age twenty and 70 per cent unmarried) found that only 18 per cent had intended their first pregnancy (Fulton and Factor 1993). The young mothers in this study may or may not be representative of unmarried mothers in Ontario. However, this finding strongly suggests that unintended pregnancies among Ontario adolescents are far more than the 50 per cent which annually end in abortion, plus the declining few in adoption placement. By 1989 only 3.6 per cent of unmarried Canadian mothers giving birth under age twenty-five placed their baby for adoption (Daly and Sobol 1993).

Prevention of unintended pregnancy among adolescents can be seen as the unfinished task of this century's family planning movement to enable choice about parenting. That was a difficult forty-year struggle in Canada to change the family planning policies of a sufficient number of churches in order to gain support of political parties to repeal the 1892 federal ban on contraceptive methods (achieved in 1969).

It is sometimes argued that family planning is a middle-class agenda or a white-racist agenda imposed on others. Population policies and processes certainly may be authoritarian and coercive, whether anti-family planning or pro-sterilization without informed, voluntary consent. Within the West, however, family planning originated as a people-based movement precisely to enable choice, in the face of religious agendas opposing any method of family planning except abstinence, even for married couples. This argument also ignores the direct benefits of family planning, regardless of class or race, to women's education and health and, in turn, their benefits to children's health and family well-being, and to women's equality in personal relationships and in society.

For humanitarian as well as democratic reasons, it is essential to reinforce the principle of informed, voluntary choice concerning sexuality and family planning and respect for the person whatever the choice. The goal must determine the process and the content of preventive programs. We must educate broadly and accurately, with a focus on personal integration of learning and ensure access to clinical services and contraceptive materials. To simply try to control, on the other hand, we give a 'one size fits all' message of chastity or undefined abstinence, and limited, biased information and negative attitudes concerning protective methods.

With increasing access to family planning services and declining rates of child mortality, the average family size has declined in Canada. Women are postponing childbearing. In 1960 (prior to the gradual availability of the 'pill' for females and legalization of distribution of contraceptives), the average age of women at birth of their first child was 23.7 years, shifting to 28.2 by 1994 (Statistics Canada 1994, 1996). These two trends towards smaller families and postponement of first birth have been accompanied by a rise in women's as well as men's post-secondary education and in women's participation in the labour force.

Why should we be concerned about pregnancy in adolescence? Pregnancy in adolescence is associated with higher health risks, both short and long term, to both mother and child, such as toxemia, premature birth, and low birthweight. (Direct determinants of low birthweight have been identified as smoking, low prepregnancy weight, poor weight gain during pregnancy, poor maternal nutrition, maternal morbidity, alcohol intake; and multiple births (Kramer 1987). Socioeconomic factors are indirect determinants, including youth, low income, low education, and unemployment (Alder, Vingilis, and Mai 1996: 175–82). Many low-birthweight babies are premature. Low birthweight is a major risk factor for infant mortality especially in the first month (McCormick 1985; Shah et al 1987). It is associated with neuro-developmental impairments, for example, mental retardation and learning disabilities (Eisner et al. 1979; Westwood et al. 1983). Promotion of planned pregnancies (and conversely reduction of unplanned pregnancies) and reduction of the incidence of low birthweight have been public health priorities in Ontario (Ontario Ministry of Health 1989).

Pregnancy in adolescence interrupts a young woman's life development – her secondary school education and/or work experience. Education is an essential strategy to avoid or escape from poverty, regardless of eventual family structure. In Canada, in 1991, two-parent families with less than secondary school education were twice as likely to be living below the Statistics Canada low-income cut-off line (Ross, Shillington, and Lochhead 1994: 66: Table 5.6). (Statistics Canada's 1994 poverty line for a two-person household ranged from $14,348 in rural areas to $20,762 in large cities with more than 500,000 population (Ross, Shillington, and Lochhead 1994: 15, Table 2.1)).

Among all female lone parents, the poverty rate was 56 per cent. It was highest for those under age twenty-five with less than secondary school education (90 per cent), and diminished in relation to increasing education and age. However, up to ten years later at age twenty-five to thirty-four, the poverty rate for this least-educated group of female lone parents declined only to 82 per cent (ibid.: 65, Figure 5.2). We do not know at what age these women became parents, but we do know that pregnancy and parenting in adolescence correlates strongly with lower education. In turn, lower education affects economic and social opportunities – even one's ability to obtain access to health and social resources in the community.

What are the risks for children growing up in poverty, regardless of family structure? The majority of children born to unmarried mothers do well, compared with those of married mothers (Clark et al. 1991). However, a direct influence on children's well-being is poverty which, as noted above, frequently besets female lone parents (ever-married or not) who have not completed secondary school. The 1983 Ontario Health Survey found that among low-income households (both two- and one-parent families) the reported rate of child health indicators was consistently higher and approximately double that for higher income households. Child health indicators included chronic health problems, poor school performance, emotional disorders, hyperactivity, and conduct disorders.

The 1990 Ontario Health Survey found that children and youth in low-income families are more likely to engage in riskier behaviours, for example, to smoke cigarettes and/or have alcohol problems. The proportion of teenage women reporting a pregnancy in the previous five years was 18 per cent for those in a household with income below $30,000, more than four times higher than the 4 per cent reported in households with income above $30,000. Similarly, fewer sexually active teenagers in lower income households (below $30,000) reported that they always use birth control (54 per cent vs 68 per cent in households with income above $50,000) or use condoms as protection against sexually transmitted diseases (18 per cent vs 35 per cent). Even in affluent households a large proportion of sexually active teenagers are at high risk. Although the Canadian school drop-out rate among youth age 16 to 17 has been declining steadily, the rate of teens in low-income families consistently has been almost double that among teens in higher income families (1981, 23 per cent vs 14 per cent; 1993, 8 per cent vs 5 per cent) (Ross, Scott, and Kelly 1996: charts 8, 9, 12–16). (Data on school dropouts age sixteen to seventeen do not tell the full story. Analysis of other administrative data for the academic year 1989–90 reveals that the national non-completion rate of grade 12 (presumably of those who stayed in school) was considerably higher, at 31 per cent (Canadian Institute of Child Health 1994)).

It is important to note that the majority of adolescents in low-income families do not drop out of school at age sixteen or seventeen, nor have a pregnancy. However, their higher rates of school leaving and teen pregnancy are strong reasons for governments to reduce, not increase, the incidence of poverty.

Moving beyond one's family, does the risk of pregnancy for adolescents partly depend on their address? Yes. When Ontario initiated family planning policies in 1975, there was a wide range of adolescent pregnancy rates among fifty-four localities studied. (Prior to 1998, the Ontario localities included the six cities within Metropolitan Toronto, plus regional municipalities, counties, and territorial districts.) The highest locality rate was four times the lowest. Higher rates of pregnancy to older teens (age seventeen to nineteen) were associated with localities of low socioeconomic status (SES), measured by post-secondary education for men and women, women's income, and women's participation in the labour force. Generally, low SES localities are rural and/or in the north. Although two of the three SES indicators (income and labour force participation) were measures of women's changing status in the 1970s, the rural–urban and north–south distribution of low–high SES localities is the same pattern as if we had averaged the rates for men and women on each of the three indicators.

Preventive programs were rare and almost all were in high SES localities which are large cities (Orton and Rosenblatt 1986). Their more educated, heterogeneous population provided earlier leadership and support for controversial prevention from citizen groups, professionals, and more democratically structured churches (e.g., the United Church of Canada and Unitarian churches). Urban affluence provided seed money for innovative programs (Orton 1993). Of course, all large cities include some low SES neighbourhoods, but pioneering preventive services gave cities a head start in reducing their adolescent pregnancy rates.

How can public programs develop and reinforce our private resources for prevention? Community levels of education, employment and income, as discussed above, affect the diversity, quality, and funding of community institutions. A larger population brings a wider cultural mix of perspectives and values and potentially greater tolerance of difference, and more eclectic approaches to issues. Multidisciplinary and multilevel research has documented that the incidence of adolescent pregnancy reflects a complex interplay of the characteristics of community, school systems, preventive programs, family, peers and friends, and the potential sexual partner, all as well as characteristics of the individual adolescent. Sexual health resources can be conceptualized as private or public: one's private or personal support network of parents, friends, potential partner, church, and family physician; and public programs (school sexuality and family life education; sexual health promotion and clinical services at public health units; and small learning groups and personal counselling at social services, for example, child welfare agencies). A network of public programs, by reaching all adolescents, can strengthen the personal support network of each one as well as reinforce responsible peer norms, in the following five ways.

They can complement and support parents as sexuality educators. Most sexual behaviours involve two people, and, although parents are important sexuality educators, they do not reach the potential friends and sexual partners of their children. Public programs can do so – especially school programs. Schools also can support parents as sexuality educators using various strategies, particularly since the current generation of parents did not have access to any formal sexuality education.

A network of public programs can strengthen preventive norms among peers. For adolescents, their peers and friends are becoming an important reference group, in addition to their parents. The perceived attitudes, values, and behaviours of friends are influential, as individuals try to navigate a sea of conflicting values. However, the potential for misperceptions in relationships is greatly increased by the large and widening double standards between male and female adolescents concerning interpersonal relations and casual sex.

These programs can recognize adolescence as a major transition in the life cycle which includes developing sexual awareness and experience. There is much for young people to integrate into their learning (Ontario Premier's Council re Health, Well-being and Social Justice 1994). The Canadian Guidelines for Sexual Health Education identify five principles: access to sexual health education for all; comprehensiveness of sexual health education (integration, coordination, and breadth); effectiveness and sensitivity of educational approaches and methods; training and administrative support; and program planning, evaluation, updating, and social development. The four major components of sexual health education include acquisition of knowledge; development of motivation and personal insight; development of skills that support sexual health (to set age-appropriate personal goals; to implement, evaluate, and modify these goals); and creation of an environment conducive to sexual health (Health Canada 1994).

These programs can ensure access to confidential sexual health clinical services focused on adolescent needs – for all youth and especially sexually active youth. Public health units can provide universal access, and they already have a link to students via their legislated role in schools to provide other health promotion services. Young people may be uncertain about the degree of support from a private physician and fear loss of confidentiality to their parents.

A network of programs would provide extra support for high-need youth. Child welfare agencies are already working with some high-need youth and could provide extra support concerning sexuality issues. The Metro Toronto Study of Young Mothers found that 24 per cent of young mothers had been in foster care as children (Fulton and Factor 1993). A U.K. study of parenting breakdown (children coming into care of a child welfare agency) in two succeeding generations (a young girl and later, in turn, her children) found the significant factor for women who avoided the second parenting breakdown was a non-deviant (psychiatrically and criminally) and supportive partner. This retrospective and prospective study controlled for other disadvantaging factors, for example, low academic achievement, first child birth occurred in adolescence, and currently deprived living conditions. Its many recommendations included follow-up support for adolescents leaving care and entering an extremely vulnerable period (either returning to a dysfunctional family or living alone with few personal supports) (Quinton and Rutter 1988).

What is the level of exposure to risk via sexual activity among Canadian youth? Research has identified three high-risk sexual behaviours correlated with both unplanned pregnancy and sexually transmitted disease (STD): first intercourse in early adolescence, inconsistent or nonuse of condoms and other contraceptives, and multiple sexual partners. (High-risk factors for human immunodeficiency virus (HIV) also include sex between men, needle use (injection of drugs), recipient of blood products and transfusion prior to 1 November 1985 in Canada, sex partner of HIV-positive person, and sex partner of person at risk for HIV). Women's reproductive tract is more susceptible to infection and the rate of reported chlamydia is high among adolescent women. Chlamydia is frequently asymptomatic and, undiagnosed and untreated, frequently leads to complications ending in loss of fertility (Tam et al. 1996). Individuals already infected with an STD are more susceptible to infection with HIV, leading to AIDS and death (Jones and Wasserheit 1991).

A considerable number, and more males than females, have experienced sexual intercourse before age fifteen (males, 16 per cent; females, 12 per cent) (Canada Health Promotion Survey 1990; and Canadian Institute of Child Health 1994: Chap. 5-27). By grade 11, average age seventeen, almost half of both male and female teens have experienced sexual intercourse (males, 47 per cent; females, 45 per cent). Sexual experience was much higher and the gender difference diminished among school drop-outs age sixteen to nineteen (males, 89 per cent; females, 84 per cent), college or university students age eighteen to twenty-one (70 per cent vs 66 per cent) and street youth age fifteen to nineteen (95 per cent vs 93 per cent). Among grade 11 students twice as many males as females (36 per cent and 17 per cent) had had two or more sexual partners. Sexual experience with two or more partners was similarly much higher among the other three groups but the gender difference remained large, except among street youth (Canada Youth and Aids Study 1988). Among street youth, rape was given as the reason for their first experience of sexual intercourse by 24 per cent of females and 5 per cent of males (see King et al. 1991: Tables 6.6, 6.15, 6.17). Three more recent but either not national or small-sample surveys (1992, 1994, 1995) found similar or different rates of sexual experience, which are not generalizable to all Canadian adolescents. (For a detailed review of research on age at first intercourse, see Maticka-Tyndale (1997) including Table 4.)

Many sexually active adolescents are either not using or not consistently using some method to protect themselves and their partner. Condoms were reported to be used 'each time' by more male than female teens (but only 66 per cent and 47 per cent), who had had one or more partners in the previous two years (National Population Health Survey 1994; see Maticka-Tyndale 1997: Table 6). In an earlier survey of women age fifteen to eighteen (note: excluding age nineteen) in three Canadian cities, only 24 per cent of those sexually active reported using both the pill and a condom (for double protection), and 26 per cent did not use any method (Ortho McNeil, Adolescent Female and Birth Control 1992; see Canadian Institute of Child Health 1994: Chap. 5-29).

What are some other influences, in addition to socioeconomic status, upon sexual and sexually protective behaviours? Parents may affect children's sexual behaviour via multiple ways: emotional closeness or deprivation (especially by a deserting parent) (Horwitz et al. 1991; Meloch and Plante 1991), religiosity (Miller and Jorgensen 1988), less supervision, exposure to parent's dating or sexual behaviours, and close proximity to non-family men.

A cross-Canada study of adolescent attitudes and values found a similar proportion of Canadian female adolescents (86 per cent) and male adolescents (88 per cent) thought 'sex before marriage is alright when people love each other.' However, only 40 per cent of female but 73 per cent of male adolescents thought 'sexual relations are okay within a few dates.' Honesty was viewed as 'very important' by 82 per cent of females but only 56 per cent of males; concern for others, by 75 per cent of females but only 48 per cent of males (Bibby and Posterski 1992). In Ontario 80 per cent of female secondary students reported they had been sexually harassed in a school setting. Among males, 30 per cent reported having been afraid of sexual harassment (by other males). There was a wide gender gap in attitudes to sexual harassment (Currie and Green 1994; see also Staton and Larkin 1993).

A common myth is that a monogamous 'going-steady' relationship is adequate protection against STD and use of condoms is then not necessary. This ignores the reality that one or both partners may already be infected by a previous partner or may become infected by a concurrent casual partner. Serial monogamy is only multiple partners in slow motion, with a possibly edited script.

A large U.S. study of girls in grades 8, 10, and 12 found that those with a history of sexual abuse were twice as likely to report high-risk sexual behaviours (Stock et al. 1997). Evidence is accumulating on experience of sexual abuse. A British Columbia study of students in grades 10, 11 and 12 found high rates of reported sexual abuse (females, 25 per cent; males, 5 per cent) and reported physical abuse (females, 25 per cent, males, 15 per cent) (McCreary Centre Society, Adolescent Health Survey 1993; see Canadian Institute of Child Health 1994: Chap. 5-22).

Sexual self-determination depends upon equal control between two people. Fear of abuse by one's partner is reported as a reason for not insisting on safer-sex practices (Aboriginal Nurses Association of Canada 1996: 34). Age difference of three or more years between young adolescent women and an older first sexual partner is also associated with high-risk sexual behaviours and self-reported pregnancy (Miller et al. 1997).

Gender differences in our socialization of adolescents do not adequately prepare young men to be nurturing and responsible in relationships, or young women for economic independence or meaningful activity outside the role of caregiver, or either (and especially young men) concerning sexuality and reproduction (Freeman 1989; Reitsma-Street and Offord 1991). For males, stronger socialization towards independence increases the need to gain peer acceptance and influence, to which sexual activity and alcohol lend themselves, and especially for school dropouts (Freeman 1989). Since consumption of alcohol and drugs diminish the ability to make careful decisions, clearly sexuality education has to be linked with health promotion addressing a range of high-risk behaviours.

Has research identified effective components of programs for sexual health promotion and protection? In spite of methodological difficulties in program evaluation, two decades of research have identified some effective components. Some major methodological difficulties in program evaluation include the need for a control group, uncertain reliability of self-reported outcomes of sexual behaviour and pregnancy, frequent inability to control for characteristics of other important influences (e.g., neighbourhood, quality of the system delivering the program, family, peer norms, friends, and especially potential sexual partners), and restriction to a brief one-time program and follow-up for short-term change.

Some of the following studies are concerned with prevention of either unintended pregnancy, sexually transmitted diseases, or both.

A review of twenty-three evaluations of school-based programs identified six common characteristics in curricula that effectively delayed the onset of intercourse, increased use of condoms or other contraceptives, or reduced sexual risk behaviours in other ways. These characteristics are: '(a) theoretical grounding in social learning or social influence theories, (b) a narrow focus on reducing specific sexual risk-taking behaviours, (c) experiential activities to convey information on the risks of unprotected sex and how to avoid those risks and to personalize that information, (d) instruction on social influences and pressures, (e) reinforcement of individual values and group norms against unprotected sex that are age and experience appropriate, and (f) activities to increase relevant skills and confidence in those skills' (Kirby et al. 1994: 358–9; see also a review of five programs by Frost and Darroch Forrest (1995), and a review of forty-seven programs in Europe and North America by Grunseit et al. (1997) for the World Health Organization's Global Program on AIDS.)

A preprogram survey is recommended to identify specific needs, behaviours, and attitudes of the group as a focus for the educational content based on a learning model of information, motivation, and behavioural skills (Fisher and Fisher 1992).

Some programs combining sexuality education with a related strategy have demonstrated greater change in knowledge, attitudes, or behaviour than by education alone. Some examples are combining sexuality educational modules with career mentorship (Smith 1991), or with peer role models (Moberg and Piper 1990; Howard and McCabe 1990). Another effective combination is with access to clinical services, either at an off-school site (Zabin et al. 1986) or school-based (Kirby et al. 1991; Ottawa-Carleton Health 1992). Clinical services using a psychosocial model (to identify and give special attention to individuals in high-risk circumstances) have demonstrated change in clients' self-reported contraceptive usage (Winter and Breckenmaker 1991). 'Many researchers conclude that ... programs should both encourage youth to delay or refrain from intercourse and also encourage them to use contraception and condoms if and when they do engage in intercourse. Published evaluations of programs focusing only on abstinence do not provide good evidence of effectiveness in delaying the onset of intercourse' (Kirby et al. 1994: 359; see also Jemmott et al. 1998; Kirby et al. 1997; St Pierre et al. 1995; and Roosa and Christopher 1990).

There is, however, no evidence from various studies that sexuality education, sexual health clinical services, or free distribution of condoms promote the onset or frequency of intercourse (Schuster et al. 1998; see also Guttmacher et al. 1997; and Sellers et al. 1994). In fact, there is welcome evidence that programs can be a positive influence for young men who universally report less communication with their parents on sexual issues and greater sexual activity, than do young women. A large national U.K. survey of all ages found that among the youngest men, age 16 to 24, a rising proportion (compared with older men) reported school as their main source of sexual information and, those who did, were less likely to have had intercourse before age 16 (Wellings et al. 1995).

A U.S. study compared four comprehensive school health promotion programs (including sexuality and decision-making skills) over a three-year period. Programs differing in focus, resources, and class-time were tested in over 1,000 classrooms in grades 4 to 7. It was found that more classroom hours were required to produce significant change in student attitudes than in either knowledge or practice. Large effects in all three areas required approximately fifty classroom hours plus full course implementation, dependent in turn upon full in-service teacher training. Follow-up through several grades dramatically increased gains in attitudes and practices (Connell et al. 1985).

Studies of the school system as a learning environment have found that the normative environment and academic organization of schools affect a range of student behaviours and thus have implications for the effectiveness of sexual health education. A comparative study of twelve inner-city London (UK) schools, found children's behaviours differed significantly by schools, while controlling for student background characteristics, including family socioeconomic status. Positive student behaviours measured by higher examination grades, lower delinquency rates, and good school attendance, were associated with schools characterized by rewards and praise for student work, better pupil conditions (school as a living space for pupils, e.g., not locked out over lunch hour), more opportunities for student participation in and responsibility for school activities, academic emphasis, teachers as models, constructive teacher management of classroom, supportive staff organization, and teacher participation in development of school policies (Rutter 1980). For the detailed study see Rutter et al. (1979). See also Comer (1985) on the Yale–New Haven (mental health) Prevention Project in a low-income primary school (K–4) serving minority children; and Lee and Bryk (1989) for a comparative study of U.S. high schools (eighty public and eighty Catholic).

What can we learn from a study of the preventive behaviour of Ontario institutions as well as of the youth population? Our Ontario Study of Adolescent Pregnancy, established in 1980 and now including prevention of STDs, was designed to promote development of provincial policies and local programs for prevention. We had to find a way to combat pervasive myths about adolescent pregnancy, such as, 'We don't have that problem here' or 'Yes, that's a problem but it's the same everywhere and it's been around since time began.' To see differences between places and over time, we need a *local* rate of adolescent pregnancy (under age twenty) and we need a *complete* rate (including live births, stillbirths, hospital abortions, and abortions in free-standing clinics).

We have twice surveyed all fifty-four localities for their preventive programs (1981 and 1991) and compared the effectiveness of policy at three ministries (Education, Health, and Community and Social Services) to achieve program development in their sectors across the province. We have retrieved previously unreported data on abortions to Ontario women at free-standing clinics in Canada and American border states and included these data in the calculation of locality rates of adolescent pregnancy. Trends in locality rates have been analysed in relation to their preventive programs, over five-year periods (1976, 1981, and 1986), and we hope to be able to analyse 1991 and 1996 data soon. Ontario's livebirth and abortion data for the necessary years have not been available because of a number of reasons including lack of government priority. Following are some of our findings.

Can programs reduce locality adolescent pregnancy rates and do so regardless of locality SES? Yes. This was evident within the first five years (1976–81) following initiation of policies at the Ministries of Education and Health. At that early stage of program development we used the following criteria in defining 'local access' to each of the two core programs: (a) access to sexuality education at school: 50 per cent of secondary school students in the locality were enrolled at boards of education that had approved inclusion of sexuality topics within their Health or Family Life curriculum; and (b) access to family planning services: the public health unit had a family planning clinic which prescribed and dispensed contraceptives. Among localities providing access to both core programs, a higher percentage exceeded the provincial mean decline in pregnancy rates compared with localities providing access to only one core program or programs that did not meet our definition of 'core.' These greater rate declines associated with access to both education and clinical services occurred in rates for both younger and older adolescents (age sixteen and under, and seventeen to nineteen respectively) and, most importantly, regardless of locality SES.

At that early stage of program development, a single core program of sexuality education in a locality had less impact on pregnancy rate than a single core program of family planning clinical services, and especially in localities of low SES which are more likely to be rural (Orton and Rosenblatt 1986). This is to be expected for a number of reasons besides the effectiveness of beginning programs in sexuality education. A higher proportion of self-selecting young people at a clinic (compared with students in a classroom) are likely to be sexually active and at risk. A clinic for young people obviously welcomes them, whereas they may be uncertain whether a doctor will assist them, may fear loss of confidentiality to their parents, may not have a family doctor, or the nearest town may not have a doctor.

Can programs make a major impact on the pregnancy rate and reduce our expenditures on the consequences of pregnancy? Yes. By the end of the first decade (1976–86) there was a 23 per cent decline in Ontario's total rate of adolescent pregnancy (1976, 54.2 pregnancies to women under age twenty per 1,000 women age fifteen to nineteen; in 1986 the rate was 41.9). The evidence is fairly strong to conclude that the developing sexual health programs exerted a major influence on this rate decline. The programs are in two public sectors, potentially in contact with the total local adolescent population. This is not a one-time demonstration project or sample study – but a universal study of all localities in one province, monitoring change over five-year periods. In Ontario's five-year high school program, for example, it takes five years for a single course to reach all its students. Policy and program development have varied among the other provinces, and at varying times their adolescent pregnancy rates (although incomplete) have also declined within the same decade 1976–86. Unfortunately, we cannot compare trends of this program decade with a preprogram decade because we lack abortion data in Canada to calculate pregnancy rates prior to 1974. It will be important therefore to study the next decade, 1986–96.

By Ontario's rate decline, adolescents avoided 31,000 pregnancies, that they would have had if the 1976 rate had continued unchanged through the decade to 1986 (Orton and Rosenblatt 1991: 2). Our cost–benefit study on only the first eight years (1976–83: 21,600 pregnancies avoided because of the declining rate), compared actual expenditures of $16.4 million on public health family planning services, against avoided expenditures of $41.4 million on avoided abortions, births, and one year of General Welfare and Family Benefits to adolescent lone mothers. In the first eight years of preventive policy Ontario saved $25 million on only the short-term consequences (Orton and Rosenblatt 1986: 126-7).

Can programs be effective with both younger and older-teens? Yes. Over the decade 1976–86 there was a greater decline in the pregnancy rate among younger teens (–33 per cent among age sixteen and under) than among older teens (–20 per cent among ages seventeen to nineteen). In 1976 there had been much less difference between localities in younger teen rates than older teen rates, suggesting a more common norm against sexual intercourse among younger teens regardless of locality SES, which could be reinforced by early educational programs. Decline in the younger teen rate actually accelerated in the second half of the decade (–15 per cent and –21 per cent). After age sixteen, an increasing percentage of teens drop out of school at each higher grade and are less easily reached by community programs. This would be a continuing factor affecting older teen rates. However, the decline in older teen pregnancy rate slowed dramatically in the second half of the decade (–17 per cent and –4 per cent) (Orton and Rosenblatt 1991: Tables 10, 11). This slowdown for older teens over 1981–86 occurred concurrently with an economic recession in 1980–81 and rise in Ontario poverty rates which peaked in 1983 (National Council of Welfare 1998: 12, 28). Nevertheless, with the rapid rate decline over the first five years, by 1981 there was no longer a correlation between low SES localities and higher rates of pregnancy among older teens.

How great a decline in adolescent pregnancy rate must we achieve in order to reduce secondary rates of abortion and unmarried birth? This will vary, depending upon a number of local factors affecting personal decisions in response to the pregnancy. How an adolescent woman responds to unplanned pregnancy depends upon her personal circumstances, and support from her personal network and community services to implement any of the alternatives (marriage and birth, abortion, unmarried birth, adoption, lone parenting). A high locality rate of adolescent pregnancy can mean wider swings among those changing choices and less predictability for community planners.

By the end of the decade 1976–86, just over half of Ontario localities (twenty-eight) had experienced a major decline in their adolescent abortion rate. Among these, seventeen localities with a group mean decline of one-third in their adolescent pregnancy rate had a group mean decline of 29 per cent in their adolescent abortion rate. The other eleven localities with an even greater decline in their adolescent pregnancy rate (group mean decline –38%) had simultaneous declines in their adolescent abortion rate and birth rate to unmarried adolescents (group mean declines of –21 per cent and –20 per cent respectively) (ibid.: 5). These simultaneous declines in pregnancy outcomes mean that a decline in abortion rate was not achieved by a rise in birth rate to unmarried teens or vice versa. When we look at trends in locality rates, we can see the process of social change across the province long before it shows up in a provincial rate.

Can preventive programs reduce the wide difference in rates between localities of high and low SES? Yes. By 1986 this geographic inequity was declining. Among the seven Ontario regions the gap between the lowest and highest regional rates declined by 14 per cent in young teen pregnancy rates and by 16 per cent in older teen pregnancy rates (Orton and Rosenblatt 1991: 23–4, calculated from Tables 10–11).

Since 1987, Statistics Canada reports a rise in Canada's rate of adolescent pregnancy. Canada's rate of adolescent pregnancy in 1986 was 41.2, rising by 1994 to 48.8 per 1,000 (Wadhera and Millar 1997: Table 1). Since 1994 Statistics Canada has revised Canadian pregnancy rates from 1978 on to include abortions performed in free-standing clinics within Canada or as reported from the United States. However, Statistics Canada does not receive such details as residence or age on these abortions and consequently the numbers of free-standing clinic abortions cannot be included in their provincial rates. Thus, Statistics Canada's rates of abortion and pregnancy are less than complete for province or territory. The sharpest rises of adolescent pregnancy were in 1988 and 1989, leading up to the next economic recession (1990–91), when family and child poverty rates began to rise. Ontario's adolescent pregnancy rate also rose from 41.9 in 1986 to 44.6 in 1992. We lack complete pregnancy rates for the intervening years. By 1994 Ontario's rate rose to 46.8, dropping to 44.7 in 1995. We should expect that fluctuations in locality rates of adolescent pregnancy will depend upon the presence of well-designed preventive programs and severity of recession in each community.

Can we achieve universal access to preventive programs, that is, in all localities? Yes. But we can do so only if the relevant ministries mandate the intervention and provide specific standards and special funding. Only the Ministry of Health did this. By 1991 there were huge differences between the sectors in local program development. In our 1991 survey of programs we also asked about prevention of sexually transmitted diseases (STDs/AIDS) and surveyed a third sector of Children's Aid Societies (CASs) who serve high need youth (Orton and Rosenblatt 1993). The response rate to our 1991 survey of Ontario preventive programs was public health units, 100 per cent; boards of education–public boards, 66 per cent; Roman Catholic Separate School boards, 67 per cent; and Children's Aid Societies, 74 per cent.

Within fifteen years (1976–91) public health units had established the basics of universal access across the province – at least one sexual health clinic in 98 per cent of Ontario localities. In 64 per cent of the localities there were at least two clinics. However, school boards had established access to sexuality education in only 30 per cent of localities. In 1991 we defined local educational access as follows: two-thirds of students were enrolled at boards that introduced the topics of STDs/AIDS by grade 8, and contraception by grade 9. Our 1991 criteria for local access to sexual health education were higher than a decade earlier (1981), but still within the suggested outline of ministry policy. The number of school boards in a locality varied from one to fourteen.

In the third sector, only 40 per cent of Children's Aid Societies offered life skills groups (including some topics of sexuality) to wards, usually those about to leave care, and only 30 per cent to non-wards. In 1991 there were fifty-four Children's Aid Societies (including several agencies under native auspices) serving Ontario's fifty-four localities. The four sectarian CASs (three Catholic and one Jewish) were located in large cities together with a public CAS, and a few rural CASs served more than one locality. CASs had no reportable data on the extent of sexual counselling or even of pregnancy among children in care. CAS attention to sexual health is largely not reported and, where reported, is minimal.

The rapid development of sexual health clinics across the province was achieved under the public health approach to health for the total population, the Health Ministry's mandate for local access to preventive services, 100 per cent provincial funding since the initiation of family planning policy (1975), increasingly comprehensive and specific standards over the years, and the energetic leadership of the provincial program director, Dr Helen McKilligin, a committed specialist in maternal and child health.

Policy resources for sexual health at the other two ministries have been either minimal (Education and Training) or non-existent (Community and Social Services). Both these ministries have a more decentralized as well as dual delivery system of public and sectarian agencies, stemming from their historical origin under local, sectarian auspices.

The Ministry of Education and Training failed to revise its 1978 guideline adding sexuality topics to the health curriculum. That guideline directed introduction of the topic of STDs by grade 8, but only suggested that topics of adolescent pregnancy and contraception might be introduced by grades 9 or 10. In 1985 a teaching module on AIDS was developed by the ministry and mandated. Only one health credit is required for the grade 12 certificate. Health is given twenty-five to thirty hours within the physical education and health course. Sexuality is only two of twenty-one topics in health. Students usually take this credit course in grade 9, when the majority of students are age fourteen or fifteen.

Vague direction and lack of resources from the Ministry of Education and Training have resulted in idiosyncratic curriculum development by each local public board of education and a narrow curriculum developed under the auspices of Ontario Roman Catholic bishops for local Catholic boards. The greater emphasis in the guidelines upon prevention of disease (STDs/HIV/AIDS) than pregnancy, is replicated strongly in local board curricula – at public boards as well as Catholic boards, and particularly at the latter. Although the majority of responding boards introduce STDs/AIDS by grade 8 (public, 88 per cent; Roman Catholic Separate School, 94 per cent), only a minority require introduction of contraception by grade 9 (public, 43 per cent; Catholic, 20 per cent). Public boards report a wider range of sexuality topics, but there is great variation among boards. Catholic boards teach sexuality topics within family life education and this, in turn, within Religious Studies. Consequently, Catholic boards provide more classroom hours and annual reinforcement from kindergarten to grade 12. Their new curriculum ('Fully Alive') in place up to grade 8, to date, teaches chastity, natural family planning, and offers negative comments concerning condoms (highly unreliable), oral contraceptives (high health risks), IUDs, and sometimes oral contraceptives (act as an abortifacient, therefore immoral). Catholic boards report more support to parents as sexuality educators.

Ontario's Child and Family Services Act (1984) does not mention sexual health, aside from child sexual abuse as evidence of a child in need of protection. The act defines prevention solely as 'prevention from coming into care,' and agency budgets have been frozen or cut since the late 1980s. Funds under the act are not available for other prevention activities in the community, for example, working with street children. The ministry has no central director of child welfare programs. Collection of data (other than for financial management) is left to the non-governmental Ontario association of child welfare agencies. Ministry resources for child protection are inadequate in general and nonexistent concerning prevention in sexual health. The only directive concerning sexual health from the Ministry of Community and Social Services requires Children's Aid Societies to report to their local Medical Officer of Health any case of HIV/AIDS among children in care.

As in the educational sector, this policy vacuum at the ministry has resulted in scattered, idiosyncratic local programs at public child welfare agencies and religious limits at the few sectarian agencies. The extent and quality of non-reported sexual counselling is bound to be compromised by long-term budget restrictions that have led to staff overload and undoubtedly contribute to the reported low incidence of CAS staff training on sexuality issues.

Some Conclusions

First, a government, by its policy resources, strongly shapes program development at its local institutions or agencies. It is the key determinant of universal access and core program content in all localities. Educational policy, by emphasizing prevention of disease and neglecting prevention of unplanned pregnancy, both of which ensue from sexual intercourse, gives the message that pregnancy and its serious consequences for young women are of minor importance. It fails to inculcate responsibility into the values of young men concerning effects of their behaviour upon women, potential children, and our communities. It contradicts and undermines other policy goals for women's equality and family health and well-being. Child welfare policy neglects our most vulnerable children by remaining silent concerning the sexual health of children in care. The inescapable conclusion from this research is that what we put into government policy is what we get in local program effectiveness.

Second, a vague and sexist policy or the lack of any policy is found in ministries with a dual delivery system of public and sectarian agencies. The absence of a mandated policy and standards may seem like religious tolerance and decentralized grass-roots democracy, but it is the very opposite in reality. Generally, only fundamentalist or orthodox religions have religious schools. Their teachings on sexuality are rooted in sacred scriptures from ancient patriarchal societies (non-democratic, sexist, and homophobic), and they are interpreted by current male church leaders and patriarchs, usually in other countries.

Consequently, the content of sexuality and family life education in publicly funded, religious schools cannot be changed by local church members and parents to serve the needs of today's youth, in spite of direct election of school board trustees. For example, the Fully Alive and AIDS Education curricula in Ontario's Roman Catholic Separate Schools have been developed under the auspices of the Ontario Conference of Catholic Bishops in accordance with Vatican teachings. These curricula do not reflect the views of Canadian Catholics, judging by a cross-Canada survey over a decade ago that found no significant difference between Catholic and non-Catholic women in self-reported contraceptive practice (Balakrishnan et al. 1985).

Third, decentralization without special funding as well as policy and mandated standards does not necessarily mean local accountability in either public or sectarian agencies, at either boards of education or child welfare agencies – because of fewer local resources in low SES localities and/or the authoritarian auspices of some agencies. Nor does it protect the individual's right of access to broadly based learning and comprehensive services. Decentralization may appear to offer incremental development of programs across a territory. However, as our findings reveal, that development is extremely slow – may never occur, especially in low SES localities – and it often lacks program elements that research has documented to be more effective.

Fourth, a ministry or departmental mandate, with standards and special funding, is compatible with a process of developing programs to serve local needs. The extension of sexual health clinics across the province 'where needed ... to ensure access' under the health ministry mandate took fifteen years. Obviously some localities took longer to recognize the need, regardless of the special funding. They did so eventually, however, because the ministry mandate specifically included a needs assessment by the broader community.

These findings and conclusions raise important ethical issues.

Ethical Issue 1: There are strengths and weaknesses in sexuality and family life education under both public and Catholic boards of education, but children in *both* school systems are being short-changed. Education is the only universal program able to reach all adolescents, and it is not doing it concerning sexual health. The public assumes high-quality sexuality education is there for all. This false assumption strongly contributes to blaming the victims as irresponsible. Lack of a mandated program and standards for prevention produces inequitable access and wide variability in program quality and effectiveness.

Ethical Issue 2: For many reasons, sexual health education should address two stages of decision making. It should promote postponement or abstinence (especially among young teens) and, for the sexually active, then double protection against both unintended pregnancy and STDs/AIDS. The concept of postponement prompts discussion of all the reasons and also what circumstances would have to change for each to review that decision in the future. If we teach a single message of abstinence or chastity, we leave everyone at risk. For those aiming for chastity, occasional lapses can have severe consequences. We fail to recognize the developmental aspect of relationships, that emotional and sexual intimacy increase over time. And we leave the uncertain or undeterred sexually active always at risk. Limited information and negative attitudes to protective strategies deny young people their right to make informed decisions within their personal values, and to protect themselves and their partner.

Ethical Issue 3: The failure of government ministries and local institutions to resolve these two issues means some young people now have both private and public resources for prevention, some have only private resources, and some still have neither. We fail to inform and influence the total adolescent peer group and thus the normative environment for each adolescent. The most disadvantaged are still disadvantaged rather than receiving extra support. *By omission or ineffectiveness in preventive policies and programs, we adults are building social inequities among our young people.*

Postscript: In January 1998 the Ontario government downloaded responsibility for total funding of public health and other core social programs to municipalities. Just before the 1999 election the government announced it would pay 50 per cent of the cost of mandatory public health programs. This is less than was taken away, however, and full funding has not been restored for the more sensitive sexual health programs. We are undermining the only sector that has succeeded in developing sexual health programs across the province and that serves as a catalyst to the education and social services sector.

A new health curriculum finally arrived for 1998–9, focusing on developing and applying 'living skills' concerning a range of health issues. It introduces topics of reproduction and abstinence in grade 6; sexually transmitted disease in grade 7; 'physical, emotional, interpersonal, and spiritual aspects of healthy sexuality (e.g., respect for life, ethical questions in relationships, contraception)' in grade 8 (a grade earlier than the previous curriculum). This is one step forward and one step back. In Protestant fundamentalist and Catholic usage, 'respect for life' refers to non-acceptance of condoms and other contraceptives, as well as abortion, on religious grounds that they defeat God's procreative purpose for sexual intercourse. Both contraception and abortion are legal in Canada. In our Ontario study, our most important recommendation was:

A Ministry of Education should mandate:
... that comprehensive sexual health education be provided within the Health course which has a scientific interdisciplinary knowledge-base and the value-base of education for a democratic society.
... that the Health course be separate from and not limited in content by the tenets of religious education at Catholic boards and other denominational schools.
... that the Health course be provided from kindergarten through grade 12, with a minimum of 50 classroom hours annually. (Orton and Rosenblatt 1993: 15–23)

This recommendation would not limit religious schools in teaching their perspective on sexual issues within Religious Studies.

In summary, through recent policies governments are:
... increasing child poverty,
... cutting funding for resources for basic human needs (housing, education, child care, health care, welfare, pay equity, women's shelters, environmental protection, etc.),
... severely undermining public health programs for sexual health by shifting them down upon the unequal financial resources of local governments,
... and failing to separate the school health course from sectarian religious rejection of condoms, contraceptives, and abortion.

All these actions and policies can be expected to increase the rate of adolescent pregnancy (and STD/HIV), which, in turn, will further increase poverty.

References

Aboriginal Nurses Association of Canada. (1996). *HIV/AIDS and Its Impact on Aboriginal Women in Canada*. Ottawa: Minister of Health Canada.
Alder, R., Vingilis, E., and Mai, V., eds. (1996). *Community Health and Well-Being in Southwestern Ontario: A Resource for Planning*. London, Ont.: Middlesex-London Health Unit.

Balakrishnan, T.R., Krotki, K., and Lapierre-Adamcyk, E. (1985). 'Contraceptive Use in Canada.' *Family Planning Perspectives* 17(5): 209–15.

Bibby, R.W., and Posterski, D.C. (1992). *Teen Trends: A Nation in Motion.* Toronto: Stoddard.

Campaign 2000. (1997). 'Child Poverty in Canada, Report Card 1997.' Toronto: Campaign 2000, c/o Family Service Association.

Canadian Institute of Child Health. (1994). *The Health of Canada's Children*, 2nd ed. Ottawa: author.

Clark, S., French, F., Dechman, M., and MacCallum, B. (1991). *Mothers and Children: One Decade Later.* Halifax: Nova Scotia Department of Community Services.

Comer, J.P. (1985). 'The Yale–New Haven Primary Prevention Project: A Follow-up Study.' *Journal of American Academy of Child Psychiatry* 24(2): 154–60.

Connell, D.B., Turner, R.R., and Mason, E.F. (1985). 'Summary of Findings of the School Health Education Evaluation: Health Promotion Effectiveness, Implementation, and Costs.' *Journal of School Health* 55(80): 316–21.

Currie, D.W., and Green, V. (1994). 'The Sexual Harrassment Project: Student to Student Sexual Harrassment in Ontario Secondary School.' Toronto: Ontario Secondary School Teachers' Federation.

Daly, K.J., and Sobol, M.P. (1993). *Adoption in Canada, Final Report.* Guelph, Ont.: National Adoption Study, University of Guelph.

Eisner, V., Brazie, J.V., Pratt, M.W., and Hexter, A.C. (1979). 'The Risk of Low Birthweight.' *American Journal of Public Health* 69: 887–93.

Fisher, W.A., and Fisher, J.D. (1992). 'Understanding and Promoting AIDS Preventive Behavior: A Conceptual Model and Educational Tools.' *Canadian Journal of Human Sexuality* 1(3): 99–106.

Freeman, E.M. (1989). 'Adolescent Fathers in Urban Communities: Exploring Their Needs and Role in Preventing Pregnancy.' *Journal of Social Work and Human Sexuality* 8(1): 113–31.

Frost, J., and Darroch Forrest, J. (1995). 'Understanding the Impact of Effective Teenage Pregnancy Prevention Programs.' *Family Planning Perspectives* 27: 188–95.

Fulton, R., and Factor, D. (1993). *A Study of Young Mothers in Metro Toronto.* Toronto: Young Mothers' Resource Group.

Grunseit, A., Kippax, S., Aggleton, P., Baldo, M., and Slutkin, G. (1997). 'Sexuality Education and Young People's Sexual Behaviour: A Review of Studies.' *Journal of Adolescent Research* 12(4): 421–53.

Guttmacher, S., Lieberman, L., Ward, D., Freudenberg, N., Radosh, A., and Des Jarlais, D. (1997). 'Condom Availability in New York City Public High Schools: Relationships to Condom Use and Sexual Behavior.' *American Journal of Public Health* 87(9): 1427–33.

Health Canada. (1994). *Canadian Guidelines for Sexual Health Education*. Ottawa: Minister of Supply and Services Canada.

Horwitz, S.M., Klerman, L.V., Sung Kuo, H., and Jekel, J.F. (1991). 'Intergenerational Transmission of School-Age Parenthood.' *Family Planning Perspectives* 23(4): 168–72.

Howard, M., and McCabe, J.B. (1990). 'Helping Teenagers Postpone Sexual Involvement.' *Family Planning Perspectives* 22(1): 21–6.

Jemmott, J.B., Jemmott, L.S., and Fong, G.T. (1998). 'Abstinence and Safer-Sex HIV Risk-Reduction Interventions for African American Adolescents: A Randomized Controlled Trial.' *Journal of the American Medical Association* 279: 1529–36.

Jones, R.B., and Wasserheit, J.N. (1991). 'Introduction to the Biology and Natural History of Sexually Transmitted Diseases. In J.N. Wasserheit, S.O. Aral, K.K. Holmes, and P.J. Hitchcock, eds., *Research Issues in Human Behavior and Sexually Transmitted Diseases in the AIDS Era*, pp. 11–37. Washington, DC: American Society for Microbiology.

King, M.A., Coles, B.J., and King, A.J.C. (1991). *Canada Youth and AIDS Study* (technical report). Kingston, Ont.: Queen's University, Social Program Evaluation Group.

– (1988). *Canada Youth and AIDS Study*. Kingston, Ont.: Queen's University, Social Program Evaluation Group.

Kirby, D., Korpi, M., Barth, R.P., and Cagampang, H.H. (1997). 'The Impact of the Postponing Sexual Involvement Curriculum among Youths in California.' *Family Planning Perspectives* 29(3): 100–14.

Kirby, D., Waszak, C., and Ziegler, J. (1991). 'Six School-Based Clinics: Their Reproductive Health Services and Impact on Sexual Behavior.' *Family Planning Perspectives* 23(1): 6–16.

Kirby, D., Short, L., Collins, J., et al. (1994). 'School-Based Programs to Reduce Sexual Risk Behaviors: A Review of Effectiveness.' *Public Health Reports* 109(3): 339–60.

Kramer, M.S. (1987). 'Determinants of Low Birthweight: Methodological Assessment and Meta-Analysis.' *Bulletin of the World Health Organization* 65: 663–737.

Lee, V.E., and Bryk, A.S. (1989). 'A Multilevel Model of the Social Distribution of High School Achievement.' *Sociology of Education* 62(July): 172–92.

McCormick, M.C. (1985). 'The Contribution of Low Birthweight to Infant Mor-tality and Childhood Morbidity.' *New England Journal of Medicine* 312: 82–90.

Meloch, M., and Plante, G.C. (1991). 'Fillettes a risques.' *The Social Worker* 59(4): 154–7.

Miller, B.C., and Jorgensen, S.T. (1988). 'Adolescent Fertility-Related Behaviour and Its Family Linkages.' In D.M. Klein and J. Aldous, eds. *Social Stress and Family Development*, 210–33. New York: Guilford Press.

Miller, K.S., Clark, L.F., and Moore, J.S. (1997). 'Sexual Initiation with Older Male Partners.' *Family Planning Perspectives* 29(5): 212–14.

Moberg, D.P., and Piper, D.L. (1990). 'An Outcome Evaluation of the Project Model Health: A Middle School Health Promotion Program.' *Health Education Quarterly* 17(1): 37–51.

National Council of Welfare. (1998). *Poverty Profile 1996*. Ottawa: Public Works and Government Services Canada.

– (1997). *Healthy Parents, Healthy Babies*. Ottawa: Public Works and Government Services Canada.

Novick, M., and Shillington, R. (1996). 'Crossroads for Canada: A Time to Invest in Children and Families.' Toronto: Campaign 2000, c/o Family Service Association.

Ontario, Ministry of Health. (1989). *Mandatory Health Programs and Services Guidelines* (Public health Branch). Toronto: Queen's Printer for Ontario.

Ontario, Premier's Council on Health, Well-being, and Social Justice. (1994). *Yours, Mine and Ours: Ontario's Children and Youth, Phase One*. Toronto: Queen's Printer for Ontario.

Orton, M.J. (1993). 'Speeding up Structural Change to Redefine the Problems: Learning from the Struggle for Resources of Primary Prevention of Unwanted/Adolescent Pregnancy. A Study of the Canadian Government and Two Provinces, Alberta and Ontario.' Doctoral dissertation, University of Toronto, 1991. *Dissertation Abstracts International* 53-8, 2986A.

Orton, M.J., and Rosenblatt, E., (1993). *Sexual Health for Youth: Creating a Three-Sector Network in Ontario* (Report 4). Toronto: University of Toronto, Faculty of Social Work, Ontario Study of Adolescent Pregnancy and Sexually Transmitted Diseases.

– (1991). *Adolescent Pregnancy in Ontario 1976–1986: Extending Access to Prevention Reduces Abortions, and Births to the Unmarried* (Report 3). Hamilton, Ontario: McMaster University, School of Social Work, Ontario Adolescent Pregnancy Project.

– (1986). *Adolescent Pregnancy in Ontario: Progress in Prevention* (Report 2). Hamilton, Ontario: McMaster University, School of Social Work, Ontario Adolescent Pregnancy Project.

– (1981). *Adolescent Birth Planning Needs: Ontario in the Eighties*. Hamilton, Ontario: Ontario Adolescent Pregnancy Project, School of Social Work, McMaster University.

Ottawa-Carleton Health Department Teaching Health Unit. (1992). *Evaluation of the Ottawa-Carleton Health Department's School-Based Sexuality Health Centre Program*. Ottawa: Ottawa-Carleton Health Department.

Quinton, D., and Rutter, M. (1998). *Parenting Breakdown. The Making and Breaking of Intergenerational Links*. Brookfield, U.S.: Avebury.

Reitsma-Street, M., and Offord, D.R. (1991). 'Girl Delinquents and Their Sisters: A Challenge for Practice.' *Canadian Social Work Review* 8(1): 11–27.

Roosa, M.W., and Christopher, F.S. (1990). 'Evaluation of an Abstinence-Only Adolescent Pregnancy Prevention Program: A Replication.' *Family Relations*, Oct.: 363–7.

Ross, D.P., Scott, K., and Kelly, M. (1996). *Child Poverty: What Are the Consequences?* Ottawa: Centre for International Statistics, Canadian Council on Social Development.

Ross, D.P., Shillington, E.R., and Lochhead, D. (1994). *The Canadian Fact Book on Poverty 1994*. Ottawa: Canadian Council on Social Development.

Rutter, M. (1980). 'School Influences on Children's Behavior and Development.' The 1979 Kenneth Blackfan Lecture, Children's Hospital Medical Center, Boston. *Pediatrics* 65(2): 208–20.

Rutter, M., Maughan, G., and Mortimer, P. (1979). *Fifteen Thousand Hours: Secondary Schools and Their Effects on Children*. London: Open Books.

St Pierre, T., Mark, M., Kaltreider, D., and Atkin, K. (1995). 'A 27-month Evaluation of a Sexual Activity Prevention Program in Boys and Girls Clubs across the Nation.' *Family Relations* 44: 69–77.

Saul, J.R. (1995). *The Unconscious Civilization*. Concord, Ont.: House of Anansi Press.

Schellenberg, G., and Ross, D.P. (1997). 'When Social Programs Disappear, Can the Marketplace Fill in the Gap?' *Perception* 20(4): 7–11. Ottawa: Canadian Council on Social Development.

Schuster, M., Bell, R., Berry, S., and Kanouse, D. (1998). 'Impact of a High School Condom Availability Program on Sexual Attitudes and Behaviors.' *Family Planning Perspectives* 30: 67–82, 88.

Sellers, D.E., McGraw, S.A., and Mckinlay, J.B. (1994). 'Does the Promotion and Distribution of Condoms Increase Teen Sexual Activity? Evidence from an HIV Prevention Program for Latino Youth.' *American Journal of Public Health* 84(12): 1952–7.

Shah, C.P., Kahan, M.I., and Krouser, J. (1987). 'The Health of Children in Low-Income Families.' *Canadian Medical Association Journal* 137: 485–90.

Smith, M.A.B. (1991). 'The Teen Incentive Program: A Research and Evaluation Model for Adolescent Pregnancy Prevention.' Doctoral disserta-

tion, Columbia University, 1990. *Dissertation Abstracts International* 51–9, 3244A.
Statistics Canada. (1996). *The Daily*. 24 May.
– (1994). *Vital Statistics, Birth and Death*. Catalogue 84-204.
Staton, P., & Larkin, J. (1993). *Sexual Harassment: The Intimidation Factor. A Project Report: Sexual Harassment as a Barrier to Gender Equity in Education.* Toronto: Green Dragon.
Stock, J.L., Bell, M.A., Boyer, D.K., and Connell, F.A. (1997). 'Adolescent Pregnancy and Sexual Risk-Taking among Sexually Abused Girls.' *Family Planning Perspectives* 29(5): 200–3, 227.
Tam, R., Macdonald, N., Feder, S., et al. (1996). 'Chlamydia Infection in Street Youth: Need for More Aggressive Screening Programs.' *Canadian Journal of Infectious Diseases* 7: 49–52.
Taylor, C. (1991). *The Malaise of Modernity*. Condord, Ont.: House of Anansi Press.
Wadhera, S., and Millar, W. (1997). 'Teenage Pregnancies, 1974 to 1994.' *Health Reports* 9(3): 9–17. Catalogue #82-003-XPB. Ottawa: Statistics Canada.
Wellings, K., Wadsworth, J., Johnson, A.M., et al. (1995). 'Provision of Sex Education and Early Sexual Experience: The Relation Examined.' *British Medical Journal* 311: 417–20.
Westwood, M., Kramer, M.S., & Munz, D. (1983). 'Growth and Development of Full-Term Nonasphyxiated Small-for-Gestational-Age Newborns: Follow-up through Adolescence.' *Pediatrics* 71: 376–82.
Winter, L., and Breckenmaker, L.C. (1991). 'Tailoring Family Planning Services to the Special Needs of Adolescents.' *Family Planning Perspectives* 23(1): 24–30.
Zabin, L.S., Hirsch, M.B., Smith, E.A., et al. (1986). 'Evaluation of a Pregnancy Prevention Program for Urban Teenagers.' *Family Planning Perspectives* 18(3): 199–26.

10

A Round-Table Discussion of Teen Parenting as a Social and Ethical Issue

The discussion was held 11 May 1996 at Oakham House, Ryerson Polytechnic University, Toronto.

Participants

Kathryn Pyne Addelson, Philosophy, Smith College, Northampton, Massachusetts
Laurie Bryden, Bay Centre for Birth Control, Regional Women's Health Centre, Toronto
David Checkland, Ethics Centre and Philosophy, Ryerson Polytechnic University, Toronto
Susan Clark, Vice-President Academic, Brock University, St Catharines
Ruth DaCosta, Executive Director, Covenant House, Toronto
Linda Davies, Social Work, McGill University, Montreal
Ian Hacking, Philosophy, University of Toronto
Beverley Leaver, Jessie's Centre for Teenagers, Toronto
Colin Maloney, Executive Director, Catholic Children's Aid Society of Metropolitan Toronto
Margaret McKinnon, Education, University of Ottawa
Suzanne Peters, Canadian Policy Research Networks
Prue Rains, Sociology, McGill University, Montreal
Peggy Robertson, Medical Services Director, Children's Aid Society of Metropolitan Toronto
James Wong, Communications Studies Program, Wilfrid Laurier University, Waterloo

David Checkland: I thought it would be interesting for us to start with a theme that all the participants touched on yesterday, and which becomes central for most of us thinking about the issues of teen pregnancy and parenting. I'm thinking of the relations between need, entitlement, responsibility, and choice. Susan Clark mentioned in her talk yesterday that often we take the notion of adulthood or age as determining our attitudes to the connection between need and dessert; it's the *youth* of early parents that is the issue. They are at a developmental stage at which full responsibility is something that some of them may reach for, but can't really achieve. Hence, having and raising children is bound to be a bad idea for most, if not all, teenagers – certainly the younger ones. On the other hand, Suzanne Peters mentioned in her discussion of the focus groups that she and Canadian Policy Research Networks have held that very often people started off with rather harsh attitudes regarding other people's entitlement to various kinds of social services, and often modified those attitudes in the light of discussion with other members of the focus groups who would point out aspects of those other people's reality or social situation. Margaret [McKinnon], Linda [Davies], and Prue [Rains] mentioned some of the quite responsible choices made by young mothers which are often portrayed as *irresponsible* choices, such as the choice to stay on welfare rather than work because that enables them to care better for their children when working would expose their children to poorer parenting. So, this theme of responsibility and peoples' responses to it was one I thought would be useful to start with.

Suzanne Peters: One of the things that I would like to point out on this issue is that the notion that people should take increased responsibility for themselves is not a new notion. Self-reliance is not a new principle. I think Canadians always expected programs to offer people opportunities that would maximize their ability to be self-reliant, that they would start from the basis of *only* helping to the point that people actually needed it, and that what people have been discouraged about is that they see programs going for years and years creating a cycle of dependency. The programs haven't, they believe, achieved appropriate levels of personal responsibility. It's not a new issue. It may be more squawked about in a sense because the people are aware there is less money to go around, they feel threatened themselves, and they feel the programs are unfairly distributed.

One of the things I didn't say [in my paper] yesterday, but I have said to some of you personally, is that single moms on welfare also have very strict criteria about who they think should be self-reliant. It may not be themselves – exactly because they see their circumstances as very difficult. But they are extremely angry at unemployed single men who are on welfare, and particularly those they see as ripping off the system, or dealing drugs when they are on the system. They see the level of self-reliance to be just below the level that they themselves are exerting. They also hold to the notion that individual effort is ideal and necessary, and they blame those who don't achieve it. So, it's not exactly as if there is an age or a gender or position discrimination on this. It's where you attach that notion [of self-reliance or responsibility], but it is there for them too. Most of them in the various focus groups that I have been in over the years have also said they would rather work if they could. It's the circumstances of being unable to work that have been difficult.

Ruth DaCosta: One of the things that is becoming more clear in terms of the kind of work that we do at Covenant House is that we are seeing an increasingly large number of young people, both male and female, using what would be the equivalent of our 'outpatient services,' coming in with very young children – the youngest being a 5-day-old brought in by a 17-year-old mother who was really bringing the child 'home,' if you will, to show it off. This was pretty sad. But it is the code of ethics among the kids that I find fascinating. My thinking on this initially was that some of these kids were having kids to love because there was nobody else around, available to them to love. I feel that this view is quite inaccurate. My sense is that, to a large extent, these kids are having kids largely as a means of being able to be cared for themselves, because the system, in their minds, has more to offer to young women with babies than they would have access to if they were 17 and on their way out of care from the child welfare agency and so on. It's a phenomenon that I don't quite know how to articulate yet, but I believe that I am on to something. In addition, you also have a code of ethics among the street kids themselves. The last thing these kids will do is give up a baby, at least at the front end, because they've been so disconnected themselves that it's just a sin to do that on the street. So you are dealing with what I feel is a very complex issue that we need to know a lot more about.

Kathryn Pyne Addelson: Is the issue a question of whether this is a federal or provincial policy with regard to welfare responsibility, or a question on the local, everyday level? In the United States – I have to talk about the United States – there are questions of what you are going to do nationally so far as welfare goes. At that level, there are a lot of questions about irresponsible welfare people, people who are perpetually on welfare, or having children to stay on welfare. But there are other questions on other levels. Many people do a much more local, engaged level of work. It may connect with policy, but the primary thrust of the work is not aimed at policy. It is aimed at people in local solutions, where the discussion of responsibility and undercutting responsibility might take a different cast, as it seemed to do when Ruth was speaking. We seem to get two different views of responsibility, according to the level where action and discussion takes place.

Beverley Leaver: There must be a continuum of what we expect in terms of 'self-reliance' in talking about a 13-year-old as compared with a 19-year-old. If I am working with a 14-year-old, if she can eat right during her pregnancy, I consider that a very positive thing. If she can take on breast feeding, then that's another plus. That is what I expect from these people. I am not expecting them to be employed and supporting themselves, because that is a mistake, given their age.

Peggy Robertson: I agree with what is said about young people getting pregnant at times of transition. I think part of our problem is lack of prevention, that we don't teach the practical skills needed, that we don't teach them how to do things – self-reliance. There is a great fear for kids leaving care. I don't know how many pregnancy tests I do and how many of those are positive. These pregnancies take place against the background of tons of sexual information, of condoms, and a whole array of community and other kinds of services to prevent pregnancies. I think these are deliberate and well timed by and large because kids are really scared witless. And of course the positive reinforcement that goes with being pregnant. Unfortunately, kids don't get the service, they don't get the intervention, they don't get the strokes, that come from *not* being pregnant. They get it when they are involved, the attention lavished on them is quite wonderful. Why can't we do that when they are not pregnant as well so *that* becomes an accomplishment in and of itself? At Children's Aid [Ontario's child social welfare agency] we set our sights lower so that success is not necessarily that someone has a job or is not in the criminal system. For instance, when they hit 18, they haven't been pregnant, they had all the sexually transmitted diseases successfully treated – not that they didn't get them – that they got treated and were responsible enough to do that. I think that when we measure outcomes as success that the level is way too high for a lot of our young people and is totally unrealistic given the services that we have to provide and prevention that just isn't there.

Susan Clark: Can I just ask, given the comments that you have made, that in some ways are you seeing the most disadvantaged young women?

Peggy Robertson: Very much so

Susan Clark: There must be a whole group out there, given how many young women do become pregnant and are unmarried, that don't come into contact – or not very much, anyway – with social services. So we are dealing with a particular group of young unmarried women , I think.

Peggy Robertson: A lot of women who have been sexually abused physically and emotionally all their lives end up in circumstances that may be harder on them than otherwise. We see a high rate of pregnancy in these kids that have been set up for victimization and have no boundaries, don't have interpersonal skills to negotiate sexual experiences that might be healthier or to negotiate not having sex. So, yes, we see the 'cream of the crop,' but looking at the cream of the crop when it comes to disadvantaged young women I think is very important; it gives clues to the rest as well.

Susan Clark: Yes it does. But I think it also speaks to the question of entitlement and how you make those arguments get skewed at times because the focus is on the most disadvantaged. But that is not necessarily characteristic of all young unmarried women. We need to get past people's notions and see that this group is not characteristic of other women. Indeed, life can go on without a lot of intervention sometimes.

Laurie Bryden: But it *is* the population that tends to get focused on. I feel there is a little confusion about how we are actually defining 'responsibility.' Yesterday, Margaret [McKinnon], Prue [Rains], and Linda [Davies] spoke about the responsibility that these women are taking. When I talk to women on a daily basis, I hear them really think through the issues of social and emotional support, their financial reality, what their goals are, whether they feel prepared to parent, and what that means to them. It's often a very well thought out decision-making process, and one which seems to be not too different from that of older women. I think there tends to be (and I don't know whether it's an age matter or a value issue) an underestimation of women's decision-making ability in terms of how we conceptualize our reality, make plans for the future, adapting and developing the skills that we need for that future.

David Checkland: Margaret [McKinnon] or Linda [Davies] made the point yesterday that many of the young women they interviewed viewed having a child as an opportunity for growth. I don't know if that conflicts with what you said, Ruth [DaCosta], but it sounded as if it was an opportunity for *them* to be cared for.

Ruth DaCosta: Yes.

David Checkland: That sounds like these views are in some kind of tension, although one might be the earlier stage of the other.

Prue Rains: It is a question of how people define the situation after they find themselves in it. It's not that they have walked into it with that in mind, but once you are in that situation, how do you view it? In one way, if you come from bad-off circumstances, one would view it as an opportunity for getting straight with your life and possibly get cared for while caring for someone. It's not that people set out with this objective in mind. Often pregnancy is accidental.

Peggy Robertson: They don't choose to not take a self-help course and to get pregnant instead. One of things I find is that our young women who get pregnant, they age overnight once they have made the decision. To some of the group, this is just astounding. Then when the babies bring the babies in, they bring them home to be looked at. I can't believe how the changes occur in a short period of time. Nine months is not very long, and these kids physically age, emotionally age, their priorities swing, and some of those changes occur once they make the decision to continue with the pregnancy. It is almost as though the hormones conspire to help the child grow up – and they are children still. They have the capabilities for growth and development and for nurturing their infant. It's scary, though, to see that happen, because they will never be the same again. They all say, 'I didn't know it would be like this, and I will never be a child again.'

Linda Davies: Exactly. The point about these 'routes-to-responsibility' is – I'm thinking of Kathy Addelson's 'good-girl life plan' in her talk yesterday – that the ground is shifting now. What we would normally conceive of as the 'right' or 'normal' sequence of events is maybe not the sequence that necessarily applies to working-class people in the same way it might apply to middle-class people. The British researcher, Anne Phoenix, has done a study on young mothers. In the communities she looked at, the age of giving birth has only gone down a year or two, but what is different is that the jobs in those communities for the fathers of those children do not exist anymore. So, they are thrown on to the welfare system, which *does* in fact provide some basis for a passage to adult status. You can move out of home, and get council housing. Some of the parents of those babies may be able to access those things in this way. But they don't have jobs, so they have to move through a different sequence to adulthood responsibility, adulthood status. We hold out this notion that responsibility is supposed to follow a certain pattern. If the preconditions are not there for you to do that, then people look to grow up in other ways. And they do. They take on 'adulthood responsibilities,' maybe younger than what they might want. What they are trying to do is grow up, to move on in their lives.

Kathryn Pyne Addelson: There is also the question of when and how you expect people to grow up. This business of expecting people to stay in school until they are 16 years old. My grandmother went to work when she was 12. My father and my aunt went to work when they were 14. They might go to night school. But they took on adult responsibilities of helping support the household at 12 or 14.

Prue Rains: Yet others expect to stay in school until they are 20, 25, or 30.

Margaret McKinnon: I would say that we aren't clear in our society about what we see as appropriate behaviour for adolescents. This whole notion of 'babies having babies' or 'children having children' suggests that teen mothers are too young to be taking on adult responsibilities when they aren't financially or psychologically ready to do so. I'd suggest that we are uncertain about what 'adult' behaviours we think are appropriate for teenagers. We expect teenagers to be in school and not have a job. However, lots of adolescents are working. They are taking on huge responsibilities at their jobs. They are working long hours, working late, and making all kinds of decisions about work.

Laurie Bryden: The work is in conjunction with school, and they are juggling that schedule. What is interesting is that they may view the future in terms of 'Well, it's not going to be too different from my life now.' They are already carrying responsibility in a lot of different areas. They may have been on their own emotionally for a long time.

Prue Rains: We can also question the notion that they don't act responsibly. Take ourselves for example. I have trouble with the notion that I am a self-reliant person and I take individual responsibility for my life. That really masks a whole lot of stuff. There are supports for education, tax subsidies, etcetera, for all kinds of things – for the way of life that generates the notion that we have got here on our own and so should other people. I am sure they would have reached the same place with the same supports. The idea is that not only should we benefit from these particular advantages, but we should pat ourselves on the back and trash other people for not having them, and act as if it was our own doing – and theirs. That idea seems an illusion to me.

Suzanne Peters: I call what you are describing the hidden issue of class. What I'd like to do is examine the conventional idea of the family and show all the social supports it has had over the years. That would reveal the amount of public education, health care, and other things that average families have had. So I think that is a really important point in breaking through some of the notions of 'self-reliance' and 'autonomy.' This kind of thing that comes out in the [focus] groups, when people soften their positions from an initial pure self-reliance position to the notion that 'well, actually collective responsibility – is a good thing and it is acceptable.'

Prue Rains: Not to mention your *family* that is supportive.

Suzanne Peters: For Canadians struggling with the issue of self-reliance and collective responsibility, the bridging factor is usually the notion that the family should take on the responsibility. They are not thinking about the cases that you are describing, the kids that are in care. They are thinking those who had an accidental pregnancy, but not necessarily those who *had* the child in care. They feel those teens shouldn't be independent – their families should support them. As much as the most disadvantaged population portrayed by media, that's not who people are thinking of. I imagine that they would say, 'If children are in care and then have a pregnancy, of course they can't go back to their family. But everybody else, their families are responsible.' That's how they construct that bridge of the family as responsible, between what could be a pure model of individual self-reliance and a model of collective state supports, or civic community support – the family is very important in their minds.

Colin Maloney: In [Susan Clark's] research, what percentage of the families that you said have not gone on child welfare – what was the percentage keeping their children?

Susan Clark: I can't pull a figure right out of my head at the moment from the Nova Scotia study, but it certainly was quite small initially. Now, again, you are dealing in Nova Scotia with a slightly different population than, say, Metropolitan Toronto. Certainly family support was quite strong for the teenage unmarried mothers when they became pregnant. We did not have a lot of children who were in care. For instance, there were certainly some but, again, not many. I could go back and try to make an estimate, but my impression is that there were not a lot.

Beverley Leaver: About a third of the families that come to Jessie's [a centre in Toronto for pregnant teens] live with their parents still, and probably half of that starts with family support, usually child care and emotional support.

Colin Maloney: What would your breakdown be in terms of those whose only support being the welfare system such as social services and elsewhere? What about those teen who don't carry their pregnancies to term? That is the first choice. The other choice is keeping the child. Those on welfare often keep them. It is one of the interesting statistics there seems to be little research about. What I know is, of three different welfare agencies, concerning the clientele they have – people of any age – over 85 per cent had their first birth as teenagers. It is an interesting and significant fact.

160   A Round-Table Discussion

Ruth DaCosta: Why do you find that significant?

Colin Maloney: Well, it is high for the general population. It is so skewed there.

Ruth DaCosta: Well, a teenager could be 19.

Colin Maloney: But they are still high compared with the general population. There is just a difference.

David Checkland: It seems to create a kind of a statistical anomaly too. Susan's study showed that compared with married mothers, unmarried mothers generally and teenage unmarried mothers too did not do dramatically poorly in many areas. They did slightly less well, but that by itself would not send their kids into care or create a social crisis. Yet, when you look at the population in care, you have a tremendous percentage of those people being kids whose parents were parents quite young.

Prue Rains: I think these kinds of quantitative questions are being addressed in the American literature. There has been a longitudinal study following particular populations and a series of studies done by Furstenberg. There are now a set of articles coming out analysing National Youth Survey (NYS) data, in which they have taken a random sample essentially of the entire population of young women and follow them at intervals of a couple of years to see how the family-generating process starts. I can't deliver you all the statistics, they are quite intricate, but those are the studies that really address those questions in the way you raise.

Colin Maloney: My concern is that there are certain groups of teenagers that are vulnerable. One factor [which helps identify them] is poverty. Are there other common factors that put them at significant risk?

Susan Clark: Our conclusion [from the Nova Scotia study] would be lack of education is a factor in terms of the *mother* – the mother of the baby, the unmarried mother. In terms of our research, whether you were 20 when you had your baby, or whether you were a teenager, those mothers tended to have less education than the general population of mothers. There is this notion of 'get pregnant, drop out of school and become dependent,' but it is not quite that simple. There is a very high correlation between the unmarried mothers having low education or not completing high school.

I think what people have been saying here is that the teens when they become pregnant and have their children, generally, make very good decisions and are very conscious of what they should do, that is, they should complete their education, they should go back to high school. What they do, I think, is underestimate the difficulties in doing that either because the one area where they can go is day care, transportation, getting themselves and the baby there, is very hard to do school work and be a young mother, and take on those responsibilities. I think the decisions they make and the ideas they have of what they should be doing are very responsible and absolutely correct. Being able to do it depends on services that are available. We don't often make sufficient services available to really keep those young women in school. A lot of our mothers certainly had a very high expectation of going back to school and they do go back, but only insofar as completing the grade they dropped out of at the time that they became pregnant, so they finish grade 10 or 11. They didn't get certified completion. Some do though. But typically it is the ones that have family support in the sense of being able to get child care support and really encourage the mother to go back into the educational system, some all the way through.

Colin Maloney: Eighty-five per cent of the children in care don't finish high school.

Susan Clark: The realities of being able to do it are quite difficult.

Linda Davies: I am not sure if this fits your study, Susan. In one study in England, they found that a lot of young women had dropped out of school first and then got pregnant. It wasn't pregnancy that caused them to drop out of school, which is what we usually think about. There is something wrong with the school system in the first place, and then they might get pregnant.

Ruth DaCosta: We found that as well. Some of the women who were pregnant certainly had dropped out beforehand. But to come back to Susan's point, the issue is what services are available in schools in order to make it possible for them to go back to and stay in school.

Laurie Bryden: I think there is also a question about the notion of the 'responsible mother.' We are trying to say, 'Well, teen mothers *are* responsible' for such and such reasons. Yet they are often viewed as being irresponsible because they chose to parent early. If you are going to ask the question, 'What does an irresponsible mother look like?' We should also ask, 'What does a responsible mother look like?' We should open the field to mothers *and* fathers of all ages.

Linda Davies: Another point on this issue is that, if you look at different concerns of middle-class women, they are told that they should be concerned that they are not at home with their children. Their children are deprived because they are out of the home working. But we reverse that when we look at working class or younger mothers, we say, 'You shouldn't be at home with your children, you should be out working.' You are irresponsible if you are at home and dependent on welfare.

Colin Maloney: Some single mothers that I've seen – they seem incredibly responsible to me. But what struck me was how few of them really were able to envisage going on to get a higher education. For them, there was a drive. But for the others, there wasn't a sense of envisaging themselves, a sense that 'I could pull this off.'

Kathryn Pyne Addelson: There may be a question about the type of support they need. Different people need different routes in education. In the United States, there is a general education degree [GED]. High school is inappropriate for some kids. The GED is not done through the high school system. It uses community teachers, and you don't have to go through the kind of classes that are very hard on people who are more practical. So they can get a diploma through GED. One of the efforts that is linked with the GED is to teach kids how to get a job and to think in terms of going on to post-secondary education as a possibility.

David Checkland: Yesterday, Kathy, you talked about how the way we now view responsibility is a vision of the person who is perpetually embedded in what you called 'a matrix of future-oriented possibilities,' or something like that. There are various ways of succeeding in future-oriented possibilities. People may work, but not necessarily view responsibility in terms of a 'matrix of future-oriented possibilities' at all. When I did inner-city work 12 to 15 years ago, a number of the people who would be classified by many others in our society as bums or outsiders, or as in some ways quite marginalized, were at times incredibly responsible. But they viewed responsibility as a kind of improvisational response to present circumstances. I witnessed people who had serious criminal records actually give away their coats at 42 degrees below zero to someone else, and just walk off to fend for themselves. Those are acts of generosity and responsibility. It would be moralistic for people to say these acts are not real. Yet the social structure imposes a kind of punitive effect on people who live their lives in a short-term kind of improvisational responsibility. You are considered really irresponsible if you are not thinking of your own retirement. I mean they are advertising for 22-year-olds to start on this. That is the way we conceive of responsibility, as thinking in terms of future-oriented possibilities.

Prue Rains: And especially for women. I notice now that many of my students will talk about 'life trajectory' and have some occupational plan. But I think that women in my generation still have a provisional notion about their futures. I think boys are raised in a way to say, 'I am going to get *there* within an array of possibilities.' But with women, how you are going to live the future role will depend on who you end up with. Insofar as that person is usually older than you and has a higher status by virtue of being in the job market sooner than you, you are more likely to follow him than he is to follow you. At some level in women's minds, you can't set out a life plan as if you could just do that without regard for who it is you end up having that life with.

Kathryn Pyne Addelson: This raises another question of responsibility which I don't think we have discussed, which is everybody needs some kind of community support, family support, family responsibility. But in a market economy, you often have to leave for jobs. My family and lots of other families are shattered, because you had to leave your community and your family to get a job.

Margaret McKinnon: In the Maritimes, for generations, people have been leaving the area to find work in central, western, and northern parts of this country.

Kathryn Pyne Addelson: Can I ask Suzanne Peters a question? In your discussion groups, do any of them raise the question about the market and the destructiveness to communities? Does that come up?

Suzanne Peters: What happens when people start reflecting on tightening ways of assistance to welfare moms is they first start talking about the fact that there are no jobs. That seems to come as the first thing. Then they talk about the mobility issues, the loss of community, the loss of extended family ties that everyone sees here, and then they sort of flesh out the facts. It is a process in which they demystify the notion about self-sufficiency for families, and therefore, they imagine themselves sufficient individuals to some degree. But mostly what they are doing is deconstructing the notion of family responsibility or family self-sufficiency. They are breaking that down and recognizing that, in a more complex social structure, what they assumed could be the case – that families would, or should step in and take over – may not be possible. That allows them to talk about a different kind of social and collective responsibility. The move is an interesting one, because first they start to think, 'Well, maybe we can just mow the person's lawn next door, maybe we can just make a sandwich and help someone ...' This is because they are resistant to the notion of state support being the first line of intervention, it goes from the family to maybe the community. Then later they say, 'Maybe that is really too complicated, so maybe the state *is* the appropriate place.'

David Checkland: But people don't have that kind of picture of self-reliance as incredibly supported.

Suzanne Peters: No, but that is the position they end up with more or less. They end up with a notion that still holds individual effort as ideally necessary, but they recognize that it takes some collective support. In the context of the discussions that I participated in, it is always a question of negotiating that boundary of what makes a person look for support, negotiating what David [Checkland] called need and responsibility. I think that is exactly the process that they are going through. It would take more discussions and more opportunity to talk about this, even for us, we can't articulate all the complexities of the issue. But that is what they are struggling with. It's the initial knee-jerk responses that focus on, more than 80 per cent, maybe 100 per cent, of the individual's responsibility. But in fleshing out the notion, they recognize that maybe it is distorted, and that there are many factors that come into play. They see support playing an increasing role. They come back to a broader sense of collective responsibility. Generally though, they don't talk that way because they are angry, they are fearful, they have lost hope, they feel these cuts coming, and there is a lot of angst.

Laurie Bryden: I don't think we emphasize the connection between what is happening economically – what the realities are – and why we have to depend on the system. We have a value system based on the concept of individuality and being able to support yourself economically, but few of the structures in support of that notion are there. That discussion is not there.

Suzanne Peters: I think that we are talking about the privatization of disadvantage or the individualization of disadvantage, which is a theme that we are all seeing and are all concerned about. We assert the notion that we want to have a sense of collective barrier or boundary to buffer us against disadvantage and that seems to be a critical notion that needs to inform the present debate. I agree that we need to start to meet people at the political level, and there have not been any political champions of late that have taken it up. Across all parties, it has been problematic to engage in that discourse. It seems to be inefficient and cost too much. How do we lead, address, and put forward what we know to be an appropriate notion of collective capacity to address disadvantage without it appearing to be a 'bleeding-heart' notion? So I struggle with the problem of how to articulate a sense of collective responsibility, to get people to think about the hidden issue of class. To me, the project on the struggle of what needs, responsibility, and entitlement are, the enterprise of collectively naming and finding a new discourse that draws people in, is very interesting and important.

Ian Hacking: I think that it is wonderful the way the discussion branched out into many different notions about responsibility. That was partly what we were looking for, since we are also concerned about developing our own notions, as well as how the public and legislators who are responsible to their constituents view these matters. It seems to me that there is a tension in the original sense of responsibility. On the one hand, both yesterday and today, there has been a heartwarming story about the way in which young women decide to carry their children. They change, they become immensely responsible, have a view of the future, often one which is a very undesirable future, one where it is clearly totally rational to stay on welfare rather than face other problems. They know what they are doing. That is responsibility. On the other hand, when the general public – which is me also – comes to think about these matters, their focus is on the issue of responsibility for becoming a mother, for becoming pregnant – maybe as high as 90 per cent decide to go for abortion, zero go for adoption from what I hear. So there is this 10 to 20 per cent, or whatever, that decide to carry a child, and they are held to be somehow responsible for what they have done, and hence irresponsible. So they are to be blamed for that. Now I think that, in my experience as a member of the public, I hear almost nothing about the later growth and responsibility, and this might well be extremely useful in public relations – the sense of responsibility just emphasized. One question to be answered by cynics is how the young women go on to get pregnant the second time and carry the second child, too. That of course is the standard anti-welfare mother rhetoric. Anyway, these are two notions of responsibility or at least two types of life for which one is responsible. I don't think that we had enough distinction between these groups. Ruth [DaCosta] said earlier that this group of young mothers not only need somebody to love, but they also know they are going to get better care if they have babies. This sounds exactly what the critics of welfare say, namely, that these young women get children in order that they will be cared for, so why should we pay for them? It is a dumb system. The critics' view is quite different, and it may be false. To sum up, there are two different kinds of questions about accountability or responsibility. I would be interested in hearing them put against each other a little bit more.

Ruth DaCosta: There is a different sort of worry for the Children's Aid Societies. One of the issues that is being dealt with there is that young women keep their babies and then relinquish them when the kids are 2 or 3 years old. It is much more difficult to place them in adoption. I am not judging that, I am reporting this.

Beverley Leaver: When Ruth said earlier that teenaged women get pregnant to stay in the system, I am reminded of the huge stigma that is still attached to teenaged parents. I don't think they feel terribly cared for outside of a service that is positive to them as parents. When they get on public transit, the driver treats them badly, and when they go to the hospital, they are bad mothers because the baby has an ear infection, it is because they are a teenager, not because their babies get sick. There is a huge stigma attached still to parents in their teens, and in the school system, there is a huge barrier to continuing school. I can't accept the desire to obtain services is a reason for teens getting pregnant.

Ruth DaCosta: That is not what I said. What I had in mind, in particular, are kids, who have been raised in the child welfare system, who have had fifteen foster homes, feel disconnected, and they are anticipating being discharged from care at 18. I am not saying that this is a conscious choice, but for these kids, my impression is that they are becoming pregnant as a means of having a continuation of care available to them because they have not had an opportunity, for a variety of reasons, to be able to anticipate the possibility of looking after themselves.

Laurie Bryden: There is also a concept of family that we have idealized and yet may have never experienced. But I wonder what is so wrong with a young woman wanting to create stability, create a family unit, create that support system that she hasn't had. Why does it have to rule out her access to education, her access to decent employment? Why does being a teen parent rule out a woman's access to what she should have access to within the society – education, health care, decent housing, and decent employment? I don't understand that. I have worked with young women who have made phenomenal changes in their lives because they became parents. This was their opportunity to alter their reality and to put into place a different way of living in the world for their child. In some circumstances, perhaps if they hadn't got pregnant and continued the pregnancy, they would perhaps not be as stable in their lives as they are now. The pregnancy was the incentive for them to go and find those things and get involved in those programs, access those resources where there were workers that were going to support them so that they could continue schooling, could do job training. Why do we challenge this? What is wrong with a woman wanting to put those things into place, earlier rather than later in her life?

Prue Rains: I have another example like that. I did a small study on an Inuit community in Northern Quebec. I went there because people wanted to know why kids were dropping out of high school, and I chose to follow a cohort that all had been in secondary school together and looked at the point at which they dropped out, the order, and what their reasons were, talking to them and their parents and from a variety of sources. What was interesting there was, first of all, virtually everyone had dropped out, so the notion that there was a deviance is misplaced, this was in fact the usual thing. Only one graduated and some had gone back to try to continue their schooling. But in that case, there were a variety of reasons which had to do with the nature of the school system. Kids were a little bit older in high school than normal, for some it took them longer to finish, and therefore they were older. Families start earlier in the North traditionally. So there was an overlap between say high school and the family-beginning process, and because the school was rather rigid, and because it was a Quebec model which does not allow for goose hunting season and a few other relevant local events – that's when exams are – so you get a choice to either go hunt geese or take your exams. There are a variety of disjunctions between the normal family-starting process and schooling assumptions. They particularly affect things like the notion that somehow now that high school is available in the community that kids would finish high school and then go south to CEGEP [the first level of post-secondary education in Quebec]. This was particularly unrealistic because it meant leaving their community and their family and all of the supports around children, and going south where they would have none of these things, or they would be separated from it all. In that community, even the notion of having children at 17 or 18 had not been pathologized by the local community as it is here. But it does raise a question of why does having a family rule out being able to continue school, or why aren't there ways of doing schooling that are consistent with having a family and, even for young men, a system consistent with hunting and a few of the other things that they do? As for the young women, all but one dropped out because they were pregnant.

Linda Davies: I think when we look at and try to unpack the taken-for-granted view of the teen mothers as a problem, we need to ask, What are the reasons that make it a problem? Is it that they are young? Is age the issue? We can point to other kinds of situations and cultures like the Northern Quebec case and like the Hasidic culture, where being a young mother is not a problem and is, in fact, encouraged. Is it age, or is it the fact that they are single, although we find that they are probably more involved with the father than we think they are? But is it the fact that they are single, or is it the combination of these two things? Is it the fact that they are dependent, like it's okay to be dependent on a man, that's good dependency, but it is not okay to be dependent on the state, that is bad dependency? When you try to unpack it then lay down what the other values are, about women, women's position, who is responsible for children, what does the decline in the bread-winning ethic mean?

All those tensions are there. When we look at teen mothers, we have to look at the whole picture – the way child care and the responsibility for children has been organized in this society, which is historically and culturally specific.

Margaret McKinnon: Isn't it that the girls are sexual or engaged in sexual activity, but that they really shouldn't have been? They have not taken proper responsibility for that and that is what they should have been doing in the first place. And secondly, they haven't taken proper responsibility because they have had a child.

David Checkland: What strikes me is, when you put together all those sorts of problematic aspects, the thing that moves people is the sense that others are disadvantaged, that it is not a level playing field, and that is why they move to respond to the needs. Yet it strikes me as if we have a simple capitalistic model of life: you get certain advantage capital; if you use it right or use it wisely, you will be fine; if you use it irresponsibly, then we won't help you, it's your responsibility. The issue then becomes what factors are relevant to the levelling of the 'playing field' – to equality of opportunity.

Suzanne Peters: I want to add to Linda's point on different factors of dependencies and David's idea of the capital to get yourself ahead. I think that one important consideration, which was alluded to yesterday, is that now we are in a situation where women are in the labour force and women with young children are in the labour force – 67 per cent now. These single moms and teen moms are being compared with a different case than when women worked largely at home taking care of their kids. I mean it is just the comparative sense of the society, of fairness, and what expectations people have. If you do have a two-income family and both are earning minimum wage, both working to struggle through, there is a resentful and blaming aspect that comes in, not only because the two are barely able to take care of themselves, but because so many other people are struggling because the labour force profile has changed so much.

Prue Rains: Why have maternal aid programs changed so much? I raise this question because of what my accountant said to me. Her point was something to the effect that you shouldn't have children unless you can afford to support them, which I think is an interesting notion. If you are poor, you should not have children. Perhaps that is the level at which the discussion really should take place. What really does that mean? That's really the fundamental issue. If you are poor, does it mean you should not have children?

Linda Davies: Poverty is not randomly distributed. Does this suggest, therefore, if you are, for example, black or native, then you shouldn't have children either?

Laurie Bryden: If we feel that younger women aren't able to manage raising a child, how do we feel about disabled women or about same sex couples having children and forming a family? There is a real lack of support for anything outside of the nuclear family, which actually is not the statistical norm. It just raises a lot of issues about what it is that we are valuing and under what circumstances.

Colin Maloney: This raises the issue for me that we in the West have privatized sex. We have also privatized the family. As David [Checkland] was saying, if you make the choice, it is yours, not ours. There is no sense of the community, like 'can we talk this out to hear where you are going?' From our society's point of view, it is an individualistic choice. If you can afford it, go ahead. You make that choice, and you live with it. It is an incredible disintegration of society. Why should I rely on anybody else? It is not a communal decision.

Ruth DaCosta: I think there is another tension, too. The common view is that it is not okay for teenagers to get pregnant and have babies. At the same time, you have middle class career women delaying having babies. There is some tension in our perception of these two groups.

Suzanne Peters: There is a very interesting study in Quebec – I take this to be an interesting example of the 'good-girl plan' that Kathy talked about yesterday (which perhaps some of you hadn't seen). The study basically said there were all kinds of ways you could be invisibly running around the problem but still end up on the 'good-girl' path by abortions, adoptions, and things like that. But in this Quebec study, they started with a cohort of women and then they looked at the various paths that women took over their lives. Some of them never had kids, some of them were married and had kids, some of them were unmarried and had kids. Then they looked at all the different kinds of outcomes that this ended in; in effect, the branching of a number of trees. What that shows you is how chequered are the paths that women take. Even if you started out married with kids, your marriage might have failed, you might have ended up in another relationship, or you might have been a single parent over a certain period, and you ended up here somewhere different than when you started. If you were unmarried and had kids, you might have been through one marriage at one time, and then that one might have ended. The study demystified in a very powerful way this notion that there is a majority of people that are in intact first marriages raising their kids because it gives you that sense of trajectory and change over the life course that is so transformational.

Prue Rains: This is especially relevant for teen mothers because they don't *stay* teenagers very long.

Suzanne Peters: Right, and you cast them in that mode forever. A lot of things happen over their lives that change them. The study shows the number of people over different points of the path and where they end up.

Colin Maloney: Well that doesn't matter. What does it matter to our society that is technologically and economically driven which says it doesn't matter if you are a teenager, if you can afford it, no one would care less if you were a teenager? If you are 34 and have a child, and you are on welfare, you experience much the same difficulties as when you are a teen mother on welfare. The perception is that when you are 34, you are marketable, you have a job that is an economic factor that we are dealing with here when you are a teenager, you will experience difficulties.

James Wong: But we believe that teenagers *as* teenagers are not supposed to have 'capital'; they are not supposed to be marketable.

Suzanne Peters: It also demonstrates to people that the stereotype of women on welfare being teen moms is false, that a lot of other people on welfare are people who have intact marriages.

Kathryn Pyne Addelson: I want to say something about research. There is quite a distance between people who do research in the academy and people who need research for their own approach, community groups especially. Some of us in the United States feel that there is a need for a different support system for researchers where they can share their knowledge on how they do this kind of collaborative research. We feel it would be helpful to have some centre that could give people advice on how to do the research and avoid pitfalls. The discussion is currently on an E-mail list.

Susan Clark: I want to pick up on the notion of collaborations in research as well. I think the reason we have so little research on the outcomes of the welfare system is the fact that we, as academics, can't get into that data (for good reasons probably), and so if it is going to be done in any way at all, it has to be a collaboration between the agencies or sometimes the government departments to get into the data bases and into those records. For good reasons people have not allowed that. Some people who are going into that research want to show the positive things that happen, the good news. Because we have never done it, we are a little nervous that, in fact, the good news is going to outweigh the bad news. So people have never really pushed it, I think, on a larger scale, and may get interested in more agencies of this sort. But without that sort of collaboration, we can't address some of the issues that do need to be addressed, or even know what they are.

Kathryn Pyne Addelson: The other side of this, I feel, is that as academics, if this is research to help out policy, then we need to help to do that. We are not policy experts, nor are we community experts. So in that sense, it needs to be collaborated as a team with people who have experience and a much better hold on things than we can.

David Checkland: Kathy has touched upon an issue that Ivan Illich called 'research by people.' The research is not necessarily generated collaboratively or within any context of academia. Sometimes that's the value; it is anecdotal because it is not done with our methodological fetishism in place. Sometimes methods are relevant, sometimes they are not. Sometimes people are asserting control.

Kathryn Pyne Addelson: Yes, and it has to change us, I think. Working this way has to change our methodology.

Prue Rains: What I found is that sometimes agencies themselves are so driven by need for funding that what they really want is evaluation research that they can hand to someone else to say what we do. Sometimes that imposes a frame that one doesn't necessarily buy into as an academic. So you have a gap between wanting to look at some other things, but the agency itself wants outcome measures for its own political or financial needs.

Colin Maloney: I think this would be very helpful for teenage pregnancies if there was this kind of research. We would see what is the reality. The public is calling into question the welfare and education systems and pulling back on funding. Most would be glad to help people if they felt this tolerance is well spent. Mike Harris's big election issue is the fraud and dependency issue. It caused tremendous upheaval in the social services system. Fraud and dependence are myths, but research doesn't say that. If we have that in the public domain, that would be the biggest help for anyone in this area.

Laurie Bryden: Yes, research doesn't tend to measure reality. Nor does it tend to capture the opinions of people accessing services and whether they feel those services have assisted them in achieving their goals. This perspective gets missed a lot, and if we don't have this perspective then it is really difficult to secure funding for support programs.

Ian Hacking: I want to make an academic remark. We are hearing about causal interactions between the investigator and the investigated. There is a whole lot of things that happen there. There may be a feedback, back and forth. So often we assume that when research works right, we are finding out the truth, the facts, the knowledge. We take the knowledge. If we have got good will and good sense, it is possible that we may be able to do something. But, I think there is another kind of interaction between the research and the subject. As researchers, especially as soon as we become quantitative, but even when we are qualitative, we have to formulate questions in certain ways, we have to use certain terms. As Kathy reminded us yesterday, the terminology of early parenting, has changed tremendously. You approach someone up the street and ask them about early parenting, they think it means bringing up children between the age of 0 and 3, that is parenting. But suddenly there is this technical word, 'early parenting,' which is supposed to take the stigma out of teenage pregnancy, and it doesn't. More precise concepts get introduced. They are created to describe this phenomenon, but they are sometimes actually crystallized as a phenomenon. Even in the case of your interest groups, they are presented as if we are finding out what Canadians really think. I am not so sure that we get at what Canadians really think. After three hours of discussion, people think differently from what they thought. Ideas are formed by this very process, concepts, descriptions. I think that in the end even kinds of people are formed in the course of research. This doesn't mean research shouldn't be done, but one shouldn't have the image of there being knowledge to be found out if only what we get is rather partly formed knowledge, and sometimes even forms of people. We seem to know a lot about a mother of 14 who is not married. We have the concept of that very person, and in the way which such a person thinks of herself has changed in the past ninety-six years. Every time we do research, and we have discussions like this, it seems that we engage, not only in making up knowledge, but also in making up new kinds of people without any clear understanding about what the consequences may be. Because the people who are thus formed often react in ways which are quite unpredictable, they often must take things into their own. For instance, yesterday's extraordinary discussion of adoption, was as vigorous a discussion as I have witnessed. A whole generation has taken the idea of adoption into itself and has made it absolutely taboo, for reasons no one well understands. That doesn't mean that there aren't reasons, maybe there is no causal story at all. But here is a case in which the people investigated – the young women – have changed the whole terrain completely on their own, and I think rather unpredictably.

Afterword: The Rhetoric of the Public Debate – Kathryn Pyne Addelson

For factions on both sides of the public problem, responsibility often involves liability: who is to blame for this mess? In our discussion, I was struck by the fact that both the 'traditional' and the 'family-planning' sides seem to rely on the 'good-girl' life plan as the model for assigning responsibility. The 'traditional side' wants sex tied to marriage and babies – though in a pinch, putting the baby up for adoption will do. The 'family planning side' moves sex up to the dating stage and recommends the contraceptive elevator, though in a pinch, any of the other elevators will do. Abortion becomes a responsible choice – and the traditionals find that shocking. For both sides adoption becomes a responsible choice – and many of the young women and their families find that shocking.

Assigning responsibility in the teen pregnancy problem is done from the viewpoint of the judging observer. The public problem is observed, the cause is uncovered, the blame assigned, the cure recommended. A different sense of responsibility is needed if we take the viewpoint of the more immediate participants – the pregnant teens, the young mothers, and, the families and communities. In our discussion, several people noted that for some of the young women motherhood was an opportunity to grow up, and others mentioned them wanting a good future for themselves and their babies. This is responsibility from the point of view of the actors rather than the judging observers, and I think that if we looked at it philosophically, it would include the families and communities, as well.

Responsibility in the actor's sense doesn't focus on blame, and it doesn't focus on the individual. It is a collective responsibility that people share for making the future together – for acting together to determine how we should live. The attitude here isn't one of blame or moral rescue, but one that involves care, forethought, intelligence, and initiative on the part of all the people involved. 'It takes a village to raise a child' has become a slogan, but it points to this kind of responsibility – a procreative responsibility. I think people on all sides understand this, but the rhetoric of the public problem puts the emphasis on the judging observer. It makes a 'them' who are the problem and a 'we' who have the solutions. Or, rather, several 'we's' with different, competing solutions.

11

On Choice, Responsibility, and Entitlement

DAVID CHECKLAND AND JAMES WONG

Describing people as the (sole) authors of their own lives is another way of punishing them.

Adam Phillips, *Terrors and Experts*

Rhetoric frequently offered in support of currently fashionable policies diminishing the welfare state makes much of the ideas of choice and responsibility. Frequently one hears expressed the idea that teen parents have been irresponsible in choosing to parent (and perhaps also in choosing to be sexually active or have a child). This notion is often coupled with the idea that it is wrong of such people to demand or expect that others (namely, taxpayers) pay for their choices or mistakes. The underlying idea seems to be, as philosopher Hillel Steiner puts it, that 'the set of entitlements should reflect the requirement that persons be held *responsible* for the adverse consequences of their own actions' (Steiner 1988). This *seems* undeniable, for to advocate otherwise seems to be to advocate wanton irresponsibility. Indeed, a common perception is that liberal welfare policies undermine initiative and responsibility because, in acknowledging the importance of 'social forces,' such policies deny responsibility.

Is it true, though, that we should be held responsible for the consequences of our actions? The answer is that this is too simple a generalization. Worse, stated baldly, the claim leads us in the wrong direction when thinking of issues of entitlement, justice, and opportunity. To see this, consider the case where one person injures another: I am fixing my roof and, in reaching for a box of nails, I knock my hammer off the edge; the hammer falls on your head as you pass beneath on the sidewalk. Who is responsible here? In this context, determining who is responsible also means settling who should bear the costs of this accident. (The case and the argument are taken from Ripstein (1994). Sagoff (1992) argues in similar fashion against the general position under consideration, but draws less far-reaching conclusions than does Ripstein).

Everyone, we trust, will assign costs to the careless repairman, and not the hapless pedestrian (at least without further conditions such as protective boarding, or signs warning of danger above). It is important to note, however, that the general principle under consideration, that one is held responsible for the consequences of one's actions, does not give that answer. After all, you, the pedestrian, chose to be where you were, too. Why should you not bear the costs of that choice (and the related choice not to wear a helmet when walking down the street)? 'Outrageous!' you say? Absolutely. But if such a conclusion *is* outrageous, it must be because there is more to the question of who bears which costs of which choices than simply the idea *that* a choice was made. The problem is that too many choices are involved in most cases; some subset must be identified as particularly deserving of blame or as implying the bearing of costs.

Here one might appeal to the idea of what a 'reasonable person' would do in the same situation. But use of that notion has two implications fatal to the simplistic view we are discussing. First, the reasonable person will have to know what *others* are likely to do. There does not seem to be any way of predicting what others are likely to do without knowing what norms they accept. Further, if we are to use the idea of the 'reasonable person' to guide one's own behaviour and not merely to predict what others will do, then the content of what is reasonable must be specified by norms one accepts as guiding one's own actions. Such norms, however, are only gestured at in the idea of a 'reasonable person'. They need to be made explicit by giving content to an idea such as that of a 'standard of due care,' through, for example, tort law in adjudicating damage claims.

Following Arthur Ripstein, the point we wish to make is that it is such standards, which are deeply and thoroughly normative in character, that settle the question of who bears the costs of a situation. Choice is not irrelevant, of course. But the conditions under which the various choices were made are also taken into consideration and assessed for their moral impact against norms like a 'standard of due care.' By itself, the bare fact of choice settles nothing. If we focus on choice alone, then everyone who made a choice that contributed to the causal history of the event would be 'responsible.' But that just means no one is responsible – that everyone bears whatever costs they suffer. At least in our usual way of deciding such matters this is an intolerable conclusion. Instead of worshipping the mere fact of choice, we actually settle *which* choice matters through articulating a standard that all are expected to live up to, assigning costs to those who fail to live up to that standard and are also unlucky enough to suffer or cause bad consequences. As Ripstein puts it, 'Some sort of balance must be struck between my interest in going about my affairs and your interest in security. Each of has the opposite interest as well – I want protection from your activities, and you want to be able to go about your affairs. A standard of care treats us as equals when it balances these competing interests' (Ripstein 1994: 8).

The fundamental idea of such a standard, then, is that it specifies or gives content to the idea of what it is to treat others as ends or persons, and not as mere means or natural phenomena. 'So long as others are treated as agents rather than objects, one is not responsible for the effects one's action have on their fortunes. But if one treats another as a mere thing, by failing to exercise due care, one becomes responsible for whatever bad luck may bring' (Ripstein 1994: 9). At first glance, such a position may seem more congenial to those who oppose welfare benefits for single mothers than to any liberal supporter of such policies. After all, is not their point that the careless sex or choice to parent of the female teen fails to meet a reasonable standard of due care, hence those teens ought not foist the costs of their actions on to society? If that *is* the point, however, the debate should then focus on whether the standard of due care under consideration is reasonable or just, and not simply on the presence of choice.

Once we recognize how little choice alone settles, it may be useful to distinguish between *responsibility* and *accountability*. We may consider a person responsible for a situation because she was an agent who made uncoerced choices, and at the same time, and with no contradiction, refuse to hold her (fully) accountable (i.e., make her bear the costs) because her choices were constrained in ways which were unfair to her.

Our ordinary uses of the term 'responsibility' are varied and subtle, but two central aspects involve the bearing of costs and the obligations one has towards others. Our distinction assigns to 'accountability' the first sort of issue, to 'responsibility' the latter. Interestingly, even if it is true, as is sometimes argued, that young women who choose to parent when economically unable to 'provide for themselves,' or in so choosing render themselves unable to provide, thereby violate some obligation to taxpayers not to 'become dependent,' it does *not* directly follow that they ought therefore to bear the costs of an 'immoral' or irresponsible choice. We might bear such costs in common because we recognize that *our* prior obligation to provide reasonably equal opportunity had not been lived up to. This failure on our part might also help explain the behaviour of the young women.

In our stipulative sense, accountability admits of degrees. In this way it mirrors liability in tort law; *what* one is liable for is specified in monetary terms. These terms are not settled by the mere fact of liability, as when a libel action is won, but damages of one dollar are awarded. Also, we might not assign full costs to someone even when she otherwise ought to bear them because the effect might be to implicate other innocent parties in some special way (e.g., the children of those held accountable).

In matters of public policy and entitlement (as opposed to tort law or corrective justice), the way we treat others as equals, we suggest, is to examine the resources and options open to them in making their choices, and assess these against standards of equal opportunity. This may take us back so far as to consider the nature of certain persons' opportunities to develop important talents and skills. If a person's set of available choices are or were constrained or limited so as to be seriously less than those of most others, then in asking such persons to succeed or even cope we are clearly asking more than we ask of others. To ask that arguably just *is* to treat them as less than equals. If we hold equality of opportunity (the notion of a 'level playing field') to be a central requirement of a just society, then justice can demand that we hold certain costs in common as a way of compensating for past inequalities or of 'levelling the playing field' prospectively. In effect, we do this in supporting public education and (in Canada) through a publicly funded health care system. For some reason, the connection between those issues and equality of opportunity is thought to be clearer than when welfare is under discussion. One reason for this, of course, is that society can legitimately expect of many of us that we work much of the time and, to a substantial degree, 'support ourselves.' Even here, of course, one must consider the complex set of policies and practices that exist and which may render certain forms of subsidy or support invisible. (See remarks on this by Peters and others, in the round-table discussion in this volume.) But once that is considered, and we do not suggest that this is any small matter, the question arises: 'Under what conditions ought society as a whole bear the costs of certain people's daily life expenses?' Our main point here is that this question is more complex and richly normative than reference to choice suggests. Moreover, this question forces us to consider how much and what we can legitimately expect of others – what the social and political analog of a standard of due care in action is. People will disagree about such matters, of course. But we make some progress if we recognize that the question at issue is not whether choices were made, but the conditions under which they were made and the appropriate normative standard to hold people to.

The position we are arguing for is very different from that of the classic 'bleeding heart' liberal (satirized in songs such as 'Gee, Officer Krupke!' from *West Side Story*). The bleeding heart accepts the same linkage between choice and accountability that the libertarian or conservative does. Unlike the others, however, the 'bleeding heart' argues that certain groups are so disadvantaged by circumstance that their apparent choices are not real. Rather, members of such groups are victims of social coercion, and so they are not responsible for their behaviour and should not bear costs. The typical response is to point out that some members of the same disadvantaged groups do better than others, attributing different outcomes to individual factors such as effort and character. The 'bleeding heart' then looks condescending and patronizing precisely because he shares with the conservative the idea that the mere presence of choice fully determines who bears the costs. In effect, the 'bleeding heart' denies too much (agency or choice) to justify a sense that it would be unjust to assign all costs to the disadvantaged. The issue is not full-blown coercion so much as constraints on opportunity.

The view we advocate, on the other hand, helps us avoid the choice of a liberalism blind to individual responsibility and initiative, and a conservatism blind to the relevance of differences in opportunity. This option is open to us once we distinguish between the questions of whether or not a choice was made and the quite different question of who should bear certain costs. This latter question, we have claimed, involves consideration of equality of opportunity, hence it cannot be answered without a fairly rich appreciation of the context in which the

On Choice, Responsibility, and Entitlement 181

people under consideration (here teen single mothers) make their decisions. This fact may tend to put any such position at a rhetorical disadvantage just because it is more complex and requires a certain degree of empathetic understanding as part of what is needed to think through questions of justice. The simple-minded linkage of mere choice and full responsibility we have been considering appears to require no such knowledge of circumstance, hence it can pretend that its clarity is a matter of being more cogent and principled. In reality, it is a matter of simplicity alone. And while it can be, in the words of an old Shaker hymn, 'a gift to be simple,' *oversimplification* would seem to be a defect rather than a virtue.

An appreciation of the circumstances in which another person makes choices allows us to see that the issue of responsibility is also much more complex. For in making a choice that would typically be one labelled 'irresponsible,' a person may well be acting responsibly. As Davies, MacKinnon, and Rains (this volume) point out, placing the central focus on the choice of some teens to parent (or its causal antecedents) obscures the ways in which acting responsibly can be manifested over time through accepting (and struggling to live up to) the implications of parenting. Indeed, when teen (or any) parents fall below a certain standard of care for their children, we attempt to protect their children through child welfare agencies, support services, and the like. This shows that there are issues of responsibility to be considered besides those gestured at in the term 'economic self-sufficiency.'

If we accept that the issue to be discussed is not whether certain choices were made, but the fairness of the conditions under which they were made we are explicitly raising the question of equality of opportunity. In the context of single parenting, this has two distinct aspects. The first has to do with the presence or absence of equal opportunity in the decision making of female teens who get pregnant and become parents. The second has to do with the range of opportunity available to the children of such teen mothers. Our focus here has been on the first aspect, but the second is every bit as important.

In this volume much has been said that makes it plausible that many young women choose to parent singly in their teens because they have (or think they have) rather limited other options. When educational and economic options are indeed highly constrained, we could say that insistence on economic 'independence' could amount to denying the poor the right to have children. But we need not assert any general right to have children in order to claim equality of opportunity has been violated and, therefore, that we should hold some of the costs of raising the children of single parents in common. Very generally, the following sorts of evidence exist to support such claims: (1) the disproportionate number of teen parents in the lower economic and educational ranges; (2) the disproportionate number of such parents among disadvantaged minorities; (3) incomplete or differential access by class and age in many places to sex education, birth control, and abortion; (4) asymmetry in power between, and perhaps different desires of, somewhat older men and teen women when it comes to the use of birth control; (5) the mere fact that these are *teenagers*. As Lea Caragata (this volume) points out, being a teen is inherently a difficult time with respect to issues of choice, self-definition, and, we suggest, accountability. Ripstein points out that the law 'exculpates adolescents more readily, because adolescence is a stage en route to maturity' (1994: note 16). Exactly what we can legitimately expect of teens will be contentious. But that we should be prepared to bear some of the costs of their choices in common as a way of protecting them as they develop autonomy-related skills seems to us undeniable. What needs further discussion is the relative merits of specific ways of doing this, but not the general idea that the standards of due care applicable to them ought to be milder than for the fully mature.

The second sort of equality of opportunity considerations concern the children of teen parents. These come into play even in cases where parents made their choices with plenty of opportunity. Contemporary practices of eliminating or reducing welfare, at least taken in isolation, clearly run the risk of passing on the costs of a teen's decision to parent to the child. This will be true whatever their effectiveness may be in deterring further teen pregnancies and teen parenting, an issue about which there are few good data (Jencks and Edin 1995.) To leave a child simply hostage to parental ability or willingness to provide is, in effect, to privatize the issue of equality of opportunity. Further, to make the child bear the costs of the folly of her parents seems to violate the moral maxim that we should not treat others as mere means, but always as ends in themselves. Falling back on the idea that parent–child relations are natural, not social, again denies any wide role for society to play in guaranteeing equality of opportunity. Since the child is thereby assigned costs – it is simply his or her bad luck to be born to a parent ineligible for welfare – surely this requires justification. State-supported child welfare laws, services, and agencies exist precisely because we have come to see that the meaning of treating the child as of value or as an end implies limits to parental authority and responsibility. But while these provide some protection against gross abuse and neglect, by themselves they cannot accomplish anything like equality of opportunity. There is, of course, a pragmatic and occasionally tragic judgment call to be made between intervention in the child's interests and sober recognition of the limitations of state resources. Indeed, it was appreciation that foster homes and adoption are limited devices with real downsides that led to current practices in child welfare.

Could radical alternatives such as a return to orphanages do better in providing opportunity? We are highly sceptical, and there is some literature about previous experience here that is troubling, for example, Levesque (1994). But whatever their merits or defects in other ways, at least such policies recognize a collective responsibility to address the issue of the child's level of opportunity.

Nothing we have said so far bears directly on welfare disentitlement schemes such as those of the Blair government in Britain, which are justified on a different basis. The British scheme is defended, not on grounds of parental choice as implying the assignment of costs, but via arguments to the effect that welfare provision is in fact disenabling with regard to initiative and opportunity. The basis for disentitlement is not that an irresponsible choice to parent has been made, but rather the wider social good served by alternative policies encouraging initiative. Here, too, there are grounds for scepticism. Even if such policies 'work' in the sense of forcing people into gainful employment or other activity, there remains the question of whether the children affected bear unduly the costs of such effects and are, thereby, treated as a mere means to an end. No doubt the story to be told about such policies will vary from place to place and with the effectiveness of related policies in a wider package. For example, effective provision of education and training and/or day care might go a long way towards mitigating the evils of welfare disentitlement. Our point has not been to argue for particular welfare policies. Rather, we are concerned to see the debate of these matters become more informed and more sensitive to concerns of equality of opportunity, both among policy makers and interest groups who work out the details, and among the general populace who provide the mandate to do various things and whose attitudes and values much depends on.

Acknowledgment

We would like to thank the following people for valuable comments and suggestions: Donald Ainslie, Jean Baillargeon, Lucia Dow, Danny Goldstick, Kevin Graham, Cindy Holder, and an anonymous reviewer for University of Toronto Press.

References

Jencks, C., and Edin, K. (1995). 'Do the Poor Have the Right to Bear Children?' *The American Prospect* 20(Winter: 43–52).
Levesque, A. (1994). *Making and Breaking the Rules: Women in Quebec 1919–1939.* Toronto: McClelland and Stewart.
Ripstein, A. (1994). 'Equality, Luck and Responsibility.' *Philosophy and Public Affairs* 23(Spring).
Sagoff, M. (1992) 'Technological Risks: A Budget of Distinctions.' In D.E. Cooper and J.A. Palmer, eds., *The Environmental Question.* pp. 194–211. New York: Routledge.
Steiner, H. (1998). 'Choice and Circumstance.' Paper read to the Department of Philosophy, University of Toronto, March.